# Dolphins, Whales and Porpoises:

## An Encyclopedia of Sea Mammals

# Dolphins, Whales and Porpoises:

## An Encyclopedia of Sea Mammals

### David J. Coffey

*American Consultant Editors*

David K. Caldwell

Melba C. Caldwell

**Macmillan Publishing Co., Inc.**

New York

Copyright © George Rainbird Ltd 1977

Macmillan Publishing Co., Inc.
866 Third Avenue, New York, N.Y. 10022

**Library of Congress Cataloging in Publication Data**
Coffey, D J
    Dolphins, whales, and porpoises.

    Includes index.
    1. Cetacea.    I.    Title.
QL737.C4C56    1976    599'.5    76–12469
ISBN 0–02–526660–8

First American Edition 1977

This book was designed and produced by
George Rainbird Ltd.
36 Park Street, London W1Y 4DE

Printed in Great Britain

# Contents

# List of Plates

# Preface

There is a trend within the evolution of animals towards the colonization of land habitats. However a number of instances are apparent where this has been reversed. Three large groups or orders of mammals have separately re-adapted to the marine environment, the Cetacea (whales, dolphins and porpoises), the Pinnipedia (seals, sea lions and walruses), and the Sirenia (dugongs, sea cows, and manatees). This adaptation is most extreme in the cetaceans which have adopted a totally fish-like form, which disguises their true mammalian features.

Sea mammals have been of significance to man over a long period of his history. Prehistoric middens have revealed cetacean bones and palaeolithic cave drawings record scanty and poorly understood information on the role of these creatures in those ancient societies. Scattered throughout the surviving art of ancient civilizations are the clearly recognizable, though embellished and exaggerated, images of these strange groups of mammals. We are fortunate to have some written knowledge of them, dating from Greek and Roman times. From their writers and historians come tales of fact and fiction. Although these are often exaggerated, to endow these creatures with greater powers, occasionally a tale, which at first sight seemed a figment of imagination, has subsequently been proved true.

In modern times, as no doubt throughout pre-history, the role played by these animals varies with the society. To some they are believed to be gods who can leave the water at certain times of the year and father human children. Such societies naturally show great reverence to them. Several, which rely on fishing, maintain that local species assist them during fishing expeditions, by driving the fish towards their nets.

The meat of all three groups is acceptable food and many tribes hunt these creatures as a source of nutrition. In most cases where the methods used are traditional and simple, the numbers killed are small relative to the size of the total population. Population dynamics ensure that adequate reproductive replacement occurs to maintain the level of the species concerned. Eskimos who rely heavily for survival on seals and to a lesser extent on dolphins and whales, were never even remotely in danger of decimating the herds that fed and clothed them. Only in the African manatee is there a suspicion that native hunting has had an adverse effect on its possible survival, and studies suggest that its decline was well under way long before the European exploration of the continent began in the nineteenth century. Today only a small number of African manatees remain and it is doubtful they can resist much longer the pressures building up for their final extinction.

Modern exploitation of the three orders of mammals began slowly and simply enough. Courageous men ventured out in small boats and regularly risked their lives in the struggle against these huge beasts. The great increase in the human population of the last two centuries, however, led to a higher demand for oil, fur and cosmetic products, and during the industrial revolution both boats and killing apparatus became more sophisticated. Hunting became a large-scale commercial enterprise: the development of faster boats, factory ships and explosive harpoons made it uneconomic to take small numbers any longer, and a period of ruthless, indiscriminate killing began.

Species after species were hunted to the verge of extinction and some were totally annihilated. The motivation for this slaughter was not survival of the men concerned, but to pander to the whim of ladies of fashion. The cosmetic industry must shoulder much of the blame, as also must the fur trade.

I have been accused by those who have read the text of overstressing the horrors of exploitation. I would claim that any appearance of repetition on my part is simply a factual reflection of man's story of wanton destruction. The story is always the same. A species is hunted until the surviving numbers are so small as to make commercial exploitation unprofitable. Then the nearest responsible government or international body rushes in to 'defend' the species with protective legislation – legislation no longer usually required since the hunters have left for pastures new. If, and when, the numbers increase to any size at all the government or body concerned succumbs to the pressure from commerce and allows so-called 'essential' cropping for the well-being of the species. If I do repeat the lack of ethics and morality in this pattern of events perhaps some will feel it is no bad thing.

Today as this sad saga is played out for many species of whale we find the International Whaling Commission, emasculated by political pressure, unable to make any positive contribution to conservation.

Living in an environment so different from our own it is not surprising that many of us are unfamiliar with these mammals. My own interest began in the Whale Hall of the British Museum (Natural History) where the model of the blue whale is breathtaking. My interest became scientific, and moved through a fascination with the evolution of these creatures whose ancestors from being land-living animals started their return to the sea in the middle Eocene period (*c.* 50 million years ago). I am fascinated by the structural and functional problems associated with mammals in water; the problems of live birth, lactation, breathing and diving. My veterinary training inevitably makes their management in captivity most interesting. Transporting, housing, nutrition and disease all present problems not dissimilar in basic concept to the husbandry of any animal under man's care.

To a student of animal behaviour the Cetacea are of particular importance. With the possibility of keeping these creatures under closer observation both in the wild, by using photography, television and telemetry, and in the more stringent confines of captivity, we have come to appreciate their natural history and great mental capacity. Studies on their brain structure, learning abilities, direction finding, special orientation and communications continue to astound.

Accepting all of the fascination these creatures have for the biological scientist, they also have great aesthetic appeal; they have a beauty of movement as well as the visual attraction of form and expression.

The text, describing each of the three orders of sea mammals is handled in two distinct sections: the general articles as an A-Z, and the dictionary of species follows. The animals are listed alphabetically in families and within each family by generic and specific names. Where a species is known by several common names, these are all given. The book ends with a description of the sea otter, which, although having its origins in a totally separate ancestry from the other three orders, is nevertheless a marine mammal and deserves mention – if only for its interest to man as a user of tools.

In writing a book of this kind one must rely heavily on the studies and researches of others. It would be impossible to mention all those who have spent hours in careful observation and scientific study to produce the many facts used in this book. I would like to recognize their efforts here.

Taxonomy is an ever-changing science: I have used the classification of Masaharu Nishiwaki, the well-known Japanese biologist, throughout the book but have on occasion indicated where main areas of disagreement lie.

Any book about sea mammals, and this one is no exception, would be incomplete without reference to that excellent volume *Whales* by E. J. Slijper (Hutchinson, 1962) to *Marine Mammals* by R. J. Harrison and J. E. King (Hutchinson University Library, 1965) and to the comprehensive work *Mammals of the Sea* by Sam H. Ridgeway (Charles C. Thomas, 1972) whose contribution to the study of these creatures is legion. Karl W. Kenyon has made a special study of the sea otter and it is from his work that a great deal of factual information here recorded is derived.

Without the tremendous help and encouragement of the production team of George Rainbird Ltd, in particular Tom Wellsted, Curigwen Lewis, Karen Goldie-Morrison and Alastair Dougall, this work would not have been completed. I would also like to thank my mother, Mrs I. G. Coffey, and Mrs S. Goble who have deciphered and typed the manuscript. Finally my thanks to my wife, Jean, who has encouraged me throughout and undertaken some of the research, particularly into the art and mythology of sea mammals.

D. J. Coffey

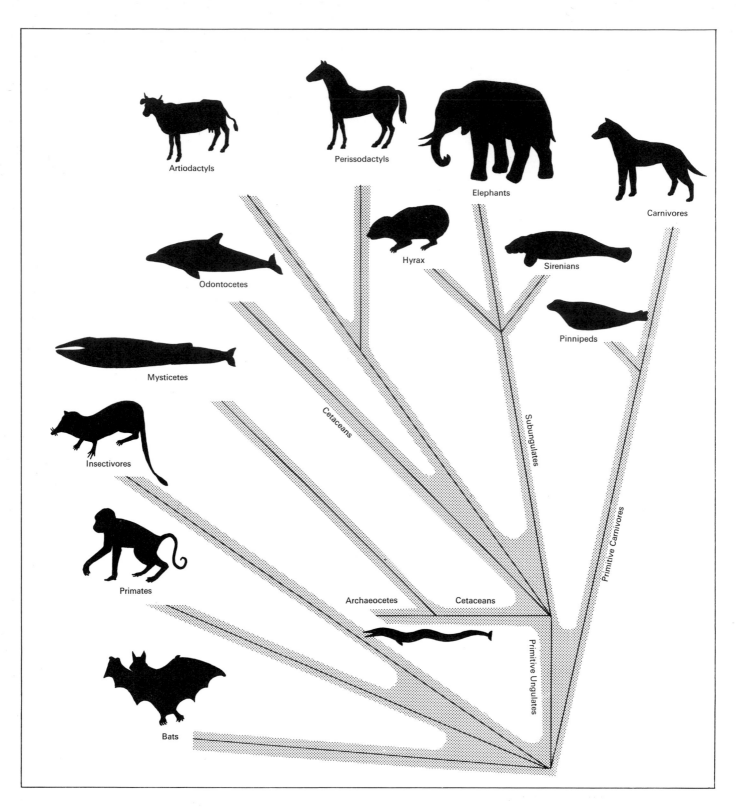

# Cetacea:
# *Dolphins, Whales and Porpoises*

The adaptive radiation of mammals has led to their exploitation of land, air and sea. The diverse origins of the three orders of sea mammals: Cetacea, Pinnipedia and Sirenia are *left* clearly shown.

## Introduction

Whales, dolphins and porpoises are mammals that have returned to the sea; their ancestors lived on land. They are therefore warm blooded and air breathing.

Some are less than 90 cm. in length, others approach a length of 30.5 m. to make them the largest animals that have ever lived. They are perfectly adapted to an aquatic life and are virtually incapable of leaving it; trained dolphins have managed to stay only a few seconds on the floor outside their tank. Their bodies are streamlined for efficient movement and their forelimbs modified into flippers. The external hindlimbs have disappeared completely and the tail has been modified to form a flat broad paddle or fluke which is used in locomotion. Other changes necessary to allow these mammals to exist in their watery home include a thick layer of blubber under the skin to protect them against the cold, altered position of the nostrils to the top of the head, and variations in reproductive and parental behaviour.

There are two living suborders of Cetacea – Mysticeti and Odontoceti – and one suborder to which only extinct species belong – Archaeoceti.

The living suborders are distinguished mainly on the structure of their teeth and skulls. In the Mysticeti the teeth, which are present as buds in the gums of the immature, never emerge. They are replaced by the baleen plates which are used to strain the food from the sea water. Odontoceti may have a full and sometimes powerful set of permanent teeth but unlike most mammals have no milk teeth.

These beautiful and fascinating creatures are sadly becoming scarce. With the advent of industry has come the introduction of technology into their environment; pollution and, more important, 'improved' methods of hunting are likely to prove their Waterloo. Without rigid controls on hunting, backed by international cooperation and enforcement, they may well become extinct.

### Mysticeti

This fascinating group includes the blue whale, the right whales, the rorquals, California grey whale and the humpback whale. They are characterized by their large body size, which may exceed 30 m. in length and weigh over 120 tonnes, the relatively large proportion of the skull which in some species exceeds one third of the body length, and the replacement of the teeth by a series of elongated whalebone plates, called baleen plates, on either side of the jaw. In some species these plates exceed 400 in number. In spite of their great size which, as far as is known, makes them the largest animals that have ever lived, most of them feed on small crustacea known as krill. A few will, however, consume small fishes. They feed by simply opening the mouth to fill it with krill-laden water; they then close it. The whalebone plates form a fine mesh strainer which traps the krill as the water is expelled between them.

The thorax has an unusual structure, only 1 to 2 ribs being fixed to the sternum. Hindleg bones are usually absent although a few species retain vestigial traces of the femur and tibia.

There are 3 families – Balaenidae, Balaenopteridae, Eschrichtiidae.

### Odontoceti

This is the largest group of whales and contains the majority of species. Several features distinguish them from the Mysticeti, primarily in that they have teeth not baleen plates. These vary in number from 2 to 250 depending on the species. All the species have 7 cervical vertebrae which are variably fused or separate, and unlike the Mysticeti, most have longer, robust sterna. The 2 parts of the nasal apparatus have joined at the external end to form a single opening.

Most members of the Odontoceti are gregarious creatures which form large herds. They keep in contact by an efficient use of sound. Their well-developed hearing apparatus enables them to pick up squeaks from within the human range to ultrasonic noises. Like bats they send out sounds and can estimate the position of objects by analysing the echo. To facilitate this, they move their heads from side to side as they swim. The great variety of sounds they make is an indication of the real development of this sense, and its importance. (See Echolocation.)

The toothed whales are carnivorous, feeding on fish and squid; with killer whales eating penguins and seals. Their daily food consumption is over 5 per cent of the body weight and in some cases as much as 20 per cent.

The Odontoceti is made up of 10 families, Delphinidae, the dolphins; Globicephalidae, the pilot and killer whales; Grampidae, Risso's dolphin; Kogiidae, pygmy sperm whales; Monodontidae, belugas; Orcaelidae, Phocoenidae, the porpoises; Physeteridae, the sperm whales; Platanistidae, the freshwater or river dolphins; Ziphiidae, the beaked whales.

## AGEING

For a scientific study of whales it is essential that an individual's age can be determined. Population dynamics, cropping rate and conservation can then be studied more accurately. No single factor can determine age accurately, but several have been examined which together offer a fair assessment.

The size of an animal is very variable at any age. It depends on nutritional planes during development, recent food supplies, time of year, state of health, i.e. presence of chronic disease or parasites, breeding cycle, and genetic factors. There is however a general, if rather crude, relationship. For example a blue whale, *Balaenoptera musculus*, measuring 24 m. in length is obviously a good deal

older than one of 8 m. which is the length of a recently born animal. Although length, an easily measured parameter, is only one dimension of size, it is interesting to record that quite accurate estimations of a foetus's age can be obtained by measuring its length. Thus in the whale, length reflects age more closely than in a land-living animal.

Baleen plates give some limited information about the age of a young individual. Along each plate run ridges at right angles to the length, the numbers of which give an indication of age. This method is limited to the young because after a few years the baleen plate is worn away and is then replaced by growth from the gum.

In the ear canal of baleen whales is found a conical plug of keratin, some 90 cm. in length. It is thought to function as a sound transmitter. If sectioned longitudinally it is seen to have a series of bands reflecting growth periods, rather like the rings of a tree, and like them can be used for age determination. The problem is that the length of each growth period is unknown, and therefore the rings reflect a relative not absolute age, since each ring may represent more than one year's growth.

In a rather similar way the age of odontocetes can be measured by sectioning their teeth.

Ovaries also provide evidence of age. Mammalian ovaries show a ripening follicle which eventually bursts to shed the egg or ovum. The space left is filled with a solid material which produces progesterone, the hormone essential for the maintenance of pregnancy. In most mammals this tissue gradually contracts and disappears. In whales the *corpus luteum*, or *corpus albicans* as it is called when well contracted, does not disappear but stops its regression at a certain point and remains through life. By counting these one can determine the number of breeding cycles the female has experienced and by then adding the number of pre-pubic years, the age can be estimated. The problem is to establish the time interval between breeding cycles.

## AMBERGRIS

This interesting substance is found in the large intestine and rectum of sperm whales, *Physeter catodon*. It is composed of various products of digestion and includes large numbers of squid

Four Russian whaledressers display a piece of ambergris weighing 70 kg. taken from the belly of a sperm whale, *Physeter catodon*. In the foreground lies the harpoon with which the whale was killed.

beaks. Ambergris is a grey waxy substance with a characteristic musty odour. Large pieces, well over 45 kg., are sometimes recovered from a slaughtered whale although the average weight is about 35 kg.

How or why this substance forms in the whale's gut is a mystery. Some believe it is formed by bowel stasis or stoppage during a bout of constipation, others that it results from a period of restricted feeding during the breeding season when there is not sufficient bulk in the gut, and it is therefore not voided.

Not surprisingly it varies in quality but at its best it is a valuable stabilizer used in perfume production. Synthetic chemicals and modern techniques have largely replaced it, but there is still a demand for it in the preparation of more expensive products. See *Physeter catodon*.

## ANAESTHESIA

Attempts to anaesthetize small cetaceans started in the early 1930s when masks over the nostrils supplied ether to the animals' respiratory system. These early attempts proved a failure: the animals died. With renewed interest in cetaceans in the 1950s, attempts were made to achieve satisfactory anaesthesia using barbiturates alone. These experiments were equally disastrous; all the animals succumbed. Nitrous oxide (laughing gas) was next tried but proved inadequate.

Success came when the potent drug halothane was used. The main advantages are that rapid recovery is possible, a very important factor in cetaceans, and there are few adverse side effects.

Modifications to this technique now make it possible to mimic fairly accurately the anaesthetic procedures used in man and domestic animals. Today, cetaceans are given a pre-anaesthetic medication, an injection, followed by an intravenous knock down or induction dose of a short-acting barbiturate, and then an endotracheal tube is passed through the mouth into the trachea and connected to an anaesthetic machine which controls quite accurately the dose of gas given and therefore the level of anaesthesia. With this control, complex surgery becomes possible and safe.

## ANATOMY

In spite of a striking superficial resemblance to fish, cetaceans are, of course, mammals. When their ancestors returned from land to water, they were obliged to modify their anatomy in order to adapt to the new medium. Their general shape closely resembles that of a typical fish, except for the tail flukes which are in the horizontal plane, shown by hydrodynamic studies to be best suited to moving through water. Cetaceans have no external ears, and the mammary glands, genital and anal openings are recessed in slits to reduce drag. Cetaceans have virtually no hair; some species do retain a few bristles around the head, particularly the mouth.

An important and necessary group of modifications to the anatomy have arisen to allow movement. The forelimb skeletal pattern of terrestrial mammals has been maintained but it has been modified to form a flipper for stabilization. Most species possess a dorsal fin which is strength-ened not by bone or cartilage but with strong fibres of connective tissue. The dorsal fin is also used for stabilization. All cetaceans have lost their hindlimbs. There are remnants of a pelvic girdle consisting of 2 very small cylindrical bones embedded in associated muscles, and with no attachment to the vertebral column. Finally, the tail has been much modified to form the propulsive organ. From the tail 2 flattened structures known as flukes have developed. These do not contain any bony or cartilaginous substance but, like the dorsal fin, are strengthened with strong fibrous connective tissue.

Apart from these structural changes, the mammalian anatomical structure is maintained. Cetaceans still breathe air and produce live young which they suckle. The various physiological systems, respiration, heart and blood, reproduction, urinary, digestive, are all basically mammalian. (See also Cardiovascular system, Digestive system, Muscular system, Nervous system, Respiratory apparatus, Sensory system, Skeletal system, Skin, Urogenital system.)

## BALEEN PLATES

Baleen whales (belonging to the suborder Mysticeti) feed by filtering huge quantities of small marine life, known as krill, from the water as they swim. The filtering apparatus consists of large numbers of baleen plates arising from the upper jaw. They are positioned vertically downwards in the huge arched mouth, and can be almost 5 m. in length, although this depends on the position in the mouth; they are several cm. wide. The outer edge is smooth and straight and the inner edge has a hairy fringe to trap the food as the water is expelled. The whale, when feeding, swims along with its mouth wide open. Water passes in and then as the pressure builds up, flows out between the baleen plates. The krill are trapped by the feathered fringe. The whale closes its mouth and, using its tongue, forces the food to the back of the throat for swallowing.

Baleen, which like hair is made of keratin, varies in colour in different species, and can be used to aid identification. It may be white, black or pale yellow, and each plate may have a similar coloured fringe or one of different hue. The plates grow throughout the animal's life, new ones re-

The six whalers *above* rest on the baleen plates in a dead whale's huge mouth.

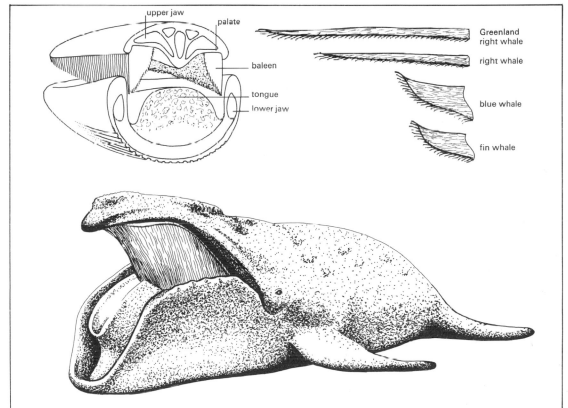

upper jaw

palate

baleen

tongue

lower jaw

Greenland right whale

right whale

blue whale

fin whale

The cross-section of the head of a rorqual (top) shows the relative positions of the baleen and tongue, while the gape of the right whale, *Eubalaena glacialis*, (below) reveals the large plates of baleen, the curved top jaw and the large tongue. The sketch (top right) gives an indication of the variation in shape of the baleen plates between species.

placing those damaged by the inevitable wear and tear of use. Young baleen whales are born with a full set of baleen plates which remain soft during lactation and harden only at weaning.

## BEHAVIOUR

To understand fully the behaviour of an animal species, it must be considered in relation to its environment. Behaviour is one of the mechanisms which enables both a species and an individual to adapt to a changing environment. For this reason it is preferable to have a wide knowledge of the behavioural repertoire of an animal in the wild, before turning to experimental situations in the laboratory for more detailed study.

The cetaceans, living as they do in an environment foreign to man, are without doubt the most difficult mammals to study. Much of our knowledge of cetacean behaviour has been compiled from a large number of widely distributed observations made over the centuries by members of the whaling industry. These men had a vested interest in learning the habits, natural movements and migrations of their quarry.

As interest in behaviour and conservation has grown, scientists have been given financial support to collate and confirm these empirical observations. Improvements in technical apparatus have done much to simplify and enhance their task.

In this brief discussion of cetacean behaviour we will follow the classical behavioural approach. We will consider, as examples, some of the species which have been the subject of naturalistic studies, and then examine some of the experimental work which has been undertaken in laboratory conditions by learning psychologists and others in controlled conditions.

Since the beginning of the twentieth century hundreds of thousands of blue whales, *Balaenoptera musculus*, have been killed by whalers. It is now feared by some that so few are left that they will be unable to recover and extinction will result. We are therefore in the unhappy position of having lost a unique opportunity of studying in any detail the behaviour of the largest living animal the world has known. We do know that these magnificent creatures live mainly in isolation or small groups, consisting of a bull, a cow and its calf. Very occasionally larger congregations of up to 20 animals have been seen. The blue whales were found in the northern and southern hemispheres close to the krill-packed waters. Today the largest populations are found in the southern hemisphere. They move to warmer waters close to the equator to breed in the winter, and after a gestation period of just under one year, spent in polar regions, they again seek the warmer waters to give birth. The young are able to swim and see at birth. Some 8 m. long when born, they reach 15 m. by the time they are 3 years old.

The migrations of these great creatures, which necessitate journeys of many thousands of miles, are governed basically by two driving forces, breeding and feeding.

In contrast to the blue whale, the sperm whale, *Physeter catodon*, has received much attention, and a reasonable understanding of its natural behaviour has been achieved.

As in the case of blue whales, sperm whales are distributed and migrate according to the demands of feeding and reproduction. Always associated with deep water, it is rare to find a sperm whale in water less than 100 m. deep; they are only seen close to land where the coast drops away sharply into the sea. These conditions off the coast of Peru, Chile and the islands of the Galapagos allow sperm whales to approach close in; so close that small numbers have been caught within a few kilometres of the shore.

Although sperm whales are widely distributed, males being found in deep water in most oceans of the world, they do exhibit migratory behaviour. Many males move into polar regions during the summer periods, leaving them again as the winter ice forms, to travel towards the equator. Female sperm whales, particularly those with calves, tend to restrict themselves to warmer waters between 40°N and 40°S, although these limitations are by no means absolute.

To a large extent, the need to seek plentiful supplies of food dictates migration. It has been found that sperm whales are most abundant where there are powerful currents or where two powerful currents flowing in opposite directions meet. Here their favourite food – squid – is most plentiful. In order to catch squid the sperm whale can dive to depths in excess of 900 m. In addition to squid they eat fish, octopus and cuttlefish. Both the fish and the squid are deep water species. A great variety of other animals have also been recovered from their stomachs, but how far these are actively pursued and how far they are accidentally taken, remains to be established.

An interesting observation, that needs to be studied in more detail, is the aggregation of sperm whales which occurs near sand banks in phase with the full and new moon; this is thought to be in response to squid behaviour.

Exactly how the squid and other food are ingested is unknown, but since the teeth do not erupt until sexual maturity, and since deformed jaws do not seem to inhibit feeding – certainly many such whales have been caught in excellent condition – and since quite large prey has been recovered from the stomach, apparently undamaged by teeth, it is supposed that even large items are swallowed whole. Exactly how squid are located at great depths is unknown but it is almost certainly by echolocation.

Reports of the social organization of sperm whales vary slightly. Most observers agree that small groups of pregnant females, nursing females, young males and females, together with calves make up small associations or schools. Depending on the season of the year there may or may not be one or more mature males associated with such a group. As the young males begin to mature they leave the female groups and form loose associations or pods which tend to remain in the proximity of a female group. Some of these young maturing males will leave these groups and migrate together with the old males to the polar regions in the summer. Groups of young males do not form tight social associations but may spread over an area of several hectares. They apparently keep in communication and move from place to place as a social unit.

Old bulls are often seen swimming in isolation. Opinions vary as to the role of these old isolated bulls. Some observers believe that they join the group of females in the breeding season, while others conclude that they have no social role at all and simply travel alone. It is also possible that

their isolation is not permanent, since several observers have seen groups of mature bulls in close association. Evidence from whalers suggests that the tendency to isolation increases as the mature bulls approach the colder water of the polar seas.

Finally it is possible that the social groupings fluctuate at different times and for different purposes since estimates of the numbers in any type of group vary considerably. Female groups of just a few individuals to several hundred have been seen, and it is suggested that small groups may amalgamate for migrating movements.

Female sperm whales mature sexually when they are between 8 and 10 m. in length, while males are probably closer to 13.5 m. Mating takes place in warmer waters during the winter months. (See Mating Habits p. 29.) Both vertical and horizontal positions have been seen to be adopted. This is followed by a gestation period of 16 months. Females in the northern hemisphere give birth from May to November, while for those south of the equator the parturition period is from December to April. The breeding area is restricted to between 40°N and 40°S. The calf, normally only one, is born tail first with its eyes open and is able to swim. Once the newborn offspring has reached the surface the mother watches over it until it has gained control of its faculties. At birth it is 4.5 m. long and weighs about a tonne. After a little search, with help from its mother, the young whale discovers the nipple. This, although normally retracted into a slit to streamline the contour of the mother, is now extruded.

The mother lies on her side with the mammary gland almost out of the water while the young whale adopts a position parallel to the mother's body and grasps the teat in the angle of its jaw.

In captivity dolphins of different species have been observed mating. Here a male bottlenosed dolphin, *Tursiops truncatus*, is mating a female white-beaked dolphin, *Lagenorhynchus albirostris* (foreground).

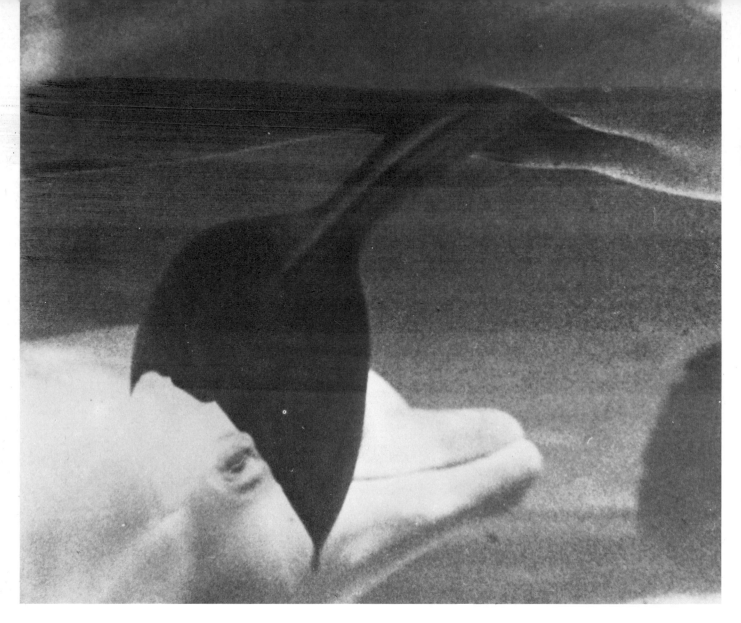

The birth of a bottlenosed dolphin, *Tursiops truncatus*, at the Miami Beach Seaquarium, Biscayne Island, Florida, showing the calf emerging tail first from its mother while her mate looks on (below). Birth took one and a half hours and the calf weighed 16 kg. and measured 80 cm.

Milk is actually squirted into the calf's mouth – an unusual adaptation, related to an aquatic way of life, which speeds up the transfer.

It has been suggested that so-called 'aunties' exist in sperm whale sociology. These are non-nursing females who adopt a role of assistant whale rearer, helping the mother to bring up the young. Although such a function has been proved in other mammals both land and aquatic, it is speculative in the sperm whale.

Following the lactation period there is a period of sexual quiescence which lasts some months. Throughout the period of lactation the re-lationship between mother and young is intense.

It is important that behavioural scientists resist the temptation to anthropomorphism. There is therefore a natural scepticism relating to tales of almost human devotion to a wounded colleague. (See Care-giving Behaviour p. 24.) Nevertheless numerous observations by whalers, who profited by their knowledge, and by behavioural scientists, do indicate remarkable social responsibility.

Reports of females remaining with, assisting and encouraging offspring wounded by a harpoon, abound. Conflicting reports, which suggest no such devotion exists, the mother simply leaving her young to its fate, may relate to a quite different situation. Most whalers report that the female will stay with a wounded calf but leave directly it is dead, and they have used this knowledge in a most inhumane way. By wounding a calf but being careful not to kill it, they can more easily catch the mother when she comes to tend it. (See Caregiving Behaviour.)

Tales by whalers of members of the group attacking boats deliberately and biting through the harpoon or line must be treated with caution. Some observers suggest that, excited by the situation to great activity, their actions occurred accidentally rather than with forethought.

Although play is often considered a prerogative of the young, most adult animals will indulge from time to time in activities which can only be described as play. The purpose of play in the young is often thought to be related to learning skills for adult life but such a function can hardly be ascribed to this behaviour in the already mature animal. Adult sperm whales are often seen to breach – jump clear of the water and fall back on their sides or belly, with a resounding crash. They also perform the mysterious activity of so-called lobtailing in which they position themselves vertically with their head down and their tail out of the water and, swinging from side to side, crash against the surface, making a noise like a cannon crack. In addition, a few observations have been made of these whales playing with floating debris.

In view of the amount of aggression shown to sperm whales by man over many years it is not surprising that our knowledge of their responses to danger is well known. Normally they consider discretion to be the better part of valour and flee when danger threatens. They either make off at speed, or sound, diving deep to swim away unseen. If however, they are harpooned or harassed they may take the initiative and attack. Their armoury includes teeth, the ramming power of the gigantic head, and the flattening effect of the fluke. So powerful are their jaws that boats have been snapped in two with a single bite.

The aggression shown to human hunters may be unremitting, but what of fights between themselves? Several bouts have been observed between mature bulls. The usual weapon used in combat is the jaw. Both males swim towards each other, jaws gaping. When they meet they interlock their jaws and inflict terrible wounds on each others' bodies. Large pieces of flesh and blubber are torn away, and on the few occasions where animals have been captured following fights, teeth and even jaws have been found broken.

The migrations of the pilot whale, *Globicephala melaena*, are also governed by the demands of feeding and breeding. It feeds mainly on squid, particularly the short-finned species, *Illex illecebrosus*, but will take cod in the absence of squid. Pilot whales are distributed in the Atlantic. They spend the summer in the Arctic, migrating southwards during the winter.

They form social groups of roughly 20 to 25 individuals, but sometimes as many as 100. In open sea they tend to form loose groups which come together in the face of danger. The structure and spacing of groups is probably dictated by the movements and spacing of the squid on which they feed. Typically the group consists of several mature females, a smaller number of mature males, and young. Females predominate in the ratio 3:1. In addition to these groups, other groups form, which mainly consist of mature males; these appear to gather temporarily during the summer months.

Females of the species *Globicephala melaena*, the Atlantic pilot whale, are sexually mature at 6 years of age, while males do not become sexually functional until they are 12 years old. Mating occurs in the northern spring from April to May. Gestation is probably about 16 months, the young being born during the summer months. The young, a little under 2 m. at birth, are nursed for 2 years but begin to take squid when about 8 months of age.

In general, this species seems to be peaceful by nature, although occasional fights do probably occur between mature males during the breeding season.

**Social Behaviour in Captivity**

There comes a time in most naturalistic studies on any wild animal when the observer feels his knowledge of his subjects' behaviour would advance more rapidly if they were confined in more controlled conditions. Captivity is not, or should not

'Aunties', which help a mother look after her young have been observed to exist in captive bottlenosed dolphins, *Tursiops truncatus*. Here an 'auntie' (left) accompanies a calf (centre) and its mother (right).

be, an end in itself but merely a scientific tool to assist our understanding of nature. As such, and providing the animals are treated with responsibility, it is probably justified.

As cetaceans live in an environment foreign to man, the problems he faces in learning the secrets of their way of life are increased. Apart from slow-swimming divers, clumsy submarines and bathyspheres, he is restricted to observing them, in an almost two-dimensional sense, at the surface of the water. He can have little knowledge of their three-dimensional existence.

The laboratory, or oceanarium, therefore, offers a relatively simple way of extending observations into this third dimension. The danger of drawing conclusions from such observations must, however, be remembered. The behaviour of animals in the wild must be re-examined and reconsidered in the light of information so obtained, but this is never easy to do.

It has not been possible to date to examine the larger cetaceans under captive conditions. The bottlenosed dolphin, *Tursiops truncatus*, is commonly kept in captivity and it is from this species that most of our information has therefore been obtained in recent years.

Captive groups are often artificially constructed so that unless the whole of a natural group is captured or the captive group is carefully made up to mimic a natural group, the resulting observations must be treated with caution. Notwithstanding these difficulties and reservations, such observations are extremely useful.

Observations on groups of captive bottlenosed dolphins tend to confirm those made on wild cetaceans that, in many species, groups of breeding females with their dependent offspring make up a social group. Within this group there is a dominance order, with usually a leader female. This female organizes the group in the face of adversity – in captivity anything from a new toy to a strange attendant. It is she who will often dominate the show in public performance and she who has the closest relationship with mature males. Mature males are less dependent on social contact. Even in captivity they spend much of their time swimming alone, only occasionally joining a member of the group – often the dominant female – for a swim. During the breeding season the male will spend much more time in close physical proximity to the receptive females. The female at this time is submissive to the male and leaves him only for very short periods to feed.

The male tends not to be aggressive but does show occasional bouts of anger. Such a reaction will be elicited if one of the group attempts to snatch his food or if a young male attempts to copulate with a receptive female. On such occasions the dominant male will bite and slap the upstart with his powerful fluke. The dominant male reserves such acts of aggression for these prospective usurpers, being usually much more gentle with the females and young.

Several groups of bottlenosed dolphins have bred in captivity. As soon as the young dolphin is born – tail first – the mother encourages it to the surface to breathe and then turns on her side to assist the offspring to find the teat. It is almost certainly at this early period, just after birth, that the firm union between mother and young is established. Their mutual recognition of each other as dependent individuals, (i.e. mother-young), rests almost certainly on sound, unlike many land mammals which often depend on smell.

The mother-young relationship is intense. Mother dolphins are very attentive to their offspring, keeping them close to them and retrieving them if they stray. They prevent the young approaching new objects or, in captivity, new attendants, and are careful that they are not injured by other adults.

*Above* A captive bottlenosed dolphin mother, *Tursiops truncatus*, 'punishes' her calf by open mouth pressure: no injury is inflicted.

*Below* A bottlenosed dolphin mother, *Tursiops truncatus*, (left) nuzzling at the genital region of her yearling calf. This active solicitation on the part of the mother forms part of the calf's long learning period of sexual patterns.

As with most maternal care in mammals the intensity declines with time. By the time the young dolphin is a year old it starts to spend more time away from its mother. It begins to take solid food in small amounts from about 6 months, but weaning is rarely completed before the calf is 18 months of age. After this the mother not infrequently actively repels any suckling attempts.

A young dolphin which resists its mother's attempts to retrieve it may be caught by her swimming on her back under it and lifting it out of the water; it can only struggle, suspended for a while between her flippers. Such admonishment usually corrects the infant's behaviour.

'Aunties' have been observed in captivity. They have been seen herding young together during feeding times or during public performances to keep them, for example, from being hit by an adult falling back into the water after a jump.

## Care-giving or Epimeletic Behaviour

These terms are used to describe all types of behaviour in which one member of a species gives care to another. They can be divided for convenience into the attentions of an adult for young and the attentions of an adult for another adult.

When a member of the cetacean group is injured, colleagues may simply remain in close proximity to the distressed animal. Whalers recognized this behaviour and termed it 'standing by'. On occasions these care-giving colleagues may approach the injured animal and, swimming around it in circles, attempt to guide or push it away from danger. They may try to bite through a harpoon line, attempt to get between the hunter and hunted, and occasionally they have overturned whaling boats. On rare occasions uninjured animals have been seen to support an injured colleague at the surface.

Care-giving behaviour among cetaceans has been observed and reported since the earliest times. Aristotle records an incident in which a group of dolphins followed their school mate, which was wounded and captured by fishermen, until the captors relented and released it. Aristotle also mentions a pair of dolphins which supported a dying colleague at the surface.

Care-giving behaviour both by the mother to its young and by one adult individual to another has been studied and recorded in a fairly large number of species, both among the odontocetes and the mysticetes.

Our knowledge of care-giving or attentive behaviour in the mysticetes is scanty. Several reports by whalers suggest, however, that the blue whale which tends to move in bisexual pairs, does show concern for its kind. Some suggest that the male is the more chivalrous and will attempt to protect an injured female while the female leaves her mate to his fate if he gets into trouble. Whalers used this information, we are told, and tried to ensure the female's capture first.

Humpback whales, *Megaptera novaeangliae*, have a well-developed maternal devotion. Whalers again used their knowledge of this species' behaviour and tried to injure or kill the offspring, to ensure that the female remained close by. Several observers have reported a female humpback manipulating the calf to safety or positioning her body between the calf and the danger. It is said that the male will turn to protect his mate and young if attacked, will attend his wounded or dying female and can be relied upon to try to frustrate the whalers in their task. The female, on the other hand, has been reported to cast a casual glance at her injured mate and go on her way. It should in fairness be said that other stories, more generous to the female's loyalty, have been recorded. Females have been said to remain attentive to their dying mate until they themselves suffered the fate of the harpoon.

Whalers from New Zealand in the late nineteenth century had the unpleasant custom of giving the right of capture of female right whales, *Eubalaena glacialis*, to the ship which secured her young, because her devotion to her offspring was legendary. She would continue to swim near her young until she too was caught. Very similar behaviour has also been observed in the white whale, *Delphinapterus leucas*.

Support for wounded young or adults has been recorded in all species of odontocetes which have been studied in detail by experienced observers. Attending adults circle a wounded colleague, become excited, may attack the tormenting boat, and

have, on occasions, broken harpoon lines. In some cases the mother has been seen to support her dying offspring at the surface, enabling it to breathe.

It is difficult to resist the temptation to lapse into sentimentality about whale behaviour. Males are most protective of females and young but according to most observers leave other dying males to their fate.

## Learning

Although the distinction between instinctive and learned behaviour is somewhat arbitrary, it is an animal's ability to learn, or modify its behaviour which allows it to adapt to a change in the environment. Very broadly one can say that learning is more important to mammals than to all other animal life. The cost of laboratory experiments in cetaceans has hindered rapid advances in this field. The presentation of public displays in dolphinaria gives some indication of their ability to learn to perform tricks. In these they are seen to respond to both sound and visual stimuli.

Evidence of mimicry or imitative learning is scanty and depends largely on casual observations, but as the evidence grows, it is likely to be shown to be of real significance.

Interest by the American navy in the possible value of the Cetacea for use in warfare (see Warfare) has been instrumental in demonstrating these creatures' ability to learn with the aid of operant conditioning techniques. Operant conditioning depends on reward and punishment. Cetaceans are trained by rewarding them with fish for the completion of a successful trick. Punishment is usually inflicted simply by the trainer leaving the side of the pool. To these friendly creatures, which apparently enjoy social and even physical contact with the trainer, this seems punishment enough.

In recent years the mental abilities of the Cetacea have been much publicized. The size of the cerebral hemispheres and the development of the higher centres in the brain have astounded scientists. The relative size of the brain suggests to some workers that its mental capacity may well be greater than that of the anthropoid apes. To others, this has not been demonstrated.

Detailed scientific experiments which tested a bottlenosed dolphin's ability to recognize a great variety of shapes and signal its interpretation to the experimenter, proved its adeptness.

It is to be anticipated that psychologists will extend the work already undertaken on the Cetacea and that comparisons will be made with other mammalian species.

It should however be remembered that intelligence is a difficult factor to evaluate since it is intimately related to an animal's relationship with its environment, and, as often as not, apparent differences in intelligence relate more to variable manipulative or memory capacities than to a particular creature's ability to assess a problem and deduce its solution.

## Mating Habits

One of the most important areas of cetacean behaviour concerns their mating habits. While it may appear strange to the layman that different species of whales, which seem to be virtually indistinguishable, maintain genetic purity and do not crossbreed, variations in courtship behaviour are chiefly responsible for their clear delineation. Thus the male's courtship display only stimulates response in the female of his species.

In captivity, however, male dolphins have been observed copulating with females of different species; this is perhaps due to the unusually close proximity of various species in the artificial confines of an aquarium, see p. 19.

Cetacean courtship display varies considerably. Exhibitions of swimming skill may be used alone or in combination with flipper waving or fluke signals. Leaps, or series of leaps, are seen in some species. The angle of leaving the water is also often of significance. Touch is extremely important to cetaceans, and they stroke one another with their flippers and brush against each other's body.

In the wild, observations of their mating habits are rare, and knowledge is, at best, fragmentary. Part of the explanation may be that the act of copulation only lasts for a few seconds. Humpback whales, however, have been seen to rise vertically from the water and appear to copulate belly to belly, though it is possible that the adoption of this vertical position is simply part of their preliminary love-play. Horizontal positions have also been observed, both animals turning on their sides.

## CAPTIVITY

In 1862 the London Zoo made its first attempt to keep a dolphin (the common dolphin – *Delphinus delphis*) in captivity. It died the day after its arrival. Since then, particularly in recent years, there has been a considerable increase in the number of cetaceans kept in captivity. In Great Britain the new fashion began in the 1960s and by the end of the decade there were about 6 dolphinaria displaying performing dolphins before the public. 2 years later the number had more than doubled and the trend continues. Figures for the United States are unknown but undoubtedly the figure is quite high and growing rapidly. Other parts of the world, including Japan, Europe and Australia, all have their own crop of dolphinaria with little legislative control and generally even less understanding. The vast majority of these watery circuses have no other function than to titillate tired crowds of humans and in so doing make a profit. The welfare of the animals is of interest only in so far as it affects the economics of the operation.

The small Cetacea usually exhibited are highly intelligent active creatures who range naturally in complex social groups over vast areas of open sea. To restrict them to the confines of a small, quite inadequate pool for our pleasure reveals the paucity of man's morality.

A survey undertaken a few years ago disclosed that the average life span of dolphins in captivity was between 5 and 6 months. Improved knowledge, more advanced technology and better veterinary attention has raised that figure to over 2 years. On any criteria this is an appalling record. It is true that some establishments have maintained animals in good health for many years but these are the exception not the rule.

Research workers have not been slow to appreciate the fascinating physiological mechanisms which members of the Cetacea have evolved in their conquest of the aquatic environment. The smaller Cetacea have become exciting new research tools. The need to keep them in captivity for research purposes has led to investigations into their care and management in captivity. Undoubtedly this has produced a beneficial spin off for the commercially confined creatures.

As with any captive animal, the greatest period of danger is the first few months of captivity. Young animals, less than 2 or 3 years of age, are more susceptible to adaptive failure than mature animals. Experience has shown that the period required for an animal to adapt to captivity may be several months. Some animals are temperamentally unsuited and never adapt. These should be released.

Although the commonest species kept in captivity are the bottlenosed dolphin *Tursiops truncatus*, and the common dolphin *Delphinus delphis*, over 15 species have been exhibited over the years. These include Risso's dolphin *Grampus griseus*, the finless porpoise *Neophocoena phocoenoides*, the false killer whale *Pseudorca crassidens*, the Pacific white-sided dolphin *Lagenorhynchus obliquidens*, the Amazon dolphin *Inia geoffrensis*, the Ganges susu *Platanista gangetica*, various species of *Stenella* and last but by no means least the killer whale *Orcinus orca*.

A killer whale was first exhibited to the public in the Vancouver Aquarium in 1964. Since then several have been shown around the world. In addition to the normal jumping and retrieving tricks which closely resemble those of the bottlenosed dolphin, it has become customary for trainers to ride on the back of these beautiful but dreaded creatures, a daring if rather sick exhibition. A pair have been kept together in Miami in the hope that they will breed. The 3-year old male when first captured was 4 m. long and weighed nearly a tonne. In 4 years he had grown to 6 m. in length and weighed over 2 tonnes.

Though named 'Sea Devil' by the Romans, the killer whale, *Orcinus orca*, is remarkably receptive to training. Here, one is being directed to turn left by its trainer who places one hand on its back and the other on its dorsal fin.

*Opposite* A dolphin performing at the Miami Beach Seaquarium, Biscayne Island, Florida.

Deep water cetaceans are caught with what is in reality a larger edition of the fishing net used by small boys. As the animal rides the bow of a ship the operator slips the net over it; this requires some skill. When the animal surfaces an attendant jumps into the water and helps to get it into a sling so that it can be swung aboard.

Coastal shallow water species, notably the bottlenosed dolphin, can be driven close to shore and encircled with a net. They are then simply lifted aboard small boats within the netted region. Killer whales are also captured by driving them close to shore and catching them individually. Unfortunately, however much care is exercized by the catchers to protect animals, many are wounded and do not receive treatment until they reach their destination.

The animal is transported to its pool. This may entail a long journey in specially designed apparatus. (See Transportation.) On arrival at their new home some animals, upset by the traumatic business of capture and transportation, are unable to swim normally. They must therefore be diligently watched until they are able to re-orientate themselves. Newly captive animals are normally kept in a quarantine pool for a period before mixing them with the other inmates to prevent the spread of disease.

A further problem is to encourage the animal to eat. While some take dead fish immediately, others will decline for several days. These must be carefully encouraged until hunger overrides their fear. Captive cetaceans are normally fed on fish. This is preferably fed fresh, but in many cases distance from source will dictate that frozen fish is used. Providing care is taken in handling it, this is perfectly adequate and consistent with good health.

Different species of fish have been used some of which are deficient in certain minerals and vitamins which must be added as a feed supplement. For practical purposes it is better to feed a variety of fish species than one alone. This helps to prevent the deficiencies mentioned above, and prevents psychological boredom on the one hand, which may lead to an indifferent appetite, and preference for one species alone on the other which is embarrassing if the supply suddenly declines. In the absence of reliable work on the nutritional require-ments of captive Cetacea, however, vitamin supplements are usually administered in the form of multivitamin capsules placed inside the dead fish.

Psychological problems associated with captivity, including refusal to feed, can be aided with a little human understanding but all too often resist therapy. The physical environment, however, is much more under man's control and it is his responsibility to ensure that nothing is spared in order to achieve the best conditions possible.

It is essential that the water in which they live is at the correct temperature, salinity and pH, and that it is physically clean and free from chemical and biological pollutants. The temperature requirements vary a little with species but experience shows that most Cetacea can adapt to a wide variety of water temperatures. It is preferable however to make temperature changes slowly, and, during the early stages of captivity the water is best maintained at the temperatures from which the animal came.

Correct salinity is essential for most captive cetaceans if they are to be kept healthy for any length of time. Needless to say this does not apply to the freshwater species. The salinity of sea water varies from 25 to 34 parts per thousand (ppt). Sodium chloride or preferably a mixture of marine salts must be added to fresh water at this rate. Similarly the pH (hydrogen ion concentration) or acidity of the water must be between pH 7.7 and 8.0.

Starting with water of the correct composition is not enough. It must be maintained in that condition. Unlike the natural oceans where the complex composition buffers the water against change – until man began to use it as a rubbish dump! – the small amount of water in a pool rapidly becomes contaminated with the animal's excreta and dead food. Micro-organisms – bacteria, fungi and viruses – gradually increase in quantity unless steps are taken to prevent them. There can also be a build up of toxic chemicals, which may be placed in the water deliberately to assist in depressing the build up of bacteria, or be absorbed from the air. The most commonly employed chemicals to control bacterial growth are chlorine and copper.

One of the simplest ways of maintaining water purity is to fence off a piece of ocean out at sea or near the shore and keep the animals in it. Naturally water flow will keep the water in equilibrium. Obviously such a situation is rarely practical and land pools are common. If these are near the coast clean sea water can be continually pumped into the tank. Care must be taken to ensure that it is not polluted by human sewage or industrial waste. In most inland dolphinaria however artificial sea water is prepared and circulated through expensive and complex filter systems. Methods of filtration vary considerably but all should aim at a complete water change every 2 to 3 hours depending on the density of the inhabiting population.

Remembering that cetaceans breathe air it is not surprising that purity and temperature of the air just above the pool is as important as the water in which they swim. The psychological stress of captivity, coupled with physically unsuitable, often biologically polluted air, combine to cause pneumonia among confined Cetacea.

Finally a word about the dangers of ingesting foreign bodies. Many animals have suffered a most unpleasant end after they have swallowed objects left in the pool by a thoughtless public. Small cetaceans have a large brain and are naturally very curious. They enjoy investigating strange objects, often taking them into their mouths. If swallowed they can become lodged in the gut, cause inflammation, secondary infection, and often death.

In view of the concern for conservation of Cetacea one is justified in questioning the value of dolphinaria which do no more than entertain. Because of the poor average record of the captive animal's lifespan and the severe restrictions placed on captive individuals in fulfilling their behavioural potential, we are right to feel disquiet for their welfare. In addition we might examine the motives and values of the spectators who derive no more than a transient period of superficial pleasure from this aquatic vassalage.

To these questions there is no simple answer. Together with the entertainment aspect is, inevitably, linked captivity for scientific purposes. The advantages to be gained from research are discussed elsewhere. (See Warfare.)

To some the spectacle of performing animals is distasteful and degrading to the watched and the watcher. Conversely it can be argued that it serves to heighten the observer's awareness of these creatures. For the first time the public at large comes into close contact with these intelligent and delightful animals. They become more than a figure on a conservation pamphlet, more even than a figure in a colour film. They become personalities, living, breathing, engaging individuals and this may do much for conservation by mobilizing public opinion in their favour.

Since we live in a world of compromise, not absolutes, it is probably simpler to accept the reality of captive dolphins. In so accepting however we must ensure adequate legislative control over those who keep them and institute research to improve their captive conditions.

## CARDIOVASCULAR SYSTEM

The cardiovascular system of the Cetacea is based on the normal mammalian structure. In spite of obvious requirements to modify its physiology to allow for its aquatic environment and the need to spend periods under water when breathing is impossible, the cetacean cardiovascular system contains no features which are not found in terrestrial mammals.

The cetacean heart is a normal 4-chambered mammalian type. It has a somewhat thicker-walled right ventricle but in other ways is unexceptional. As might be expected the fast-swimming, active species have a relatively larger

The heart of (left) a porpoise, (right) a fin whale. The different shapes are governed by the shape of the thorax. The porpoise heart tends to the longer shape found in a more active animal. (Neither heart is drawn to scale.)

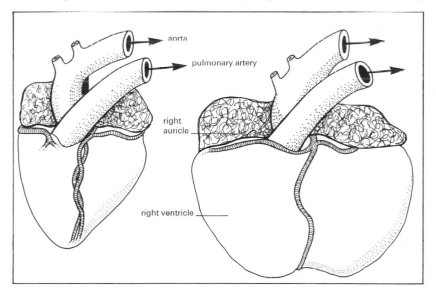

33

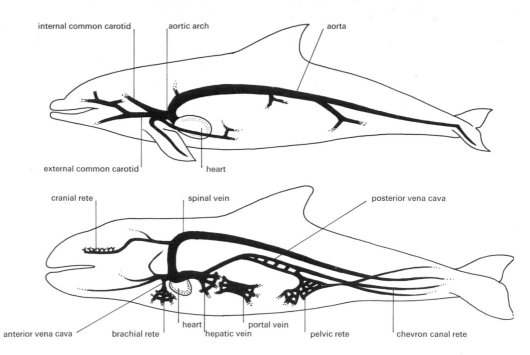

internal common carotid    aortic arch    aorta

external common carotid    heart

cranial rete    spinal vein    posterior vena cava

anterior vena cava    brachial rete    heart    hepatic vein    portal vein    pelvic rete    chevron canal rete

The main arteries (top), and (below) the veins and brachial and abdominal *retia mirabilia* in a dolphin.

heart-to-body weight than the larger, more sluggish species.

A feature of the cetacean cardiovascular system is the large structures known as *retia mirabilia*. These are networks of blood vessels embedded in fatty tissue. *Retia mirabilia* are not exclusive to Cetacea; they are also found in land mammals, principally the primates and the sloths. Retial tissue may vary in structure and composition with species and siting in the body. It is fairly widely distributed and is found in the cranium below the brain and around the optic nerve; in the cervical region it surrounds the neck bones; the largest single mass extends dorsally to the lungs, from the anterior part of the thoracic cavity to the lumbar region. It is found surrounding the spinal cord. It is associated with the gonads, both male and female, and adjacent to the pelvis. Finally in the tail the *rete caudale* runs in the haemal canal.

The function of the *retia mirabilia* is not fully understood. Since they occur in other land mammals they clearly cannot be a specific adaptation to an aquatic life. They act as a blood reservoir but not in sufficient quantities to be of significant advantage during a prolonged dive. They may well help to ensure a regular flow of blood which, without them, would be affected by pressure changes or muscle move-

ment. In certain areas of the body they may have a heat-control function. It seems likely, however, that their main function is to prevent sudden pressure variations to vital organs during a deep dive.

The cetacean arterial system is little modified from the mammalian design (see diagram). The carotids are slightly unusual in dividing into the internal and external branches as soon as they leave the aortic arch; thus there is virtually no common carotid. The internal carotid forms the carotid sinus and then diminishes in size. It retains a minimal function but is not the main blood supply to the head, a task assumed by the vertebral arteries.

The Pinnipedia are noted for very large veins. The Cetacea have no such distinction. Considerable variation between species is apparent in the posterior vena cava. It may be duplicated quite far anteriorly, or several pelvic veins may unite to form a single vessel posteriorly. Several anastomoses join the posterior vena cava to the extradural veins in the vertebral canal. Two large veins, or in some species one, run below the spinal cord.

Comparing the situation with Pinnipedia, the hepatic veins show some dilation in the odontocetes but not in the mysticetes. No hepatic sinus has been identified. Again, in comparison with many of the Pinnipedia, there is no caval sphincter, although some muscular control may be exercized on the posterior vena cava by muscle bands from the diaphragm.

Most of the blood returning from the cranium passes through the intravertebral vessels. Some drains via a venous plexus to the jugular vein. (See Diving.)

## CLASSIFICATION

Taxonomists divide the Cetacea into 3 suborders: Archaeoceti, Mysticeti and Odontoceti. The Archaeoceti became extinct in the Miocene epoch (*c*. 25 million years ago). The living cetaceans are clearly differentiated. The Mysticeti include all of the baleen whales, and the Odontoceti the more numerous toothed whales. The relationship between them in evolutionary terms is uncertain. (See Evolution.) The mysticetes are divided into 3 families – Balaenidae, Eschrichtiidae, Balaenopteridae – while the odontocetes are considered in as many as 10 families by some authorities    Del-

phinidae, Globicephalidae, Grampidae, Kogiidae, Monodontidae, Orcaellidae, Phocoenidae, Physeteridae, Platanistidae, Ziphiidae.

## CONSERVATION

It would be foolish to pretend that man is the only enemy of the whale. For reasons which are still not entirely clear, the dinosaurs succumbed to environmental pressure. Something like 70 million years ago man appeared on earth. Environmental changes outside the control of man could take place, and indeed many have in recent years, which would ensure the decline of whole populations. It is equally clear to any interested individual who examines the facts impartially, that to excuse man's complicity in the modern catastrophe would be naïve. Pollution disturbs the ecosystem and interferes with food chains and interspecific balance to challenge the whale's environmental adaptation. Consideration of the facts, however, shows that man's exploitation of

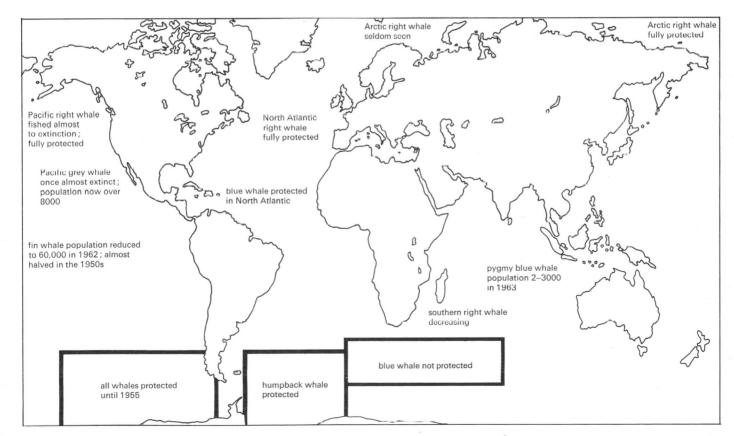

Whale map.

the whale populations for short-term profit threatens the survival of these noble beasts.

The only world organization which has any direct responsibility for controlling the whaling industry is the International Whaling Commission (IWC). This is a voluntary body set up over 25 years ago by interested nations to consider the problems of whale consumers, the whaling industry, and whale conservation. There are some 15 member countries represented, including Japan and Russia both of whom still hunt the 'great' whales. Critics of the IWC suggest that its very constitution commits it as much to protecting the interests of the whaling industry as to the interests of whale conservation. Inevitably in such an organization which has no powers of enforcement and from whose decisions member nations can dissent, there has been a long history of politically expedient compromise. Such a voluntary body remains in existence only by the grace of its members. In order to retain the interest and membership of Japan and Russia it has been necessary to make so many damaging compromises that respect for IWC's influence has markedly declined.

In 1972, at the Stockholm conference on the human environment, a resolution was passed calling for a 10-year moratorium on all whaling activities. Pressure continued and in 1974 the annual meeting of the IWC held in London considered the proposal, not for the first time.

The scientific committee of the IWC advised that no such total ban was necessary, indeed they suggested that catching of some species may be essential in order to maintain a balance between species and allow for the rarer ones to increase their numbers. The IWC adopted an Australian amendment to the proposal which defined the basis of future whaling activities, dividing the whales into 3 categories. The first – 'protection stocks' – will not be hunted at all. The second – 'sustained management stocks' – may be taken at controlled levels. Thirdly – 'initial management stocks' – which are said to be abundant, are subject to commercial whaling where the stock is above the maximum sustainable yield, 'providing there is no risk of over-exploitation', whatever that means.

The adoption of this amendment effectively placed the control of whaling with the scientists on the scientific committee. The scientific committee bases its calculations on the quantity of harvest the whale population can withstand on the maximum sustainable yield (MSY). This concept has been extrapolated from the studies on fish population and the fishing industry. Basically it assumes that the size of any animal population fits the environment in which it finds itself. At that density, deaths equal births. The reproductive level is controlled by a variety of psychological and physiological mechanisms to ensure stability. If such a population is hunted then the reproductive effort will be increased to restore the balance. This situation is however dynamic. If the population is reduced below a certain level, i.e. there is over-hunting, the reproductive ability of the remaining population cannot make up the losses and the population declines. The MSY is the highest number of animals which can be taken from a population and still allow the remaining population to make good the deficiency. Figures for these calculations suggest, for example, that the MSY level for many fish populations is 50 per cent of the original population. Statisticians have produced figures based on population models for whales which also suggest an MSY of 50 per cent.

It will be remembered that the calculation of MSY requires a knowledge of the original population size. This figure is totally unknown for the pre-whale hunting era and to pretend that estimates are more than wild guesses is ludicrous. It is equally ludicrous to suggest that there is any real knowledge of present populations. Guesses are made based on sightings by whalers and by the number of whales caught compared to the effort involved. By using statistical methods of one kind or another scientists claim accuracy, but so do statisticians associated with opinion polls and the world is aware of their validity. The truth is that the calculation of the MSY is based on unsubstantiated information.

Far too many respected and informed scientists are sceptical of the deliberations of the IWC's scientific committee for one to have any confidence in its figures. The concept of MSY was worked out in fish and here it has some substance. Fish populations are larger and the potential for increased production infinitely greater and quicker. Even here, however, serious errors have been made by the scientific advisers. The decimation of the Peruvian anchovy population to a point from which it may never recover is a classic but not isolated example. When one considers whales, one is immediately aware that a very different situation exists. Fish can more easily rectify a mistake by the scientific world. Whales have a slow reproductive replacement, producing only one offspring per female every 2 or 3 years. A miscalculation by the statisticians may therefore be devastating in its implications. It has also been shown that serious social disorder within an established whale group which effectively reduces reproduction, may be a result of hunting activity. In addition, a serious depletion in the density of a whale species may upset the dynamics of the ecosystem to such an extent that it would be impossible for the whale to recover its original status, its ecological niche being filled by other species of whale or indeed by different animal groups.

The degree of extrapolation usually necessary when calculating the MSY gives rise to a great deal of justifiable concern. There is little doubt that the risk of error is not only possible but probable. The example of the Peruvian anchovy should not be ignored. There is no evidence, with the possible exception of the California grey whale, *Eschrichtius gibbosus*, that a total ban on hunting once the population has dropped to dangerous levels results in an increase to former levels.

Even if the calculations of population size and the resulting MSY were correct for a stable population, there is no evidence that whales conform to this pattern. While some species of animals in some environments have relatively stable populations, others are subject to great fluctuations. If the latter proved to be the situation in whales it would make nonsense of the MSY.

There is, all too clearly, insufficient hard fact for the scientific committee of the IWC to recommend annual harvest numbers.

Critics of the IWC claim it is inaccurate in its scientific assessment, ineffective in enforcing its dictates, that only part of its energy is directed to conservation while the rest, many feel most, of its effort is concerned with complicity in the commercial exploitation of whales. They call for the establishment of a new body with more effective powers. The expectations for such a new body are sanguine. Such anticipation is misplaced. It would be under the same political pressures and vested interests as the IWC. If it proved a political embarrassment it would be emasculated. The only real hope is that the whaling nations develop a conscience.

## DIGESTIVE SYSTEM

It is surprising that apart from obvious differences in the mouth region between odontocetes and mysticetes, the rest of the alimentary canal is very similar.

The staple diet of the mysticetes is krill composed mainly of small crustacea. In order to obtain sufficient quantities of this plentiful material the baleen whales have developed a unique method of sieving them from the sea. From the upper jaw hangs a series, sometimes several hundreds, of long thin plates known as baleen plates (see Baleen Plates). These are fitted quite close together so that the fringes of adjacent plates act together to prevent the krill escaping. To accommodate the plates the jaws of mysticetes are well arched (see diagram on page 17). The lower lip is structured to ensure adequate closure of the mouth.

Interestingly there appear to be 2 methods of filtering the krill. Right whales swim through the water with their mouths open. The krill enter the mouth with the water. The build up of pressure in front due to the whale's forward movement causes the water to be continually forced out between the baleen plates. As this occurs the krill are trapped by the fringes of the baleen plates. At intervals the mouth is closed and the tongue collects the trapped krill and forces them to the back of the mouth where they are swallowed. Other whales, notably the rorquals with much shorter baleen plates, open their mouths, take a mouthful of sea water and then close the mouth again. The water is immediately forced out between the baleen plates and the krill swallowed.

Odontocetes have teeth (see Teeth) with which to secure their prey. These are not used for chewing as the prey is swallowed whole. Odontocetes therefore restrict their choice of food to suitably sized prey, mainly the smaller sizes of fish. The killer whale, *Orcinus orca*, however, has no inhibitions and eats anything which moves, from fish and sea turtles to other Cetacea, seals, penguins and inevitably large amounts of squid. Other odontocetes concentrate their predatory efforts on the slow-moving cuttlefish.

From the mouth the food passes into the oesophagus, the muscular tube which carries food to the stomach. Cetacean stomachs are divided into 3 compartments. The forestomach is really an enlargement of the lower end of the oesophagus, a fact easily recognized by examining the cellular lining or epithelium, which is composed of squamous cell epithelium. There are no glandular or digestive juices produced here. In the odontocetes stones are often present in this compartment, which, it has been suggested, may help to grind food as does grit in birds' digestive systems. Beaked whales, which feed primarily on soft cuttlefish, have a reduced number of teeth and a functionally less important forestomach since no crushing is needed prior to digestion.

The second compartment or true fundic stomach corresponds to the normal mammalian glandular stomach. Here digestion really begins. Digestive juices in the form of enzymes are poured into the cavity and mixed with the food. From the fundic stomach the food passes to another separate cavity, the pyloric stomach, sometimes called the connecting stomach. It also produces digestive juices but is rather narrow and tubular in shape. From this structure follows the duodenum, the first part of which is dilated to form a cavity known as the duodenal ampulla. Into this, in common with most mammals, passes the bile duct carrying bile from the liver, and the pancreatic duct which transports important secretions from the pancreas. As so often is the case with mammals, both ducts unite to form a common duct before finally entering the duodenum.

The liver is a bilobed organ and does not have a gall bladder associated with the biliary system. In this feature it resembles the horse. The pancreas closely resembles the normal mammalian pattern.

From the duodenum the food passes through the very long intestines. These can be over 150 m. in length as in sperm whales. The mysticetes usually have a well defined caecum and the large intestine

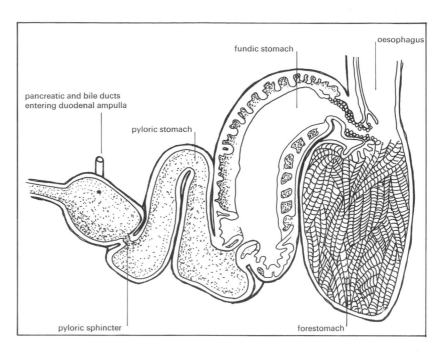

can easily be distinguished from the small intestine. Odontocetes however have no caecum and the change from small to large intestine is not easily identified, except in the beaked whales.
See also Ambergris, Baleen plates, Skeleton, Teeth.

A longitudinal section of the stomach of a bottlenosed dolphin, *Tursiops truncatus*.

## DISEASE

Until recently our knowledge of disease in cetaceans was restricted to casual field observations and haphazard reports from whaling expeditions.

One area of study which has received a good deal of attention since the middle of the eighteenth century is cetacean parasitology. This is not surprising since early biologists were great collectors and namers, and of course parasites taken from slaughtered whales could easily be popped into preserving fluid in small bottles and examined at leisure.

Clinical studies, diagnostic techniques in live animals, medical and surgical treatment had to wait for the technology enabling these creatures to be kept in captivity. Great advances have now been made possible by the interest taken in the Cetacea by the veterinary profession and allied disciplines. Management and disease are intimately related and it is the responsibility of the veterinary surgeon in charge of animals to ensure that every effort is made to maintain them in a suitable physical environment, to provide adequate food of the right type, and to cater for their social and behavioural needs.

The identification of sick animals remains the same whether the animal flies, walks or swims, is a bird, mammal, fish, reptile, amphibian or an invertebrate. The first indication of trouble is often evinced by changes in behaviour. This makes it imperative that animal attendants and veterinary surgeons familiarize themselves with the animal's normal behavioural repertoire. Any form of aberrant behaviour should be investigated at once. Animal attendants should also be instructed to report at once, any abnormal breathing, loss of appetite, vomiting, changes in the consistency of faeces or urine, discharges of any unusual kind from the eyes, blowhole, mouth, mammary glands or urogenital opening. Particularly important in the identification of disease is abnormal movements. Slow circling, head forced into corners, stiffness of flippers or flukes, loss of stability or simply a reluctance to move, often indicate disease problems.

It is at once obvious that simple methods used in clinical diagnosis on land animals present enormous problems in marine mammals. Taking temperatures, listening to the lungs and heart with a stethoscope, palpating parts of the body, collecting urine and faecal samples, taking blood samples are just a few of the techniques which take on a new perspective in aquatic mammals.

The normal body temperature of most cetaceans is about 37°C (the same as humans). As in most animals the best reading is obtained from the rectum. It is common to use one of the more modern thermometers depending on a thermocouple. The useful but older glass and mercury design are rather short for use in cetaceans. It should be noted that unless special provision is made to counteract the environmental change these animals will have a raised body temperature out of water.

Once controlled, in or out of water, auscultation and palpation become possible. An interesting technique, developed in relation particularly to the bottlenosed dolphin, involves placing the hand and arm of the clinician into the oesophagus of the patient and thereby enabling the palpation of such thoracic organs as the lungs and heart and the anterior abdominal organs including stomach and liver. It of course also provides a ready method of removing foreign bodies swallowed in error, an all too common problem of captive Cetacea who are assisted ably by the thoughtlessness of litter spilling humans.

Several methods of collecting faeces have been devised. By far the simplest is to have an attendant watch the animal in a small tank and collect it as it is produced. An interesting tip here is that faeces are in most cases passed 3–4 hours after feeding. Faeces are examined for colour and consistency. The most common reason for collecting faeces is the routine examination for parasites.

Urine samples not surprisingly are rather difficult to obtain. It is always necessary to catheterize the animal, that is, pass a fine tube through the external opening along the urethra and into the bladder. For this the animal is removed from the water.

The patient must come out of the water again for blood collection. Veins in the fluke or the flipper are commonly used.

Clinical techniques of diagnosis have moved further in all branches of medicine. Highly complex electronic methods are now used routinely. Radiography (X-ray), electrocardiography (heart readings), electroencephalography (brain readings), and radio telemetry, are all disciplines which have been applied to cetacean medicine.

Cetaceans suffer from a wide variety of diseases in all systems of the body. They sometimes have to endure heart disease, respiratory disorders, gastrointestinal upsets, disfunction of the urogenital system, and cancer. They suffer injuries and arthritis, have eye and ear diseases, and develop cirrhosis of the liver. There are however a few conditions which, whilst not specific to cetaceans, are of particular significance in them. The bacterial infection, erysipelas, is a common problem and in most well-run collections the captive cetaceans are vaccinated against it. Pneumonia is also a serious danger and where it proves a persistent difficulty in a collection poor management is indicated. The problem can often be traced to poor ventilation of the air levels directly above the water. It sounds a little bizarre but tonsilitis has been reported.

Fungal infections of the skin commonly result from skin disease or skin damage, just as with fish.

Foreign bodies have already been mentioned. It seems a normal part of cetacean behaviour to play with strange objects, manipulating them with their mouths and, inevitably, they are sometimes swallowed. Such behaviour creates problems for captive cetaceans who continue such behaviour and not infrequently swallow the odd-shaped objects made of a variety of substances which have been thrown into the dolphin pools.

At least 2 diseases, usually considered man's penalty for civilization and affluence, are found in cetacea – stomach ulcers and dental caries. Stomach ulcers are known to occur in several species of animal, including man, when they are placed in conditions of psychological stress. It would indeed be useful ammunition for those who abhor the keeping of cetaceans in captivity if this condition proved to result from the stress of captivity. Unfortunately it has been found in wild cetaceans. Dental caries have been often reported in sperm whales and in the Amazon dolphin *Inia geoffrensis*.

Finally, staying in the general area of the gums and teeth, a condition unique to the suborder Mysticeti is whalebone disease. This, in scientific terms, is an inflammation of the gums (gingivitis) resulting in the gradual loss of baleen plates.

Dosing cetacean patients causes problems for the clinician. So long as the animal is eating, medicines as tablets or fluid can be placed in the animal's food. Thus a succulent fish can secretly harbour a belly full of antibiotics inserted before presentation. Trained dolphins may be induced to open their mouths to allow manual administration. Failing this a stomach tube becomes necessary. If the oral route fails, or if clinical necessity demands, injections of medicines are possible. All the normal routes are available to the clinician including the muscles, blood vessels, and peritoneum.

Members of the veterinary profession have little more influence over the principal of keeping and using captive sea mammals than other citizens. Indeed opinion within the profession concerning the ethical and moral rights of the discussion are varied. The profession does have the duty as the responsible specialized group within society to ensure the health of all animals over which man assumes control. For this reason we can but applaud the efforts made by this small profession to discharge its social responsibility.

## DISTRIBUTION

It is not possible to generalize about the distribution of the Cetacea. Some species, the river dolphin *Lipotes vexillifer* for example, are very restricted in their distribution while others, like the killer whale *Orcinus orca*, are found in all oceans of the world.

There are two principal requirements which face an animal in any environment. It must have a sufficient supply of food and it must be able to reproduce its kind. To satisfy both these requirements, many cetaceans must migrate.

Cold water supports a good deal more microscopic life, in the form of plankton, and more krill than warm water. This is partly due to the fact that cold water carries more dissolved carbon dioxide. Naturally, krill-eating whales are found in greater abundance where krill is most plentiful. Similarly, fish- and squid-eating species are governed in their distribution by the availability of food. However, as ice closes over the polar regions, particularly the Antarctic, whales are forced to move to warmer ice-free water.

Reproduction is the other factor governing the movements of many species. Much evidence has been accumulated which shows that breeding adults migrate to mate and give birth. A newly born animal, being small, presents a larger surface area compared to body volume than does an adult; it also has less body fat to protect it and therefore will lose more heat than an adult. The fact that pregnant females of some species move to warm water to give birth, may be related to heat conservation in the young.

The wide distribution of the food of many of the Cetacea means that some species are found in several different parts of the world. Others are restricted by temperature to, for example, tropical and subtropical seas, and the freshwater dolphins by necessity are restricted to certain river systems.

In recent years one method used to investigate

migrations of land mammals and birds – by marking them – has been used for cetacean studies. A marker dart which can be fired from a harpoon has been developed. When a marked whale is killed it can be identified and the marking authority can record details of its movements. Unfortunately this takes a great deal of time and money and it will be many years before a general picture emerges.

Since the discovery of transistors, telemetry has also been used to track whale movements. A small lightweight transmitter can be attached by surgery to a creature so that its movements can be followed by the research workers over many miles. Such a system, however, needs a battery of technicians and scientists, and is also time consuming and expensive.

Further evidence of distribution and migration comes from a study of marine micro-organisms carried by a captured animal. By identifying these microscopic creatures scientists can often deduce the host's sea of origin and the course of its journey.

In general the study of distribution requires a knowledge and understanding of, in this case, cetacean biology as a whole, and a detailed knowledge of the natural history of each species and the relationship it enjoys with its environment. The more information on distribution and migration available, the better equipped we will be to conserve endangered cetaceans by preserving their feeding grounds and, if necessary, policing the seas to prevent poaching.

## DIVING

One of the most difficult problems facing air-breathing animals which take the return path to an aquatic environment is respiration. It would not be inconceivable that nature would provide them with some kind of breathing apparatus to enable them to extract the oxygen dissolved in water, such as gills. This has not happened. All aquatic mammals retain the terrestrial pattern of air breathing which means that if they are not to remain constantly at the surface, modifications are required to allow for longer periods of submergence.

Cetaceans appear to have a low respiratory rate. At the surface the animal takes a short breath, completed in less than half a minute, followed by a few minutes rest. It takes several such breaths and then may take a deep dive. Relative to body size the volume of air inhaled is no greater than in land mammals. To compensate for this situation some 90 per cent of the air is changed at each breath (tidal air), in contrast to land mammals where the percentage is approximately 20 per cent, and again in contrast to land mammals, most of the oxygen is extracted from the inhaled air. These large percentage air changes are facilitated by the anatomical structure of the respiratory apparatus (see Respiratory Apparatus). In particular the diaphragm and the thorax are efficient and specially modified to ensure maximum inhalation and exhalation of the air. In addition, the lungs contain considerable amounts of elastic tissue so they can respond more quickly to pressure changes.

One of the problems facing human deep sea divers is the atmospheric nitrogen which under pressure becomes dissolved in the blood. Too quick a return to the surface causes the gas to bubble, like the gas in lemonade, and produces the painful and dangerous condition known as the 'bends'. It is clearly of great importance that such a condition is prevented in cetaceans, particularly deep-diving species. Human divers are continually breathing air while diving. This provides a constant supply of nitrogen for solution under pressure in the blood. Cetaceans have no such constant supply, taking down only the nitrogen of one breath. In the bron-

In sea mammals, a greater proportion of air in the lungs is changed at each breath. The maximum capacity, by volume, of the lungs and the tidal air per 100 kg. of body weight are compared in a terrestrial mammal and a range of sea mammals.

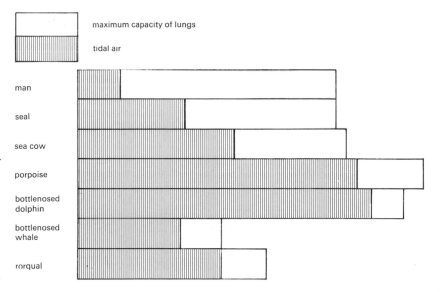

maximum capacity of lungs

tidal air

man

seal

sea cow

porpoise

bottlenosed dolphin

bottlenosed whale

rorqual

chioles, between the bronchi and the alveoli, are a series of valves which can effectively section the tubes into separate compartments. As the animal dives, the alveoli collapse, and the bronchiole valves close, effectively preventing high pressure in the alveoli and thereby stopping most of the nitrogen dissolving in the blood. It has been suggested that these valves remain closed during the deeper parts of the dive. Other functions of the valves have been postulated. They may in some way assist in the circulation of air in different compartments of the lung.

The lung capacity, as already stated, is no greater proportionately in the cetaceans than in land mammals and, since some species of cetaceans exhale before diving, it would seem that other factors are important in allowing a cetacean to dive deeply. Experimental work has shown that lung oxygen, even in species which have inflated lungs when they dive, is of little importance after the first 2 minutes of a deep dive. Indeed below 100 m. the alveoli will have collapsed, effectively preventing gaseous exchange. Therefore there must be other mechanisms to deal with the oxygen restriction.

**Heart and Blood Modifications.** As soon as the cetacean dives and stops breathing it is faced with a problem of restricted oxygen supplies. Taking priority for the available oxygen are the essential organs. As soon as the animal dives the heart rate slows down. In Cetacea this is less marked than in pinnipeds but it is still quite apparent. In addition there are alterations to the blood circulation. The brain in particular continues to be well supplied with blood, but the supply to muscles and less essential parts of the body is stopped. The amount of blood pumped by each heart beat declines. As well as conserving oxygen the restriction of supplies to the extremities prevents a good deal of heat exchange with the colder surrounding water and therefore also functions to conserve heat. With periodic interruptions to the muscular blood supply, adaptations had to be made by cetaceans in order that the muscles could continue to function. Cetacean muscles contain very large amounts, up to 10 times that found in land mammals, of a pigment called myoglobin. This acts as an oxygen store and provides a low level of oxygen

for muscle activity during the dive. A waste product of muscle activity is a substance called lactic acid. Experimental work has shown that during a dive the lactic acid content of the blood remains constant. As soon as the animal surfaces and the normal circulation of the blood is resumed the muscles pour their accumulated lactic acid into the blood so that it can be transported to those areas of the body where it can be disposed of. Blood samples just after a dive show a marked increase in blood lactic acid.

Body function, or metabolism, produces the waste product carbon dioxide. There is evidence that cetacean tissues are less sensitive to this substance than the tissues of land mammals. The need for its prompt removal is therefore diminished and the dive can be prolonged.

Another important adaptation is the large amount of blood relative to the size of the body compared to terrestrial mammals. This allows for increased storage and transport of greater amounts of oxygen within the body.
See also Cardiovascular System, Respiratory Apparatus.

## DRINKING
There is adequate experimental evidence that cetaceans take in sea water daily, although experiments also show that it is not essential for the animal to drink sea water. Smaller species probably consume up to 1500 ml. in every 24 hours. Figures for the larger species are not available. The cetacean kidney is efficient at concentrating urine and can easily deal with the sea water consumed. Indeed it may be taken in almost incidentally while feeding although there has been a suggestion that it does fulfil a nutritional need by providing essential minerals.

This is clearly an area which needs further physiological study.

## ECHOLOCATION
In the last three decades improved technology has allowed man to investigate the complex system of underwater hearing used by cetaceans. Using the basic mammalian apparatus, developed on land, cetaceans have adapted it for use in water so efficiently that hearing has become their primary

sense. Unlike the sharks and rays which have a well-developed sense of smell, the cetaceans have virtually dispensed with olfaction as a method of gaining information about their environment. Sight is moderately developed in some species, while the sense of touch is restricted to close contact.

The cetacean emits sound waves which create echoes used to furnish information about the general topography of an area, and to locate food. Sounds are also used to give warning of enemies and to keep in contact with members of their own species. This system resembles the Asdic or sonar used by navies to locate submarines or to gain information about the sea bottom. Basically three broad groups of sound are used. For information about the topography, low frequency clicks, which have great penetrating power, are used. For communication between members of the same species, somewhat higher frequency whistles are used, while the location of food may depend on higher frequency clicks. Coupled with these variations in frequency must go direction-finding. Both ears receive information independently, thus giving a directional fix which is then interpreted by the brain.

In order that the cetacean ear could be used for the reception of underwater sounds, modification of the land mammalian pattern, unsuitable for hearing underwater, was necessary. The middle ear has become much enlarged, and is more rigid since the pressures involved are greater while the movements of the enclosed structures are much less. The inner ear has also been modified to receive much higher frequencies since the same resolving ability requires frequencies four times higher in water than air.

When the normal air-adapted mammalian ears are placed in water they lose their direction-finding ability since the vibration caused in the skull by sound waves does not allow the animal to separate the reception of its two ears. In cetaceans the ears are surrounded by air-filled cavities which re-establish separate function and allow directional interpretation by the brain.

Experiments have shown that as well as gaining a great deal of information about the size and position of underwater objects, including the topography, cetaceans can probably decipher their form and even their structure. Such an ability is essential if food is to be identified. The experiments show that *Tursiops truncatus*, the bottlenosed dolphin, is able to distinguish between a piece of dead fish and an object of exactly the same shape using sound alone. It is assumed that cetaceans can detect differences in the reflection and absorption of sound waves by different materials.

The variety of sounds used by some cetaceans is legion. The bottlenosed dolphin has been the subject of much study and in this species clicks, quacks and whistles have been described. In addition, these animals may use both left and right nasal sacs independently; thus the right hole may whistle as the left clicks. The sperm whale, *Physeter catodon*, appears only to use clicks but has been postulated to identify itself with a signature sound enabling individuals to recognize each other.

It is now clear that the use of sound is of primary importance to the Cetacea and they have developed a wide series of different sounds and sonic techniques which allows them to exploit fully the physical apparatus. In addition the brain has evolved a very complex structure in relation to the reception and interpretation of sound. Structurally the cerebral cortex is similar to that of man. The sounds transmitted between animals of the same species are extremely complex. It seems probable that communication has reached a high degree of sophistication in the Cetacea. It should be stressed that most of our knowledge of sound communication comes from the Odontoceti and that it is not possible to attribute similar sophistication to members of the Mysticeti.

## EVOLUTION

At a first casual glance it is true to say that whales, dolphins and porpoises resemble fish. It is not surprising therefore that observers of nature from Greek philosophers to Linnaeus classified them thus. Linnaeus however eventually rectified his earlier mistake and placed the Cetacea with mammals. That the Cetacea are mammals rapidly becomes apparent if one examines their anatomy and physiology. Studies on cetacean behaviour also clearly delineate them from the simpler fish. In addition females nurture their young in their womb, feeding them through the placenta. Finally they suckle their young. All of these factors are so classically mammalian that a brief examination will convince even a sceptical observer.

Evidence that the Cetacea have their origins among land mammals comes from embryology. Although all traces of external hindlimbs have disappeared from modern cetaceans, examination of the developing whale in the womb of its mother shows quite clearly the early beginnings of hindlimbs, exactly as one sees them in land mammals. In land mammals these continue to develop into hindlimbs. In the Cetacea they disappear again very early in the embryo's life. All that remains in the adult are very small vestigial bones.

Having decided they are mammals, it is interesting to examine the pathway their evolution took. It is most unlikely that they evolved within a watery environment in isolation since studies have shown that mammals themselves evolved from land-living reptiles. It would be too great a coincidence for the mammalian pattern to have evolved independently on land from reptiles, and in the water from fish or primitive amphibia. It is therefore to the land mammals that we look for cetacean ancestors.

A good deal of conflicting evidence exists which has caused much scientific discussion. Some discoveries suggest close links between the Cetacea and primitive carnivores. The earliest known fossil, *Protocetus atacus*, which can definitely be classed as belonging to the cetacean line has features resembling the early carnivores but also shows early changes to the pattern of the cetacean skeleton. Other evidence however, including studies on chromosomes and proteins, gives weight to the theory that cetaceans developed from the ungulates and in particular the even-toed ungulates (artiodactyls) of which the cow, pig, and sheep are the best known examples (see p. 12).

Lack of adequate fossil record means that our evidence of early cetacean evolution is incomplete. We know that the earliest mammals, from which all other mammals have ultimately evolved, were primitive insectivores. The exact relationships and evolutionary pathways from these early mammals to the beginning of our fossil record, when the various groups were well defined, are for the present unknown. We can do little better than propose that from the primitive insectivore a line evolved which eventually divided into carnivores, ungulates and cetaceans. When and how these lines developed, and the exact relationship between them awaits further research.

It is equally unclear how the three suborders of Cetacea, Archaeoceti (now extinct), Mysticeti, and Odontoceti, evolved. Possibly they derive from separate but closely related insectivore-like mammals which each took to the water separately. The available evidence however suggests that all developed from one insectivore line which, once aquatic, rapidly branched.

Fossil records of the Archaeoceti have been found from the middle Eocene (*c.* 50 million years ago); they were extinct by the Miocene (*c.* 25 million years ago). Early archaeocetes retained many of the features of their land-living ancestors. From these early forms several branches developed. One line, a fossil of which was found in the southern states of America, was a long snakelike animal originally (in 1832) thought to be a reptile, and named *Basilosaurus*. Further study showed it to be an early cetacean *(Zeuglodon)*. Its length suggests that it moved with an undulating movement of the body. A second line produced several branches of smaller Cetacea which may have resembled modern dolphins in general features. The early snake-like *Zeuglodon* line seems to have become extinct in the upper Eocene while the smaller dolphin-like form persisted well into the Oligocene (*c.* 35 million years ago).

The evolutionary path of the baleen whales (Mysticeti) is incompletely understood. The first fossils positively identified as baleen whales are from the Upper Oligocene, very much later than the emergence of primitive toothed whales (Odontoceti). This, together with the evidence from embryology that baleen whale foetuses have teeth which are later absorbed as the formation of the baleen plates begins, strongly indicates that the baleen whales developed from the toothed whales. The divergence of pathways however must have been early since the Mysticeti retain some primitive characteristics now lost by the more specialized odontocetes. Just to stress the complexity of the relationships there is one fossil *(Patriocetus)*

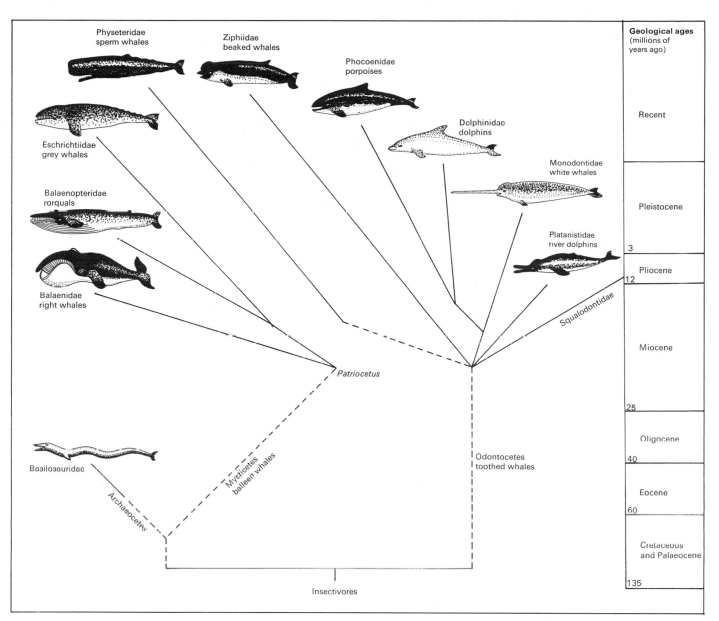

Physeteridae
sperm whales

Ziphiidae
beaked whales

Phocoenidae
porpoises

Delphinidae
dolphins

Eschrichtiidae
grey whales

Monodontidae
white whales

Balaenopteridae
rorquals

Platanistidae
river dolphins

Balaenidae
right whales

Squalodontidae

Patriocetus

Basilosauridae

Mysticetes
baleen whales

Archaeocetes

Odontocetes
toothed whales

Insectivores

Geological ages
(millions of
years ago)

Recent

Pleistocene

3

Pliocene

12

Miocene

25

Oligocene

40

Eocene

60

Cretaceous
and Palaeocene

135

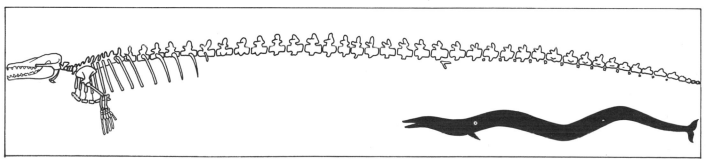

45

from the Oligocene which suggests that the Mysticeti may have developed from an offshoot of the Archaeoceti.

The earliest toothed whales were small cetaceans first identified in the Upper Eocene. It is possible that these primitive toothed whales originated as a branch of the Archaeoceti but there is no fossil record to support it. After a great deal of specialization, they eventually became extinct in the Oligocene. All showed a degree of telescoping of the skull similar to that found in the modern Odontoceti.

By the Lower Miocene early representatives of 6 modern odontocete families have been identified – Delphinidae, Monodontidae, Phocoenidae, Physeteridae, Platanistidae and Ziphiidae together with the now extinct Squalodontidae.

The Squalodontidae continued to develop along 3 main lines of evolution but eventually became extinct in the Pliocene (3 – 12 million years ago).

The Platanistidae, the freshwater or river dolphins, probably developed from early squalodonts. They have retained many primitive cetacean structures, such as a sternum and separate neck bones.

There is some fossil evidence which suggests that the modern ziphiids developed from the early squalodonts. The most primitive ziphiids – genus *Mesoplodon* – are found in the Upper Miocene and these developed into the modern genus *Mesoplodon* and also branched to form the genus *Ziphius*; *Hyperoodon* was an earlier and separate branch.

The origins of the Physeteridae are unknown. Already in the Lower Miocene members of this family can be identified with the structural provision for the spermaceti well established.

Origins of the Delphinidae, Monodontidae, and Phocoenidae are again shrouded in uncertainty. Some observers believe them to have originated somewhere along the branches which passed through the squalodonts and platanistid development. Others are equally convinced that they were differentiated earlier in the Eocene or Oligocene directly from the small toothed cetaceans mentioned previously.

It is apparent that many gaps remain in our knowledge of cetacean evolution. Fossil records are of great importance in filling in the missing information, but new techniques in science are also coming to the aid of the evolutionary scientist. Evolution of serum proteins, cytogenetics, embryology, geography and geology are among the many sciences that disclose slowly the secrets of the past.

Cytogenetics – the study of chromosome number and structure in the body cells of a species – has for example already cast serious doubts about some of the long-held beliefs of those who study cetacean evolution.

Patience and painstaking scientific detective work will hopefully complete, in time, a picture at present somewhat sketchily drawn.

## EXPLOITATION AND USES

Whales are hunted primarily for their blubber which produces oil, their meat, baleen or whalebone, and the 2 specialized products spermaceti and ambergris.

Man has exploited whales since very early times. Prehistoric middens of coastal people contain whale bones providing fairly firm evidence that they caught and used whales.

The Japanese have a long tradition of hunting the whale. Exactly how long it is impossible to say. It is thought that the primitive method of slaughter used possibly by neolithic man consisted of simply harpooning with hand spears, a dangerous and skilful operation. Later groups of whalers in boats cooperated to chase whales sighted from the coast into nets, there to weaken the victim with spears. Finally a brave soul would jump aboard the weakened whale and drive a spear into the beast so that it could be drawn ashore. These methods were used to catch the right whales, grey whales and the humpback.

European whaling began quite early in the eleventh century when the Basque coastal inhabitants caught them primarily for meat and oil. These coastal operations were gradually extended further out to sea. Since meat would not keep if the animals were caught far away from the coast it was fortunate for the hunters that oil and whalebone were valuable enough products to justify the effort.

Great developments in European whaling occurred in the seventeenth century. North-western

*Above* The early days of whaling, before the technological revolution of the 19th and 20th centuries led to the development of factory ships and sophisticated hunting methods.

*Above right* The industrial revolution led, by the 19th century, to steam-powered whaling vessels and harpoon guns replacing small boats and hand-thrown harpoons, making killing safer and quicker.

The capture of a whale is seen as a cause for general excitement in the Dutch 16th-century print *right*. The workers efforts are spurred on by the bagpipe player and flagbearer (left). In the background less fortunate whalers fall prey to fearsome monsters.

European countries began hunting Greenland right whales, *Balaena mysticetus*. They are relatively slow swimmers and were easily caught. Participants in this industry gambled their lives on huge profits. The cost of building and equipping a boat then was between £1000 and £2000. One whale would yield a profit of several thousand pounds in whalebone and oil and since 60 to 70 animals were an average annual catch it can be appreciated how easily man could be persuaded to venture to the icy northern waters.

Whalebone was of great value before the discovery of modern alternatives. It was used, classically, for female undergarments and the stiffening in crinolines, but its uses were far more extensive. Modern alloys have largely replaced its use.

Hunting activities decimated the arctic stocks of right whales, but with improved equipment, the slaughter continued well into the nineteenth century even though the animals were scarce. No thought of conservation for its own sake, or controlled cropping moderated the whalers' commercial greed.

Settlers on the east coast of America began whaling in the seventeenth century. They too concentrated on the right whale and later the humpback. Although the humpback is a rorqual, it is a good deal slower than most other rorqual whales and it migrates close to the shore – a convenient behavioural pattern from the whalers' point of view but definitely maladaptive as far as the whales were concerned.

The Russians set up whaling stations along their Pacific coast in the late nineteenth century, and the Australian and New Zealand settlers began whaling at about the same time.

Sperm whales, *Physeter catodon*, have unpalatable flesh and no whalebone, being odontocetes. They were left alone by the early whalers. However the growing demand for oil to make candles which developed among the early settlers in North America led the enterprising whalers to turn their attention to this vast natural source. It started in the late 1700s and reached its peak in the middle of the nineteenth century.

Hunting sperm whales from small rowing boats was a hazardous occupation and the men who pursued the work were tough and brave. From these dangerous times came the inspiration for the great whaling adventure *Moby Dick*. In general it was the bulls which proved so dangerous. They would lash out with their flukes and upset their tormentors, spilling them into the bubbling briny. Sperm whale hunting began to decline as other forms of lighting were discovered.

Indeed economics caused a decline in whaling generally in the late nineteenth century. Whalebone had been generally superseded. Oil from whales was no longer essential, being replaced with other lubricants, and the increase in transworld trade completely changed the economic structure of which it had once been a part.

Sadly the decline was transient. Modern technology was used by a new whaling industry. Fast ships meant that the rapidly moving rorquals, previously out of grasp, could be hunted. Explosive harpoons meant easier and quicker kills. Increased demands for soap and fat and meat for food again made whaling profitable. The important discovery of the food technologists which allowed whale oil to be hardened thus removing its unpleasant flavour and permitting its incorporation in margarine together with vegetable fats started the slaughter again. Longer range ships meant that the antarctic as well as the arctic waters were within reach. A European whaling revival was under way. Norway, Germany and Great Britain were soon joined by Japan and the United States in southern polar waters. In the early years of the twentieth century many nations exploited the whales of the southern seas. After the Second World War Russia sent a team of ships to join the bonanza. Today international whaling is subject to some limitations (see Conservation) imposed by the International Whaling Commission. The main products are still oil for soap and food and very specialized machine oils. Japan uses whale meat for food. To a large extent, until recently imposed bans by the United States and Great Britain, whale meat was used for pet foods. There are suspicions that it may still be so used.

Sperm whales are today still taken in some numbers to provide basic ingredients for cosmetics. Other whale products are used in small quantities.

Concern for conservation was rather late in emerging. Only in 1946 was the International Whal-

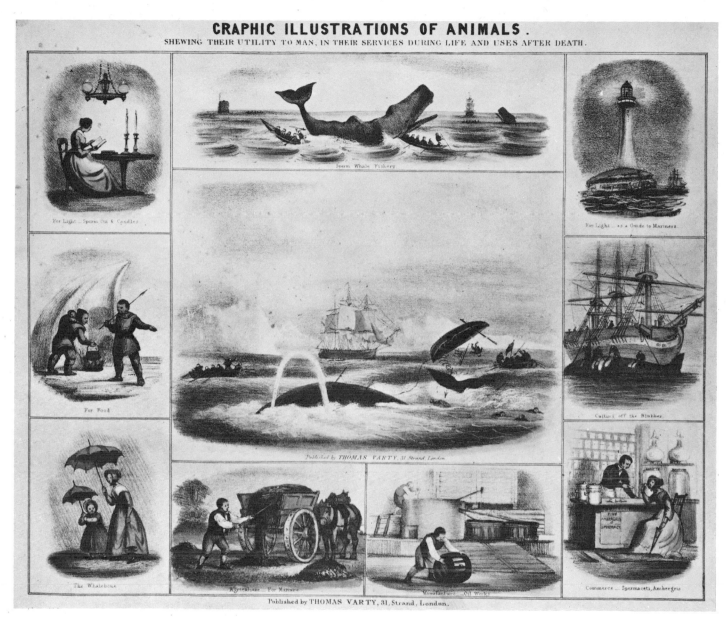

Published by THOMAS VARTY, 31, Strand, London.

ing Commission set up as a voluntary body by interested nations. Unfortunately it has no real power and has generally proved ineffective in control. This is a pity because properly harvested, the heritage provided by the whales, which belongs to all men not just the nations currently endowed with sufficient technology to exploit it, could be used as a continuing source of animal protein and fat. Proper control would also ensure the continued existence of these truly superb creatures.

The dramatic population increase of the 19th century led to a rise in demand for oil and cosmetics. This lithograph shows (centre) the perils of hunting from small boats, and the many uses to which whale products were put by civilized society, ranging from manure (centre bottom left) to scent (bottom right). It is only the primitive Eskimo family (centre left) who depend on the whale for food.

## GROOVES

Members of the family Balaenopteridae character-istically have a series of parallel ventral grooves running longitudinally along the throat, thorax and onto the abdominal wall. The grooves vary in width, depth and length with age and species. They are often 5–7.5 cm. deep and the same in width with a separation of several centimetres between grooves. Some species have a few grooves while others have over 100.

The function of the grooves has not been satis-factorily established. Experimental work has shown that when the throat is expanded the grooves disappear. It has been suggested, there-fore, that they enable expansion during feeding. In those species which eat krill such a mechanism would increase the volume of the intake. It also explains why right whales, which have modified jaws to increase capacity, have no grooves.

*Above* The gigantic tail of a whale is hauled aboard a factory ship.

*Opposite* Hunting from small boats is still carried on off the west coast of Portugal. Here one closes in for the kill as the harpooner in the prow prepares to throw a second lance.

*Left* A baleen whale being cut up by the crew of a Russian whaler, and showing distinctive grooves which run along much of the animal's length. These increase the capacity of the mouth when it is opened.

Right whales are slower swimmers than fin whales. This southern right whale, *Eubalaena glacialis*, is skimming the surface water for food. When sufficient has been filtered out by the baleens, the whale will dive, close its mouth and swallow the contents. Photograph taken in San Jose Gulf, Argentina.

Scientists interested in hydrodynamics have tried to show experimentally that the grooves help to reduce friction. Certainly species in the family with grooves are fast swimmers while those without are slow.

The most likely function is to allow distension of enclosed structures, whether this is the mouth for feeding or, as has also been suggested, the chest for breathing.

## HAEMOGLOBIN, MYOGLOBIN

Haemoglobin is a chemical carried by the red blood cells which acts as a transporting agent for oxygen. As the blood passes through the lungs the haemoglobin becomes saturated with oxygen; the oxygen loosely links to the haemoglobin, when it is known as oxyhaemoglobin. In the tissues the oxygen is released, and the haemoglobin takes up some carbon dioxide; the balance of the carbon dioxide is carried in solution in the blood serum. When linked to carbon dioxide, the haemoglobin is darker in colour and known as carboxyhaemoglobin.

In the muscles of many animals oxygen is taken up from the blood by a substance chemically very similar to haemoglobin of the blood which is called myoglobin. It stores oxygen for rapid use by the muscles. See also Diving: Cetacea, Pinnipedia, Sirenia.

## LOCOMOTION

Cetaceans, unlike fish which move their tails from side to side, get their propulsion by an up and down movement of the tail and fluke. The body is fairly rigid and the tail moves from a point about the vent. The flukes also move, continuing through the movement of the tail, to produce the thrust, which produces the forward motion. Their stability comes from the dorsal position of the lungs, to a lesser extent from the dorsal fin, and, particularly at speed, from the forelimbs. Turning is effected partly by the flippers but mostly by sideways movements of the tail and flukes.

Speeds attained vary considerably with the species. In general larger whales rarely exceed 5 knots, while the smaller dolphins and porpoises can move at over 25 knots. Some species can show great turns of speed over short distances while others maintain somewhat slower speeds for longer. Humpbacks, grey and right whales belong to the slow movers, keeping generally to between 2–5 knots although, if chased, able to top 10 knots for short periods. Surprisingly sperm whales have been observed moving at over 20 knots. Sei whales seem to be among the champions reaching over 30 knots for short sprints. Smaller dolphins of several species on the other hand can keep up a 25 knot average for quite long periods.

The design of the body has been adapted over geological time to improve locomotion. Basically there has been a reduction in the length of the cervical vertebrae and, in most species, fusion, thus reducing the length of neck, and allowing a more streamlined shape. The increase in the length of the lumbar and caudal vertebrae accommodates the powerful muscles necessary for tail movement. With the lengthened back has come an increased flexibility. The number of vertebrae has increased compared to land mammals, but they remain short. The flexibility derives from the increased number and enlargement of the intervertebral discs. It is interesting to note that the increase in length of back and the number of vertebrae can be traced through fossil records.

The particular properties of the cetacean skin and its relationship to the thick layer of blubber allow the shape of the body to vary dynamically as it passes through the water, thereby ensuring an

*Far left* The common porpoise, *Phocoena phocoena* (top), Risso's dolphin, *Grampus griseus* (centre) and the Atlantic white-sided dolphin, *Lagenorhynchus acutus*. Drawings by Archibald Thorburn.

*Below* Two common dolphins, *Delphinus delphis*, in the Cook Strait leave the water in a series of high speed leaps.

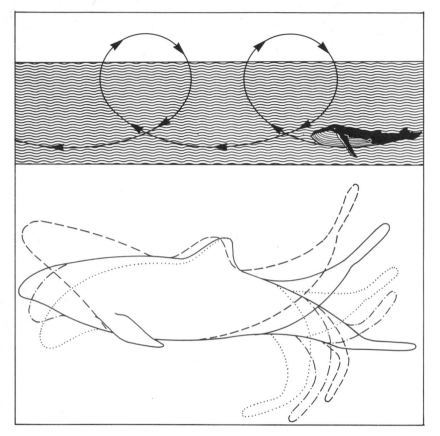
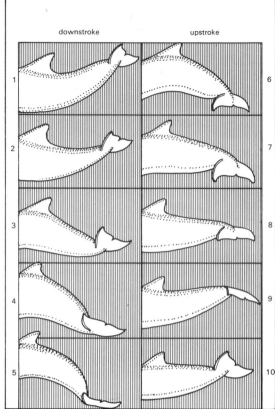

| | downstroke | upstroke | |
|---|---|---|---|
| 1 | | | 6 |
| 2 | | | 7 |
| 3 | | | 8 |
| 4 | | | 9 |
| 5 | | | 10 |

optimum streamlining at all times. A major impeding force to an animal is the resistance of the medium in which it is moving. Cetacea moving in water have to minimize the resistance of the water to their body. The mobility of the external shape ensures a laminar flow of the water past most of the body rather than the creation of turbulence.

Armed with these physical attributes the mechanics of movement become clear. Watching cetaceans jumping and diving, rolling and somersaulting however is not just a scientific study in movement. It is an aesthetic experience.

## LONGEVITY

Information about the age to which animals live in the wild is small indeed. Details of captive animals are more accurate but often bear little real relationship to the situation in the wild where environmental conditions vary considerably. The table below gives information about some of the species for which records are available.

| | |
|---|---|
| Sei whale, *Balaenoptera borealis* | 70 yr |
| Blue whale, *Balaenoptera musculus* | 95 yr |
| Fin whale, *Balaenoptera physalus* | 95 yr |
| White whale, *Delphinapterus leucas* | 40 yr |
| Common dolphin, *Delphinus delphis* | 30 yr |
| Killer whale, *Orcinus orca* | 40 yr |
| Sperm whale, *Physeter catodon* | 75 yr |
| Striped dolphin, *Stenella coeruleoalba* | 30 yr |
| Gill's bottlenosed dolphin, *Tursiops gillii* | 30 yr |
| Bottlenosed dolphin, *Tursiops truncatus* | 25+ yr |

## METABOLISM

Metabolism or the metabolic rate can best be thought of as the rate at which the body uses fuel or the processes associated with it. Metabolism is the name for the whole body working process. Anabolism is the term used to describe the building up process – the formation of new structures and repair of old, while katabolism is the breaking down for removal of old or damaged structures. The process is dynamic, both anabolism and katab-

Movement in Cetacea: (Top left) Humpbacks somersaulting off the coast of East Australia. (Below left) shows the flexibility of the body of a porpoise and (right) gives the analysis of tail and fluke movement in a bottlenosed dolphin: 1–5 downstroke; 6–10 upstroke.

olism proceeding at the same time. The rate at which these processes occur can vary considerably. They vary from species to species and from time to time.

The metabolic rate is largely controlled by the hormones of the body; in particular, the thyroid gland exercises general control.

Marine mammals in general have been found to have an increased metabolic rate compared to land mammals of similar body proportions. The reasons for this are interesting to consider. Cetacean and pinnipedian diets are basically protein and this itself increases the metabolic rate. This factor cannot however be the total explanation or their metabolic rate would not be greater than that of land carnivores. One of the problems facing aquatic mammals is the heat loss which results from continual immersion in a medium – water – which is a much better conductor of heat than air. It follows that there are advantages to an increased metabolic rate with the inevitable increase in heat production which accompanies it. There appears to be a dynamic relationship between the physiology and the environmental conditions. Several marine mammals have been shown to have enlarged thyroid glands and an increased thyroid hormone circulating in the blood, presumably in response to the aquatic environment. In addition animals in arctic or subarctic water have higher metabolic rates than those from warm seas.

A further interesting observation relating to their aquatic way of life is the great and quite sudden variations in metabolic rate of which marine mammals are capable. As they dive marine mammals have been shown in experiments to reduce their metabolic rate to half that of the resting animal. This is to conserve the available oxygen during the breath-holding process. See also Thermoregulation.

## MOULTING see Skin

## MUSCULAR SYSTEM

The basic mammalian musculature is retained although considerable modifications have occurred to adapt to the aquatic way of life. Clearly limb musculature is much reduced in importance in the forelimbs and totally absent in the hindlimbs.

Perhaps the most important general modification is that associated with the muscles of the tail used for propulsion (see Locomotion). The length of the back has been greatly increased to afford adequate attachment for the powerful caudal muscles. (See Skeletal System).

## MYTHOLOGY

The cetaceans have perhaps rather surprisingly been associated with man's history for thousands of years. Stone Age rock drawings depict the first record made by man of these creatures. Exactly what the relationship, or what the significance of the cetaceans to these primitive people was is not known. Rock drawings in Norway show probably the first record of whaling. A simple outline of (the proportions suggest) a whale is surrounded by several boats. Dots not unlike those in the palaeolithic wall paintings in south west France are arranged near the tail. Speculation tempts one to wonder if this is the point at which spears should be thrust. Alternatively the picture may simply portray one of the dangers of the deep for primitive sailors. More recently, Bronze Age and Iron Age figurines and ornaments depict dolphins quite frequently. The Mediterranean civilizations, who had emerged from prehistory earlier than the northern Europeans, were no strangers to the cetaceans. Their art abounds with dolphin decorations. The Greek poet Arion saved himself from death at the hands of sailors by playing music to attract dolphins who then carried him to safety when he jumped overboard to escape his persecutors.

Riding dolphins was a favourite theme in early mythology. The Roman Pliny relates the story of a little boy who rode a dolphin. A famous Roman mosaic floor at the Fishbourne Roman Palace in Great Britain illustrates a similar theme, where Cupid rides the dolphin.

Dolphins are constant attendants at the side of the sea god, whether he be the Greek Poseidon or the Roman Neptune. In general the Greeks regarded all cetaceans as special animals and did not hunt them.

The famous biblical myth of Jonah and the whale is too well known to be repeated, but it does illustrate that ancient peoples had a knowledge of these creatures and also a real idea of relative size.

One of the most interesting myths to emerge from later centuries is that of the fictitious unicorn. Whether the animal originated as a sea horse or not is unknown. It may have been based on the factual evidence of a narwhal tusk or as some would have us believe, had its roots in the oryx which, with straight twisted horns can, in profile, appear to have only one horn. Whatever the source of the tale there is no doubt that the narwhal tusk has often been exhibited as a unicorn horn in an attempt to prove the latter's existence. For centuries the horn has also been attributed

with magical properties. Again these may be in the narwhal's own right or derive from confusion with the unicorn.

Many stories, some undoubtedly true, of a close relationship between men and dolphins abound. Some dolphins have won worldwide fame by guiding ships through difficult sea passages. They have also been attributed with saving people's lives. Plutarch says of the dolphin that it is the only animal who chooses to associate with man with no other thought of reward than his company. Several ancient tales tell of dolphins helping to chase

Arion astride a dolphin. (J. A. Muller 1571–1628.)

fish towards fishermen so that they might be caught by net or spear. Both the ancient writers Oppian and Aelian record such stories and tell that the fishermen rewarded them with titbits later. In our less romantic days scientists have other explanations but in this section at least let us be romantic and forget factual reality. The scientist of course could be wrong because more recent tales of dolphins cooperating in the capture of fish come from Australia, Burma and Brazil, and are not so easily explained by sceptics.

It seems strange that animals which live in an environment so far removed from that of man could be so well recorded in the art and mythology of nearly all periods of his history, from the most ancient for which we have records to the most modern. From Stone Age man through far, near and middle eastern civilizations, across the Atlantic in the Americas, examples of Cetacea myth and art can be found. It is sad that modern man seems only to think of killing them or training them for acts of war. Far better Greek philosophy.

## NERVOUS SYSTEM

With the tremendous current interest in the behaviour and learning abilities of the Cetacea, which have been considerably investigated under scientific laboratory conditions in recent years, it is not surprising that there has been a concurrent interest in their nervous system.

The history of the investigation of the cetacean nervous system shows how difficult were the practical problems facing investigators. The literature is scanty. Early reports come from the seventeenth century. John Hunter, the intrepid anatomist, published an account in the late eighteenth century, and his nineteenth-century admirer, Frank Buckland, also took considerable interest in the Cetacea. In the twentieth century, even with the technical advances of modern science, there has not been what could be described as a flood of new literature.

The brain of the cetacean giants exceeds that of all other mammals in absolute weight and it this relatively large size of brain which interests and excites behavioural scientists.

The 2 living cetacean suborders differ in the shape and relative development of the brain and cranial nerves. Mysticete brains have cerebral hemispheres of moderate width while the odontocete brain is much wider than it is long. In both, the olfactory or smelling apparatus has markedly decreased in importance. In mysticetes it is still present, but reduced, while in the odontocetes it has disappeared completely.

The marked development of the trigeminal cranial nerve or fifth nerve in the mysticetes relates to the very sensitive area around the mouth. Odontocetes have the enlargement above the upper jaw known as the melon and this is thought to have a tactile as well as an acoustic function. Certainly it is well supplied by the trigeminal nerve. The eighth or auditory nerve is of importance in the odontocetes. It is the telencephalon, the most recently evolved forebrain, which shows such marked development in the Cetacea. The folding of the surface of the cerebral hemispheres is little short of that seen in man. Part of the development of the forebrain is due to increased needs for muscle control and coordination.

The reduced demand for balance in animals well orientated and structurally suited to their medium is reflected in a reduction of size in relevant parts of the cerebellum, the more primitive part of the brain.

The importance of hearing to Cetacea is reflected in the enlargement of those parts of the brain controlling this sense.

Much controversy still exists about the visual abilities of the order. Observations show that members can see well both in and out of water, although relationship to a brain structure needs more study.

The spinal cord is at variance with the typical mammalian pattern which shows enlargement for the 2 sets of paired limbs. The anterior swelling, however, remains surprisingly large in spite of a reduction in limb function. The lumbar swelling is certainly reduced but not entirely absent.

## REPRODUCTION see Behaviour

## RESPIRATORY APPARATUS

The external openings of the respiratory system — the nares — in all cetaceans have migrated to the top of the head. This allows the animal to breathe

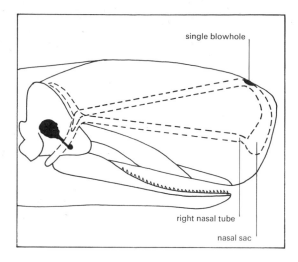

single blowhole

right nasal tube

nasal sac

without exposing much of its body above the surface. Baleen whales, like most mammals, have 2 external openings visible as 2 slits, but the odontocetes have a single crescent-shaped opening with the body of the crescent pointing forwards.

The external nares in odontocetes can be closed at will by means of a plug of connective tissue. There is a pair of tubes which pass from the external nares to the larynx. Surrounding the upper part of these tubes are several pairs of sacs, the purpose of which is not understood, which form complicated connections with the nasal tubes. Baleen whales similarly have 2 nasal tubes but without the complexity of the nasal sacs.

The larynx of the cetacea, in common with other mammals, is composed of a series of specialized cartilages and associated internal and external muscles. There are however considerable variations and modifications between species. It is surpising in view of their ability to make sounds that the cetacean larynx has no vocal cords.

From the larynx leads the windpipe or trachea; a wide tube surrounded in mammals by rings of cartilage. The shortened neck of all cetacea is reflected by the short trachea which is surrounded by several strong cartilaginous rings, many of which join together to provide very powerful protection. The trachea, as in other mammals, divides first into 2 bronchi which subdivide into a series of much branched bronchioles; these end in small sac-like alveoli. In many whales before the bifurcation of the trachea there is an extra bronchus

known as the accessory – which leaves the main trunk of the trachea giving an asymmetrical appearance to the lungs.

The structure of the cetacean and indeed pinnipedian lung tissue is modified for diving. The large airways – the trachea, bronchi, and fine bronchioles – are well supported with the cartilaginous rings and elastic tissue to assist the rapid movement of air in and out of the lungs. Compared to land mammals the supportive elastic tissue is much increased even in the finest bronchioles. In addition each alveolus has a double blood supply. There appears to be a relationship between the depth to which a species dives and its lung structure. The deeper diving species have the largest amount of elastic supportive tissue.

There can be little doubt that these modifications are part of the essential evolutionary adaptations which allow the Cetacea to exchange air efficiently during breathing and thereby extract such a high proportion of its constituent oxygen. See: Diving.

## SCRIMSHAW

This is the art of scratching or carving pictures on sperm whale *Physeter catodon* teeth and sometimes on whalebone, other kinds of teeth, or on shells. Many of the scenes produced by whalers themselves depicted the dangers of the hunt. Several classical examples show the mighty sperm whales spilling the contents of the small open hunting boats into the sea.

## SENSES

**Sight.** It is clear from behavioural observations that cetaceans do use sight but the importance of the sense is not completely known. They do move their heads; they move their eyes to attend and the pupils respond to bright lights by contracting. In animals that are primarily hunters it would be expected that the vision is stereoscopic. However physical examination of dolphins certainly suggests that, at best, their vision is only partially stereoscopic. The little experimental work that has been done with dolphins tends to be confusing rather than illuminating.

**Hearing.** There can be little doubt that this is the most important sense of cetaceans. It is used for

The odontocetes have one blowhole. In the sperm whale *far left* the 2 nasal tubes lead into a single nasal sac.

Intricate decoration on a whalebone stay busk of the first half of the 19th century, *below*.

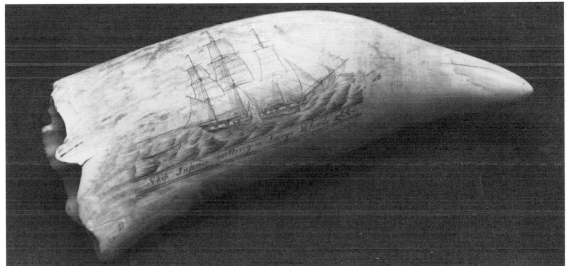

*Above* Whales, like all mammals, breathe air. Here two whales fight for air in a hole left in a frozen Antarctic channel.

The scrimshaw on this 20 cm.-long sperm whale tooth depicts the vessel *Japan*, registered in London, 1831, on one of its voyages to the South Seas.

communication between individuals over quite long distances.

There are the sounds which are usually within the human range and these are thought to be used for normal vocalizations, corresponding to the noises made by other mammals. They give an indication of the animal's emotional state.

Sounds like repetitive pulses, of very high frequency and above the human range are used for echolocation, somewhat like those used by bats. This has been developed by the Cetacea into a very sophisticated spacial sense (see Echolocation).

**Smell.** It would be premature to make definite statements but all the evidence suggests that cetaceans either do not smell, or that the sense is of very little significance.

**Taste.** There is anatomical evidence that the relevant areas of the brain are well developed. Behavioural observations confirm this evidence. Captive dolphins, particularly *Tursiops truncatus*, show definite food preferences. Even if the fish is chopped or finely sliced they can distinguish, suggesting that it is the taste or texture which is important.

**Touch.** Anatomically the evidence is against a sense of touch. The skin is thick and apparently quite ill-suited to sensitive reception. However the behaviour patterns exhibited, at least by the species of Cetacea kept in captivity, suggest otherwise. Many of them spend considerable time in physical contact with their colleagues. Certainly this is not surprising behaviourally since physical contact is a common feature of social behaviour. Some of this could be explained in terms of sexual behaviour but not all. The contact takes several forms. Sometimes there is gentle rubbing; sometimes there is mouthing and play biting, or occasionally head or snout bumping. Not infrequently several animals will swim round the tank keeping in constant contact, with flippers touching. All in all the behavioural evidence belies the anatomical expectations. Touch would seem to be important.

## SKELETAL SYSTEM

The skeletal system of Cetacea is based on and derived from the typical four-legged land mammal. It consists of a skull, a vertebral column, a pectoral girdle and forelimb and a vestigial pelvic girdle which has rarely any bones of the hindleg remaining; those that exist are very small.

The skull shows considerable modification. Particularly significant is the changed position of the external breathing holes or nares which moved to the dorsal part of the head. In the odontocetes the cranium is rounded and the beak or rostrum elongated. The maxillae and premaxillae form the rostrum. The lower jaw forms a straight bar fusing at the mandibular symphysis. The most significant modification of the Mysticeti is the absence of teeth and the presence of the characteristic baleen plates attached to the great arched jaws. The mysticete skull is also much telescoped. There is not such a distinct division between the cranium and the rostrum and the external nares are not quite so dorsally positioned as found in odontocetes.

Skulls of extinct and modern sea mammals show the migration of the blowhole, (arrowed) to its position on top of the head, and the clearly different jaw structures of the odontocete (toothed) and the mysticete.

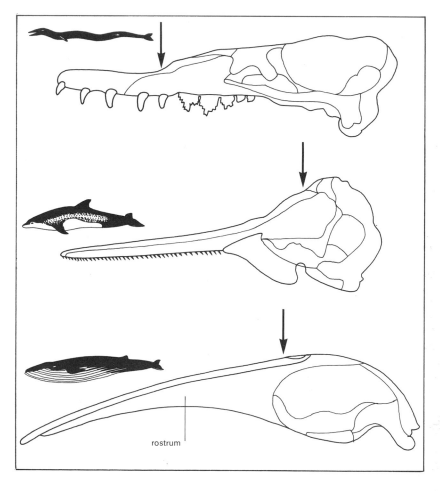

rostrum

62

The cervical vertebrae are an interesting feature of the cetacean skeleton. They are much shortened to form discs, and in many species several or all may be fused to form a rigid rod in the neck. The remaining vertebrae are shorter too with generous intervetebral discs giving flexibility, particularly in the back and tail. The neural spines and transverse processes are long, providing good areas for muscular attachment. The number of vertebrae is much larger than in most land mammals. The increase is mainly in the lumbar region. There are strangely no sacral vertebrae. The caudal vertebrae are identified by the chevron bones which are found on the ventral surface. Chevron bones exist in some land mammals but are usually small and difficult to find.

The scapula is a broad flat bone with large forwardly projecting acromion and coracoid processes. The scapula articulates with the humerus distally. The remaining bones of the forelimb are fused and therefore rigid. The radius and ulna are easily identified, being somewhat shorter and flatter than land mammals'. The carpus supports the typical 5 fingers although the first is very much reduced in length. Each phalangeal bone is a flat oblong and each digit can be lengthened by increased numbers of bones. Commonly the second digit is elongated in this way producing a long thin flipper. There are no claws on the flippers. The carpus of mysticetes is composed of cartilage.

Cetacean ribs are typically long and slender. Interestingly the ribs of the mysticetes are very loosely articulated indeed and in some species many of the posterior ribs do not articulate at either end.

The pelvic girdle is reduced to a non-articulating rod which is buried in the associated musculature. Hindlimb bones are absent.

## SKIN
The skin of Cetacea consists of 3 basic layers—the outer layer (epidermis), the middle layer (dermis) and the blubber (hypodermis). Externally it is very smooth and has no hairs apart from a few tough bristles around the mouth in newborn animals.

The epidermis of cetaceans is very thin, being less than 1 cm. in thickness. The cells contain

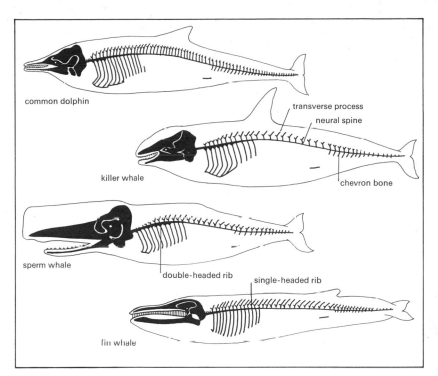

common dolphin

transverse process

neural spine

killer whale

chevron bone

sperm whale

double-headed rib

single-headed rib

fin whale

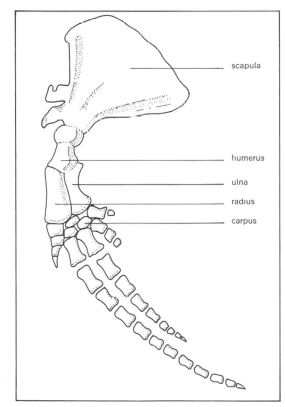

scapula

humerus

ulna

radius

carpus

*Above* Skeletons of modern Cetacea. The ability to expand the thoracic cavity during respiration is heightened by having loosely articulated ribs: In the mysticete skeleton (bottom) they are unattached to the sternum (floating) and have single-headed articulation with the vertebrae. For increased muscle attachment, the spinal processes are elongated and there are chevron bones to provide anchors for the muscles moving the tail up and down.

The extreme modification of the mammalian arm for fin-like movement: A flipper of a pilot whale (left) with the elongated second digit and lack of flexibility in the fused carpus.

63

nuclei much closer to the surface than is usual in land mammals. This rather thin covering renders them more liable to scarring than terrestrial mammals.

The dermis is also thin and sends dermal papillae infiltrating into the epidermis arranged in lines parallel to the long axis of the body. This acts to anchor the epidermis in place. The dermis consists of fibrous connective tissue and, where it merges into the hypodermis, fat cells.

The hypodermis or blubber is very thick indeed. Up to 60 cm. thick in some species, it may weigh nearly half of the total body weight of the animal. The blubber acts as an insulating layer and as a food reserve. It is principally the blubber which streamlines the animal since it varies in thickness to fill in dents and smooth over the ridges. When an animal loses weight as it does at various seasons of the year and during different stages in the reproductive cycle, it does so differentially to maintain the streamlined body shape.

Chemical structure of cetacean fat varies in different parts of the body, in animals from different parts of the world and with the 2 living suborders Odontoceti and Mysticeti.

It is principally this characteristic substance – the blubber – developed by whales in response to their environmental conditions that has proved so useful to man, and therefore so disastrous to many species of the Cetacea.

## SLEEP

Cetacean sleep is only poorly understood. Observations by several investigators on a variety of species tend to confuse rather than clarify the picture. While, for example, the Amazon dolphin, *Inia geoffrensis*, appears to indulge in deep sleep for quite long periods, the same observer watched both bottlenosed dolphins, *Tursiops truncatus*, and Pacific white-sided dolphins, *Lagenorhynchus obliquidens*, for nearly 2 days without seeing them do anything resembling sleep. One must conclude that there may be considerable differences in the pattern of sleep in different species, or at least among different age groups within a species.

By far the commonest sleep pattern appears to be the so-called surface sleep where the animal hangs, apparently suspended horizontally, just below the surface. The fluke hangs flaccid, but 2–3 times a minute it is moved to bring the animal to the surface to breathe. In another resting or sleep pattern observed, the animals swim slowly and almost mechanically round in small circles, often touching fellow dozers as they pass. Both eyes are thought to be closed.

So-called bottom sleep has been seen on occasions when the animal rests on the bottom and surfaces to breathe at intervals. There are suggestions however that this relates to water density and is mainly seen when the animal is in fresh water or water containing low quantities of salt.

An interesting suggestion made by one observer proposed that half the cetacean brain sleeps at a time. Noticing that one eye only is closed during sleep it means that half the brain remains active to control surfacing for respiration.

Most of the detailed observations on sleep in cetaceans have naturally been made on captive animals, but field observations have confirmed the surface sleep in several larger species as well. Sperm whales, several species of right whale and fin whale have all been caught napping, sometimes to their own detriment. On several occasions ships have collided with a slumbering sperm whale with disastrous results for whale and ship. It is also a field observation that whales sleep less in colder waters. This is undoubtedly related to metabolic activity and the need to maintain body temperature.

Sleep and its mysteries, even in land animals, creates great problems for the scientific investigator. In aquatic animals the problems are greatly increased. As the secrets of sleep in terrestrial mammals are revealed the path may clear to enable us to understand cetacean sleep better.

## SPERMACETI

This is an oily substance found in cavities in the heads of some toothed whales. Some species such as *Hyperoodon ampullatus* and *Physeter catodon*, are better endowed than others. During life the substance is fluid, but after death it gradually becomes solid. It gets its name because early whalers thought it was a store of male sperm cells. The function is not entirely understood but it is thought to be important in that it allows the whale to dive deeply.

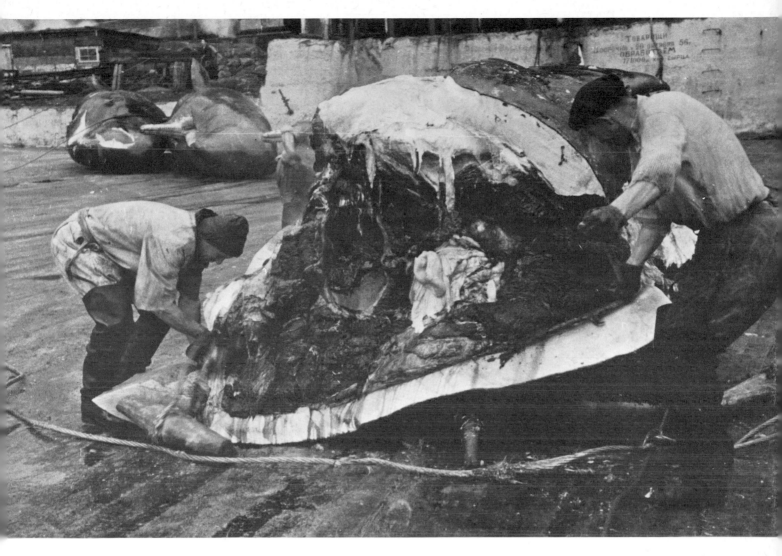

Spermaceti can be processed and separated to form a clear high quality oil and an opaque wax. The oil was used primarily in the cosmetic industry and the wax to make high quality candles. Today it has largely been replaced by synthetic chemicals but is still used for the most expensive perfumes and for other specialized manufacturing processes, including watchmaking.

## TEETH

Modern mysticetes have no teeth. Their feeding habits – the ingestion of large quantities of krill and/or small fishes – have made teeth obsolete. Fossil evidence and a study of their embryology,

however, suggest that baleen whales originated from toothed stock. The branch must have originated well over 30 million years ago since fossils show that mysticetes of the Middle Oligocene had already lost their teeth.

During development within the womb all mysticetes have tooth buds. These can easily be identified by the dissection of a foetus. As the baleen begins to develop, however, the tooth buds completely disappear and no modern baleen whales show even a trace.

Modern odontocetes have teeth which are quite unlike the teeth of the land mammals from which they descended. Early archaeocetes (see Evol-

The head of a sperm whale, *Physeter catodon*, is cut open to reveal the spermaceti.

ution) had teeth very similar to terrestrial mammals, with incisors, canines, pre-molars and molars in both jaws. Modern odontocetes have evolved with teeth ideally suited to the food they consume (see Digestive System). They are single rooted with a small pulp cavity which degenerates when the tooth stops growing. Structurally the teeth are typically mammalian, being basically composed of dentine covered with cement and capped with enamel. There are however species variations, the most important of which is the absence of enamel in some cases. Interestingly there are no milk teeth. The structure and number of teeth depends on the species and the type of food consumed. Fish eaters ideally have long thin conical teeth, a shape structurally suited to the capture of fish. Other species have flattened spatular-shaped teeth better suited to crushing invertebrates. The odontocetes usually crunch down on larger food before swallowing it whole. They therefore rarely have grinding teeth that resemble structurally or functionally the molars of most mammals. An exception is the Amazon dolphin, *Inia geoffrensis*.

One modification worthy of note is the absence or virtual absence of teeth in the beaked whales (Ziphiidae). See Digestive System.

## THERMOREGULATION

In their re-adoption of the watery environment aquatic mammals have had to face several problems not encountered by land mammals. Not least of these difficulties is the greater loss of body heat in water than on land, as water conducts heat much more efficiently than air. For this reason one becomes colder more quickly in water than in air of identical temperatures. Marine mammals need adequate food supplies in order to keep warm but this often means that they have to live in cold polar waters, which naturally increases the heat-loss problem. A variety of methods has been adopted by marine mammals in accommodating themselves to their environmental dilemma.

For short periods of immersion – probable in the ancestral pinnipeds and cetaceans – thick fur, which held a layer of insulating air, was adequate. This is the principal insulating method adopted by the modern sea otter, *Enhydra lutris*. The pinnipeds retain a good fur coat and this will inevitably hold

air for long periods. In addition, however, they have a very thick layer of subcutaneous fat which offers very good thermal insulation. The Cetacea, however, have dispensed with fur altogether and have evolved a very efficient layer of fat in the hypodermis known as blubber, a substance which acts as an excellent protection against heat loss (see Skin).

Heat loss depends on the ratio of body volume to surface area. In order to move through water at speed, the body assumes a spindle shape and all protuberances are reduced to a minimum. Just such a plan is also desirable to reduce the surface area. Hindlimbs of the Cetacea have completely disappeared and the forelimbs, as flippers, are much reduced in size. Pinnipeds have gone a good deal of the way, also having a spindle body shape and reduced extremities and protuberances.

The effects of metabolism have been discussed more fully under Metabolism but the increase in the metabolic rate with the extra heat it provides is also an important factor in the regulation of the body temperature.

Respiration has undergone modification in response to the aquatic environment, 2 aspects of which have particular bearing on heat conservation. The respiratory rate is lower. In land mammals, notably dogs, a high respiratory rate replaces sweating as the main way of losing excess body heat. In addition it has been shown that some cetaceans expire drier air than normal which again considerably reduces the heat loss.

The bodies of all mammals, land and marine, have control of the circulation of blood. This control is a major function of heat interchange with the environment. If the animal body temperature rises, the peripheral blood circulation, that is the blood supply to the limbs and skin, is increased. This brings more blood in contact with the external environment – air or water – and heat is lost. Conversely if the animal is cold the peripheral circulation is reduced, less blood, and therefore less body heat, is exposed to the cooling external environment and heat is conserved. It has been shown that during dives to the deeper and notably cooler waters there is considerable reduction of peripheral circulation in both Cetacea and Pinnipedia. Heat is conserved.

Whalers examine the huge teeth of a dead sperm whale, *Physeter catodon*, which are each the size of a man's fist.

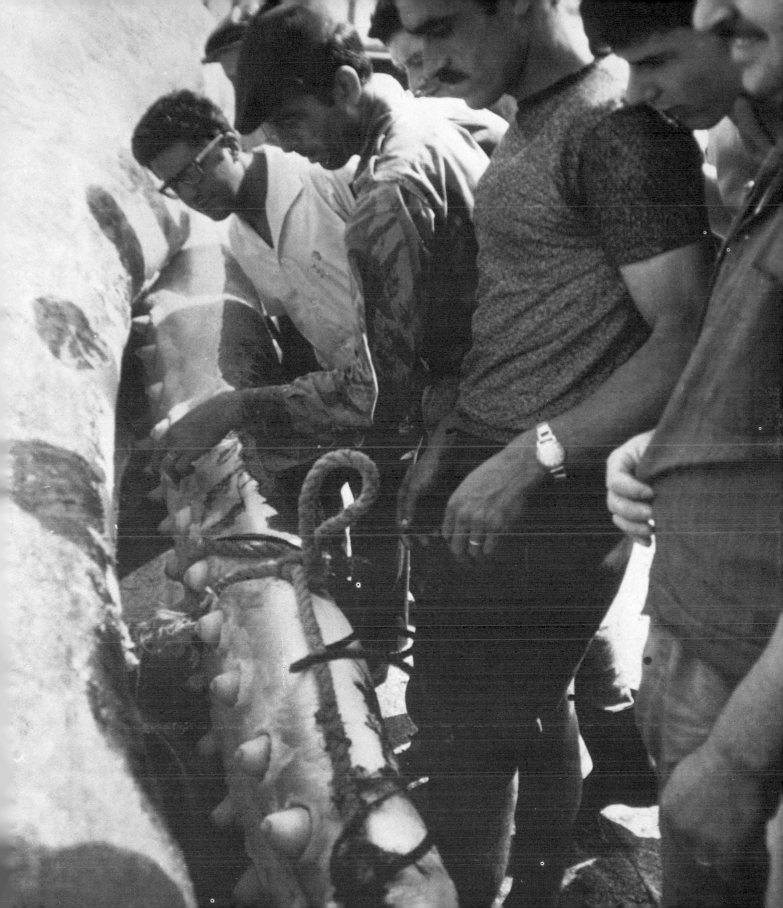

A further important mechanism has been described for the circulation of flippers, fins and flukes of Cetacea. This interesting heat exchange/conservation device is simple but effective. The arteries supplying the structures are surrounded by veins draining the area. Thus a percentage of the heated blood coming to the area is passed to the blood in the veins draining the area. Much of the heat is thus retained by the body rather than being dissipated at the skin. A similar arrangement is found in the pinniped flippers.

## TRAINING

Civilized communities throughout the world continually debate what justification there can be for training animals for public exhibition.

Cetaceans normally live in an aquatic world far from the gaze of man. Their very remoteness ensures that for most people concern for their welfare and conservation are of low priority. For the majority of the public exhibitions of performing dolphins are the only close contact with this group of creatures they are ever likely to have. To delight in their personality and ability heightens the spectator's awareness of these animals and the necessity of conservation.

Conversely the public exhibition of trained animals is abhorrent to a large percentage of people for several reasons. Animals physically so confined must be frustrated and unable to express their full physical and behavioural potential. What statistical evidence is available suggests that in many of these aquatic circuses there is a good deal wanting in care and management. Finally, to many the spectacle of wild creatures performing banal tricks is degrading both to the trainer and more importantly, since they have no choice, to the animals concerned.

As with all wild animals, dolphin trainers vary in their methods and in the kind of animal they choose to train. Cat trainers may prefer the rather sluggish acceptance of male lions, or the deviousness of the female tiger. For close work and complicated tricks lion cubs are preferred, while for showy displays needing little real action captive wild adults are probably better. Similarly for the smaller cetaceans many tricks of a spectacular but simple nature can be learnt in a short time by captured adults. Complex tricks require time and therefore money if they are to be perfected, and for this young animals with a longer and more worthwhile life span are essential. A further advantage of young animals in some trainers' opinion is the exploitation of the close social bond which exists between a young animal and its mother. Trainers believe, and some experimental evidence exists to support the belief, that these behavioural responses are transferred to them. In other words the trainer adopts the role of the juvenile's mother. Learning psychologists tell us, however, that older animals learn more rapidly. Differences in temperament between the sexes are also exploited by cetacean trainers, as they are in other species. Some like males while others have a preference for the female temperament.

Undoubtedly the species most commonly used for the performance of tricks in public is the bottlenosed dolphin, *Tursiops truncatus*. Others commonly employed are the pilot whales *Globicephala spp.*, Risso's dolphin *Grampus griseus*, the false killer whale *Pseudorca crassidens* and the killer whale *Orcinus orca*. Being one of the most ferocious of animals and certainly one of the most feared by all marine life, it is strange that the killer whale should so readily take to captivity, should be so amenable to training, and be so respectful of human swimmers who commonly swim with it and ride in splendour, if uncomfortably, on its back before an incredulous public. The first killer whale in captivity was saved from death by the sentimentality of her artist captor. Moby Doll, as she was called, was harpooned in 1965 by a sculptor who wanted a model for a statue he had been asked to execute of a killer whale. Having, after much patience harpooned her, he could not kill her so he took her into captivity and with careful nursing secured not only her recovery from the injury but also her confidence. From that moment the 'killer of the deep' has been much sought after by commercially minded men from oceanaria.

A variety of other species has been captured and induced to perform simple tricks but these less readily accept captivity and often die before training can be completed. At best their exhibition life is short and rarely repays the time spent on their education.

There is evidence that animals trained to perform have a reduced life span. The factors which cause premature death are not fully understood but comparisons of longevity between animals simply exhibited and those which have undergone training disclose advantages to the former.

Manipulation of an animal's behaviour during training is achieved by operant conditioning – the technical term for the combination of punishment and reward. All trainers of wild animals conscious of the animal welfare lobby claim that only reward is used. How true this is is open to question but facts are hard to prove. In one sense it is quite untrue since, if an animal fails to perform a required task and is denied its reward, then that becomes a punishment. However, common usage inevitably means more active, even physical punishment. One of the restrictions on punishing cetaceans is the problem of getting close enough to inflict it. There is however at least one report of an animal actually physically beaten for its lack of cooperation and the result, we are told, was an aggressive dolphin.

It is true to say that most dolphin trainers have the welfare of their aquatic charges at heart. Long hours of patience over many weeks are necessary

A bottlenosed dolphin, *Tursiops truncatus*, jumps through a hoop held by its trainer.

69

for success. The natural exploratory activity and playfulness of cetaceans need only to be harnessed and in most cases reward is probably all that is necessary. Indeed some animals are so enthusiastic that a congratulatory pat on the head is reward enough and food rewards, commonly used, can be dispensed with.

No animal can be expected to perform tasks for which it is not physically constructed. It is up to the trainer to exploit to the full the natural movements and behaviour of the trainee. Thus we see dolphins swimming, jumping clear of the water at balls or through hoops, somersaulting, collecting a variety of toys in their mouths, and walking along the surface on their tails.

An observed fact worth mentioning is the good memory shown by cetaceans for a display routine even after a long lay off. Several examples have been recorded where animals given the correct signals by the trainer have performed faultlessly after months or even years without practice.

Opinions continue to differ about man's moral and ethical right to train wild animals to perform tricks for public amusement. It is, however, probably fair to comment that, as far as can be ascertained, it is the physical and psychological welfare of the animals with causes concern rather than any cruelty involved in the training methods.

## TRANSPORTATION

Sensitivity, care and considerable animal sympathy are essential for the successful capture and transportation of any animal. The removal of totally committed aquatic mammals from water for transportation is perhaps the most demanding of all forms of animal transportation.

The usual way of capturing the smaller cetaceans is to surround them with nets until they are in a confined space, and then for a skilled diver to manipulate them, taking care to avoid holding the fluke or the end of the flippers, which are easily damaged. When using nets it is essential that divers are available to prevent the animal getting entangled in the net and drowning. The captured animal is placed carefully in a sling while still in the water. The sling should be of sufficient length to cover the body from the flukes to and including the head. In smaller cetaceans the flippers can be folded back against the body or, preferably, as in the larger flippered specimens, holes are cut in the slings through which the flippers can protrude.

Once out of the water it is absolutely essential to keep the animal moist. At all times responsible attendants are kept near by to ensure that the blowhole remains unobstructed and to protect the eyes from drying or excessive exposure to sunlight. During prolonged stays out of water there is real danger of overheating and this too must be anticipated.

Slings should fit well, the body weight being evenly distributed. The flippers, preferably hanging through holes, are protected at their base to stop rubbing. The body is covered in a thick towelling material, with holes for the genital openings, anus and blowhole. This is kept moist with water at all times. Great care should be taken to pad the animal. Careful attention is given to body temperature. Any suggestion of over heating should be countered by applying iced water or by packing the fluke and flippers in ice.

Dedication and diligence with careful attention to detail are the keywords for successful transport of cetaceans. Even so there may be problems. The lower parts of the body actually in contact with the sling and bearing the weight are likely to get overheated and to suffer pressure sores in extended travel. In addition the lungs, unused to having to expand in air, are placed under physical stress and become susceptible to respiratory diseases.

No cetacean should be transported without adequate justification, adequate preparation, an adequate number of competent attendants, and suitable sympathy among those concerned.

## UROGENITAL SYSTEM

The cetacean pattern of both the urinary and reproductive systems closely follows the basic mammalian pattern. The paired kidneys, however, situated dorsally in the abdominal cavity on either side of the vertebral column, are not the usual bean-shaped organs. They are subdivided into several smaller lobes and form a roughly ovoid structure. Each small lobe or renule acts, in fact, as a separate kidney with its own blood supply, cortex and medulla. Each renule drains into a duct shared by several other renules. These ducts all

The little piked whale, *Balaenoptera acutorostrata*, has submerged to swallow the krill.

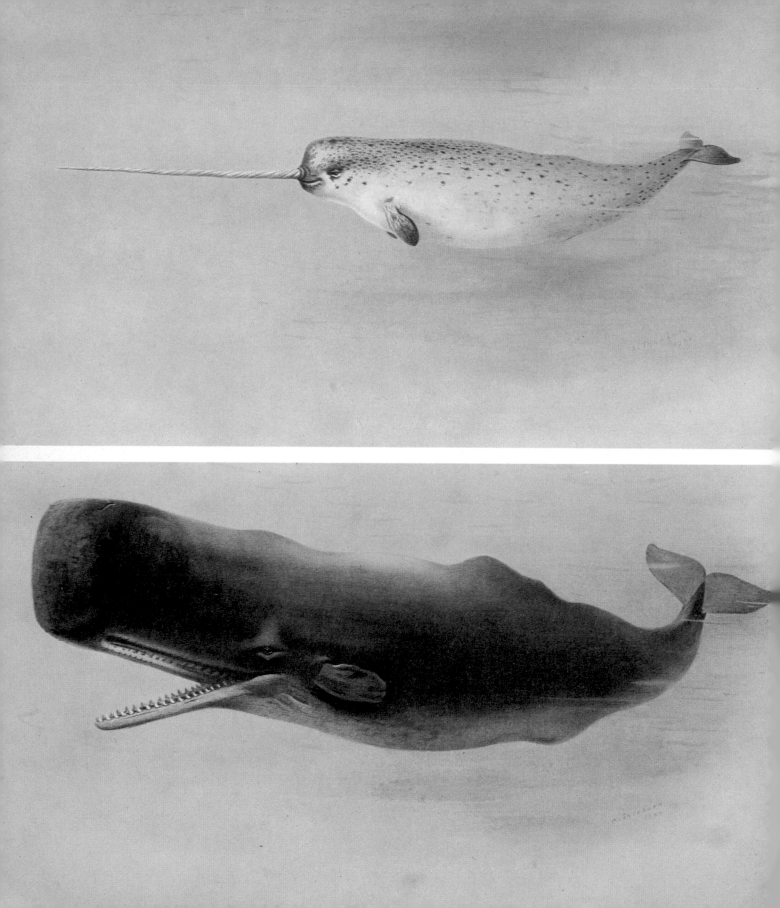

The tusk of the narwhal, *Monodon monoceros*, measures up to 3 m. in length. In medieval times traders mistook them for the horns of the unicorn. The tusks were prized for their supposedly medicinal properties.

amalgamate to form the ureter which passes to the bladder. There is a very poorly developed subcapsular renal plexus of veins which leave the kidneys at the same point as the ureters.

There is more kidney tissue relative to body weight in the cetaceans than in land mammals and it has been argued that this is an adaptation to marine life and the large quantities of urine thought to be produced. Certainly in freshwater cetaceans the ratio is lower, being intermediate between land mammals and marine cetaceans.

The ureters, after an extra peritoneal journey just ventral to the lumbar muscles, turn ventrally to pass through the lateral walls of the bladder. The bladder is small for the size of the animal. This may reflect the little need for long storage of urine in an aquatic environment, or be a result of the anatomical narrowing of the cetacean pelvis. Urine composition is similar to terrestrial mammals.

From the bladder the urine passes to the exterior via the urethra. In the male the urethra passes through the prostate gland before entering and passing through the penis. The cetacean penis is housed in a small invagination, the penial slit, which is situated between the anus and the umbilicus. The tip of the penis has tissue resembling the glans penis of terrestrial mammals. On erection the penis which, in some of the larger cetaceans can be up to 3 m. long, is protruded for up to four fifths of its length. The testes are internal and lie close to the kidneys.

Ovaries of both odontocetes and mysticetes resemble the typical mammalian pattern. Eggs pass to the fallopian tubes through a large funnel. Each fallopian tube merges with a uterine horn. The 2 horns unite to form the body of the uterus. The cervix separates the uterus from the vagina. The walls of the vagina are thick and well supplied with blood. It opens to the exterior at the vulva which is housed in a common recess with the opening of the urethra, the clitoris, and the anus.

The mammary glands are situated beneath the blubber on either side of the genito-anal recess. During lactation the elongated nipples can be seen protruding from their slits, (see Behaviour).

## WARFARE

One of the most sinister results of scientific research

*Below* The sperm whale, *Physeter catodon*. Drawings by Archibald Thorburn.

into the Cetacea is the application of that research for warfare.

Man's earliest 'gain' from a study of cetaceans was in the design of the shape of ships' hulls, and more particularly the shape of submarines. From this emerged the shape of modern nuclear submarines.

Not content, scientists turned their attention to other abilities which could be exploited. Their often incredible speeds – over 30 knots in some species, their ability to dive deeply, their well-developed hearing apparatus, and their general ability to learn and be trained.

In the late 1960s the United States Department of Defense, it is widely believed, began recruiting these obliging creatures and training them to retrieve objects from the sea bed. They found some of the smaller species eminently adaptable, notably the bottlenosed dolphin, *Tursiops truncatus*. They were taught to retrieve practice torpedoes and other more dangerous lost apparatus, using operant conditioning. They were also trained to propel deep sea divers by pushing them along, thus saving the diver's energy and increasing his efficiency.

Excited, their military masters quickly trained them not only to locate and even fetch lost objects, but to carry offensive weapons to the enemy ships. Once the problems of controlling them over long distances were overcome, they began to be used for patrol missions into enemy waters. They were trained to carry limpet bombs and to attach them to the enemy ships' hulls.

In 1971 the Department of Defense released the information that an experimental naval unit had been established in Vietnam and, using dolphins trained by behavioural engineering techniques at the Naval Undersea Research & Development Center in San Diego, was sending them on 'surveillance and detection missions' there. In addition they have placed chemical bugs in enemy harbours to establish types of fuel being used in enemy ships, later retrieving the bugs for analysis.

Again in Vietnamese waters, dolphins have been used to protect the sea surrounding allied harbours and ships from attack by enemy frogmen. It is said by frogmen used in their training that the dolphins forced them to surface and then herded them until they were picked up by human patrols.

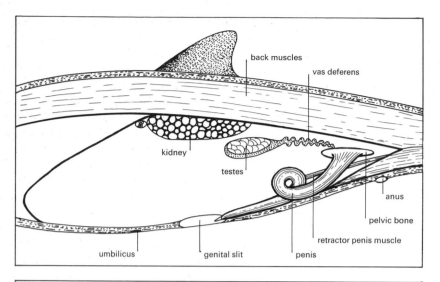

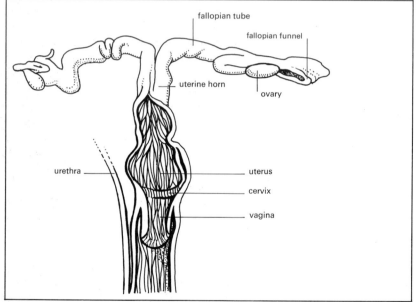

Using similar training dolphins were used to protect individual ships in Cam Ranh Bay from underwater attack. The friendly ships were identified to the dolphins by a metal plaque welded to the hull.

There is widespread concern about the methods used in training. Undoubtedly many are kindly enough, but there are thought to be less acceptable methods in use. Operant conditioning, the method used, employs both punishment and reward. The reward is usually food, the punishment an electric shock. It is well known that in attempting to so condition any animal there comes a time when it can no longer differentiate between say 2 similar tones of bell, 2 similar shapes or 2 very similar colours. The result of expecting too great an ability is neurosis. Such a psychological condition is manifest by refusal of food, lethargy and gross behavioural abnormalities. Examples have been observed during dolphin military training.

The use of these delightful and friendly creatures in the pursuance of man's greatest folly, war, cannot be condoned on any level by thinking people. Many respected scientists reject absolutely this dreadful activity. Perhaps no more suitable conclusion can be worded than the remark by Jacques Cousteau 'No sooner does man discover intelligence than he tries to involve it in his own stupidity'.

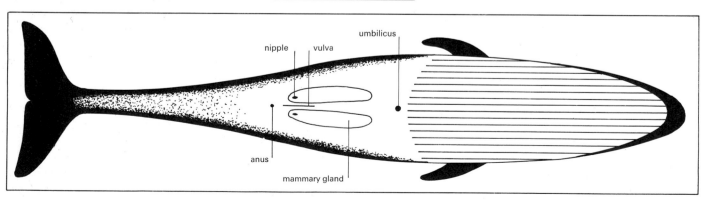

# Dictionary of Species

## BALAENIDAE

There are three living genera in this family – *Balaena*, *Eubalaena* and *Capera* – each represented by only one species. All have very large heads relative to the body size. There are no creases or grooves in the skin of the throat, or on the abdomen. Over 200 long narrow whalebone or baleen plates are situated on each side of the mouth. The cervical vertebrae are fused together into one unit. They are commonly known as the right whales because in the early days of whaling these were the 'right' whales to catch. They were recognized by the double jet of their blow. See *Balaena*, *Caperea*, *Eubalaena*.

### *Balaena mysticetus*  Linnaeus
### BALAENIDAE
GREENLAND RIGHT WHALE, BOWHEAD,
GREAT POLAR WHALE, ARCTIC RIGHT WHALE

Named in 1758. This magnificent if somewhat grotesque creature grows up to 20 m. in length and weighs over 122 tonnes. The skin colour is a dark black or bluish grey with a pale throat and underbelly. It has no dorsal fin. Its huge curving jaw bones help to make up the immense head which extends over one third of the total body length. The whole body has a solid chunky appearance. Its fluke is up to 7.6 m. wide. There are 2 slit-like blowholes, 45 cm. long, situated half way along the head. The small, superficially insignificant eyes are placed well down the side of the body at the corners of the mouth. The lips are very thick and the body is protected against cold by a layer of blubber over 30 cm. thick. There are over 350 baleen plates on each side of the mouth. Each one is over 3.7 m. long and has a feathered edge.

Greenland right whales, as the name suggests, are found in the northern hemisphere. Previously their range was more extensive but hunting has reduced it to areas off the coast of Canada, the Bering Sea, the Hudson Bay area, and around the coast of Greenland. Its movements are to a large extent dependent on the ice of arctic seas. In the warmer summer months it can be found far north in the Arctic Sea but it migrates south as the ice forms in winter.

It is a social species which forms small groups. These small groups occasionally unite into larger loose herds. They travel at speeds of up to 3–4 knots, keeping in touch by sound communication. They spend a few minutes on the surface during which time they take several breaths, then they dive for longer periods of about 20 minutes, but this can extend to last as long as an hour. They dive vertically showing their fluke and often return to the surface close to the point where they started to dive. Their blow can reach a height of 6 m.

They feed on krill, a form of crustacea found in the cold waters close to the ice.

Mating takes place in the latter part of the summer months. Pregnancy lasts about 10 months, after which it is usual for a single calf to be born, although twins have been recorded. When born the calf is up to 4.5 m. long. It is suckled for about a year during which time it grows rapidly, reaching up to 7.5 m. in length.

Even before its devastating enemy, man, appeared on the scene with his harpoon, the Greenland right whale was often a victim of the killer whale, *Orcinus orca*. However with these creatures it lived in ecological balance. Since the sixteenth century man has so depleted the population of Greenland right whales that the species is reduced to very small numbers and totters on the edge of extinction. Apart from a large quantity of oil, the whalebone was used for several purposes, including foundation garments for women, and household brushes.

### *Caperea marginata*  Gray  BALAENIDAE
PYGMY RIGHT WHALE

Named in 1846. This small whale is very rare indeed and little information exists about it. It is known primarily from stranded specimens found mainly around the coast of New Zealand. About 6 m. long and weighing 5 tonnes, it has a small dorsal fin, and small narrow flippers placed relatively far back, containing only 4 fingers, or phalanges. The body colour is black with, in some specimens, a fine white band running along the belly. The baleen plates are white with a dark brown or black outer edge and a fine pale fringe. Each jaw has 230 such plates with a maximum length of 75 cm.

A drawing of the sexual organs of a male porpoise (top) and of the female (centre). All external features of the urogenital system are drawn into the body for extra streamlining – as shown in the male (top) and the female (bottom).

A right whale, *Eubalaena glacialis*, showing the distinctive V-shaped blow. The line attached to the whale's back is connected at the other end to a monitoring device, enabling the path of the whale to be followed and plotted.

Pygmy right whales are found in the southern hemisphere, in temperate and possibly sub-antarctic waters. Stranded specimens have been recorded in Australia and New Zealand, southern Africa and the southern coasts of South America. They live on krill.

Information about reproduction is virtually non existent. They probably live in pairs or very small groups, and calves, thought to be some 3 m. long at birth, are possibly born in late spring or early summer.

### *Eubalaena glacialis (Balaena glacialis)*
Müller  BALAENIDAE
RIGHT WHALE, BLACK RIGHT WHALE, SOUTHERN RIGHT WHALE

These magnificent whales, named in 1781, are easily distinguished by the presence on their heads of the so-called bonnets. These crusty, horny outgrowths, the function of which is unknown, are infested with small parasitic crustacea. The most conspicuous is placed far forward in the midline of the upper jaw. On the lower jaw, close to the lip margin, are a series of small raised areas which surround bristles, presumably used to gain tactile information. The body, 15 m. in length, is a blue-black colour with occasionally a small whitish grey area close to the umbilicus. These whales have no dorsal fin. The head is much smaller in proportion to its body than that of the Greenland right whale, *B. mysticetus*, and extends over only about one sixth of the body length. The flippers are relatively large with 5 phalanges or fingers giving them structural support. The 250+ black baleen plates adorn either side of the mouth, each plate reaching a length of up to 2.7 m.

Right whales are found in temperate waters of the Atlantic, Indian and Pacific oceans. Some appear to inhabit the arctic seas particularly in summer, and some have been seen in the Bering Straits. They are usually found in pairs although small groups have been reported, and they seem to prefer to inhabit water close to island clusters.

Right whales have a maximum speed of 5 knots, but more commonly swim at 2–3 knots. They are rather high in the water when at the surface, where they lie taking 2–3 breaths a minute for a few minutes; they then dive deeply for up to 20 minutes. During exhalation there is a double V-shaped blast from the 2 nostrils which rises to 5.5 m.

They feed on plankton mainly composed of copepods.

Reproductive behaviour is not known in detail, but gestation and suckling each last about a year.

Like the Greenland right whales they fall victims to groups of killer whales, *Orcinus orca*, but undoubtedly it is man who has proved their downfall. These creatures have been ruthlessly hunted until today but a few hundred are thought to survive. They are now officially protected from hunting by international agreement which is, unfortunately, impossible to enforce, especially when non consenting countries are determined to continue the slaughter.

## BALAENOPTERIDAE

These great whales are easily distinguished from right whales by the series of longitudinal grooves running along the lower jaw, the throat and onto the chest. These allow great expansion of the mouth during feeding. Members of this family are streamlined, fast swimmers with a relatively small head for their suborder Mysticeti; it is less than one quarter the length of the body. The upper jaw is not so markedly curved as in right whales. The baleen plates are short and wide; more than 200 situated on each side of the mouth. A small dorsal fin is present. The top of the head is flat and streamlined. This family contains the most commonly known of the baleen whales including the magnificent blue whale, *Balaenoptera musculus*, which may be the largest animal that has ever lived on earth, larger even than the great dinosaurs. See *Balaenoptera, Megaptera*.

### *Balaenoptera acutorostrata*  Lacepede
BALAENOPTERIDAE  LITTLE PIKED
WHALE, LESSER RORQUAL, MINKE WHALE,
LITTLE FINNER, PIKED WHALE

This attractive whale grows up to 9 m. in length and weighs over 10 tonnes. The body colour is black above and white below from the chin to the tail. The flukes are white underneath. The narrow flipper is relatively long and has a distinctive white patch on its outer surface. The piked whale resembles the fin whale, *B. physalus*, but is less

A little piked whale stranded in the River Dart, Devon. Print from the *Illustrated London News* c. 1850.

streamlined. There are about 300 + pairs of baleen plates which are pale yellow with white fringes. They are up to 30 cm. in length. About 60 throat grooves extend back to a point in front of the umbilicus. There is a prominent dorsal fin which slopes backwards. It was named in 1804.

This species is widely distributed in both the northern and southern hemispheres. It inhabits the Atlantic and Pacific oceans and enters both the arctic and antarctic seas during the summer months. Some scientists have recorded small differences in form between the Pacific and Atlantic types. In the northern hemisphere the migration is to the arctic and colder waters in the summer, and back to the warmer waters for winter. Many observers have, however, seen the head of one of these whales poking through a breathing hole in the ice during the polar winters. Presumably they sometimes get stranded under the ice and must await the thaw.

Piked whales form small groups of either adults or adolescents. In the North Atlantic large herds have been reported but these seem to subdivide in the warmer subtropical waters to make groups of 5–10. They swim well, up to 15 knots if necessary, although they cruise at around 6 knots. Several breaths are taken between shallow dives to be followed by a very long deep dive of up to 20 minutes' duration. The blast reaches 2 m. in height. They have frequently been observed following ships and apparently diving under them as they move along. They also occasionally jump out of the water at an angle, falling back with a tremendous splash.

While they do feed on krill, many small fish such as herrings, anchovies and sardines are taken together with squid.

Mating takes place in the spring – February and March in the north, August and September in the south – and gestation lasts about 11 months. Calves, 3 m. long when born, weigh over 220 kg. and are nursed for 8 months.

In spite of man's endless attempts at the destruction and final extermination of this whale by hunting, the numbers remain healthy and total some tens of thousands, both in the Atlantic and the Pacific oceans. It certainly is relatively common around the coasts of the British Isles. The annual catch of these whales for years ran into several thousands but is now subject to some control by the IWC. It is fortunate for the survival of the species that their reproduction rate is high.

### *Balaenoptera bonaerensis*  Burmeister
BALAENOPTERIDAE   NEW ZEALAND
PIKED WHALE, ARCTIC MINKE WHALE
This was distinguished from *B. acutorostrata* in 1867. In fact it is closely related to *B. acutorostrata* and is probably a colour or racial variation, rather than a distinct species, no more distinguished than the Atlantic and Pacific types of *B. acutorostrata*. The main distinction is that the white patch on the flipper is missing. The baleen plates are pale yellow with a pale brown outer edge.

### *Balaenoptera borealis*  Lesson
BALAENOPTERIDAE   SEI WHALE,
RUDOLPHI'S RORQUAL, NORTHERN RORQUAL,
POLLACK WHALE, JAPAN FINNER, SARDINE
WHALE
Named in 1828. The sei whale is rather similar in appearance to the fin whale, the blue whale, and particularly to Bryde's whale. The dark back fades through grey to an almost white belly. It grows to a maximum of about 18 m. and weighs some 25 tonnes. The 40–60 throat grooves run backwards to a point half way between the flipper and the

umbilicus. The flippers are quite small, while the dorsal fin is relatively large. The 320 to 340 baleen plates are black with a very fine white fringe, the longest plate being some 60 cm. in length. They live for about 70 years.

Sei whales are widely distributed in the southern and northern hemispheres. They migrate from the colder temperate waters where they spend the summer, to the warmer tropical waters during winter. They swim at speeds in excess of 8 knots and can, for short periods, travel at 30 knots. Frequent breaths and short dives are followed by a longer dive of up to 15 minutes. They frequent both shallow coastal waters and deep ocean areas. Social groups of 2 or 3 are normal but larger groups of up to a hundred form in areas where the food supply is plentiful. Krill and small shoaling fish are the usual foods.

The migration to warmer waters is for the purpose of reproduction. Mating and birth take place in these tropical and subtropical areas. Gestation is thought to take about 12 months after which, usually, a single calf, although occasionally twins, are born. Each calf is over 3 m. long and weighs about a tonne. It is suckled for 6 months. Observations suggest that a male stays with the single female of his choice throughout the breeding season.

Because of their wide distribution and their speed they were not hunted by most whalers who concentrated on the blue and fin whales, although before the First World War several hundred were killed by land stations. They also used to be an important part of the whaling industry, now defunct, which operated from the west coast of the British Isles. Today, however, with international restrictions in force which control the hunting of the blue and fin whales, and with improved equipment, the whaling industry is taking a heavy toll of sei whales and recently tens of thousands have been taken. In spite of this the species does not seem to be in danger, though a careful watch must be kept.

### *Balaenoptera edeni*  Anderson
BALAENOPTERIDAE   BRYDE'S WHALE
Named in 1878. Bryde's whale is so similar in external appearance to the sei whale, *B. borealis*,

that only detailed examination can distinguish them. It is, however, more streamlined than the sei, and the dorsal fin differs slightly in shape being, if anything, smaller and more triangular. Bryde whales do not exceed 16 m. in length or 21 tonnes in weight. The grooves of the chin and chest number about 40 to 50, and extend to the umbilicus. The Bryde whale has 3 ridges on top of the head while the sei has only one. The baleen plates, about 250 to 290 on each side, are short, wide and thick; they shade from pale grey in the front of the mouth to a dark grey or black at the rear.

This species is restricted to tropical and subtropical waters of the Pacific, Atlantic and Indian oceans. It is not found in water of a temperature below 15°C.

Reliable information about the present numbers of this species is scarce. The population is not large but in some areas may be on the increase.

These whales swim at about 5 knots, with a top speed of 7 or 8 knots. They have a series of short breaths between deeper dives. They are seen in pairs, but more commonly in small groups or shoals of up to a hundred – a sight worth seeing.

The main food of Bryde whales is small shoaling fish, sardine and mackerel, and they are particularly fond of squid.

Reproductive information is scarce. The breeding season is unknown; some say calvings occur throughout the year. The young are about 3.7 m. in length when born.

### *Balaenoptera musculus*  Linnaeus
### BALAENOPTERIDAE   BLUE WHALE,
SIBBALD'S RORQUAL, GREAT WHALE

Named in 1758. This magnificent beast, possibly the largest animal ever to have lived on this planet, is nearing the end of its existence. The only step which offers it any hope of survival is a complete and total ban on all hunting. As a result of excessive hunting the blue whale has declined from a world population numbering over 100,000 to a few thousand. Nothing can justify killing the remaining members of this species. Indeed it is possible that even now it is too late. Population studies in many kinds of animal have shown that if the numbers become too small, recovery of the species is impossible. Some scientists believe that that low figure may have been reached in the case of the blue whale.

The blue whale gets its name from its slate blue colour, with pale spots. The body reaches well over 30 m. in length and weighs over 152 tonnes. It has up to 400 black baleen plates with black fringes. The grooves on the throat and chest extend back beyond the umbilicus; the longest are over 1 m. in length and are about 7.5 cm. apart. The flippers are relatively small and a very small dorsal fin is present. It lives for about a century.

Blue whales have a wide distribution in both the northern and southern hemispheres. In the north they were found in the Pacific and the Atlantic oceans and in the south from New Zealand through Africa to South America. During the summer they move to the Arctic and Antarctic seas, close to the ice. In the autumn they migrate to warmer, even subtropical waters, for breeding. Because of differences in seasons and migration time little if any mixing of the northern and southern population occurs.

These whales swim in small, close groups of no more than 3 or 4, but may form larger widely spread herds which communicate by sound. They swim at 10 knots with a maximum speed of 15 knots. Their normal breathing pattern is several, up to 20, shallow dives at very short intervals followed by a deep dive lasting about 30 minutes. The blast can reach over 12 m. They rarely expose their flukes when surfacing.

Blue whales feed on krill but inevitably some small fish are swallowed along with this diet.

Mating takes place in warm waters during the winter months in each hemisphere. The calf is carried for 11 months. The female returns to warm waters for the birth. Young whales can swim as soon as they are born and probably suckle for about 8 months. One calf is normal although twins have been reported. The young whale is about 7.6 m. long and weighs 7 tonnes. The mammary glands lie on either side of the mother's genital opening and during lactation are over 2 m. in length. The male's penis is 3 m. long. Soon after the birth of the calf, the adults mate.

In the early 1960s the Japanese claimed to have discovered a new species, the pygmy blue whale, *B. musculus brevicauda*.

## Balaenoptera physalus  Linnaeus
### BALAENOPTERIDAE  FIN WHALE,
FINBACK, COMMON RORQUAL, RAZORBACK

Named in 1758. To date this whale has been a little more successful in resisting man's inexplicable mania for whale extermination.

It is a fine big whale, over 24 m. in length and weighing as much as 71 tonnes, rather similar to the blue whale but dark brownish black on the back fading to white underneath. There are several dark lines and patches which distinguish it clearly from the blue whale. Strangely, the lower jaw is black on its left side and white on the right. It has a large number of tactile hairs on both jaws and a small beard of hairs clumped well forward on the lower jaw. The ventral grooves, characteristic of the family, number up to 80 and run from the lower jaw to the umbilicus. The 260 to 450 pairs of baleen plates are unusually coloured. The left baleen plates are blue grey while the anterior half of the right plates are pale yellow. It has small eyes just above the corners of the mouth. The 2 blowholes are well forward. It has small flippers and tail, and a small dorsal fin. It lives to be about 100 years old.

Fin whales are found in all of the world's oceans. They keep away from coastal areas. They move into the arctic and antarctic waters during the summer and to the warmer subtropical seas for the winter when breeding takes place.

These graceful beasts are the most numerous members of this family of great whales. Undoubtedly their wide distribution and habit of keeping some hundreds of miles off shore, together with their speed, give them greater adaptability. However, records show that hundreds of thousands have been slaughtered during this century and they remain one of the major targets for whalers. A population whose reproductive replacement time is as slow as is these animals' cannot maintain its numbers for long in the face of such abuse. Common sense and international cooperation to resist commercial plunder must rapidly emerge if this species is not to go the way of many of the other great whales.

Fin whales are fast, accomplished swimmers, a factor in their survival. They move at more than 14 knots for long periods with a maximum of 20 knots.

They were given the name razorbacks by whalers because of the long length of back and distinctive dorsal fin shown when blowing. During shallow diving periods they blow every 2–3 minutes. The blast reaches a height of 6 m. Deep dives of up to 20 minutes are started rather gently without the fluke leaving the water. They will sometimes jump straight out of the water, falling back on their sides with a huge splash. They form small groups of up to 3 in close proximity, but larger loose herds up to 200 in number are common.

Fin whales, like blue whales, feed mainly on krill and prefer it composed of euphausiids. While a number of small fish are swallowed by accident, there is evidence to suggest that they consume some small shoaling fish by design.

Mating takes place in warmer waters during the winter. There is said to be social play or courtship behaviour prior to mating and it has even been suggested that this species pairs for life although this would be very unusual. Young are carried for nearly a year and are born in warmer subtropical waters during the winter. Suckling continues for several months. Sexual maturity is not reached until they are 10 years old.

## Megaptera novaeangliae  Borowski
### BALAENOPTERIDAE  HUMPBACK WHALE

There is considerable variation of colour in this species. The back is black and in most cases shades to a white belly. The amount of black varies in different populations according to locality. The ventral grooves are characteristically few – about 15 – and reach as far back as the umbilicus. About 300 baleen plates of a slate grey colour are situated on each jaw. Close to the upper lip on the upper jaw are a series of hairs thought to be used for touch. Each has a small raised area around its base. The flippers are rather long and have serrated leading edges which indicate the fingers. The body is covered in raised areas. The flukes are notched on the trailing edge. The dorsal fin is relatively large and is placed half way down the back. It is followed by a series of hillocks which end at the tail. It is 15 m. long and weighs up to 51 tonnes. Its chunky rather amusing appearance is matched by its apparent *joie de vivre*.

This species, which was named in 1781, has a

*Tursiops truncatus*, the bottlenosed dolphin shows off the distinguishing feature of its genus, the short, well-defined snout.

*Over left* When trapped under the ice, the white whale or beluga, *Delphinapterus leucas*, rams the ice from beneath. The rounded head acts as a cushion and lessons the shock to the body.

*Over right* Western Eskimo sealskin eyeshade.

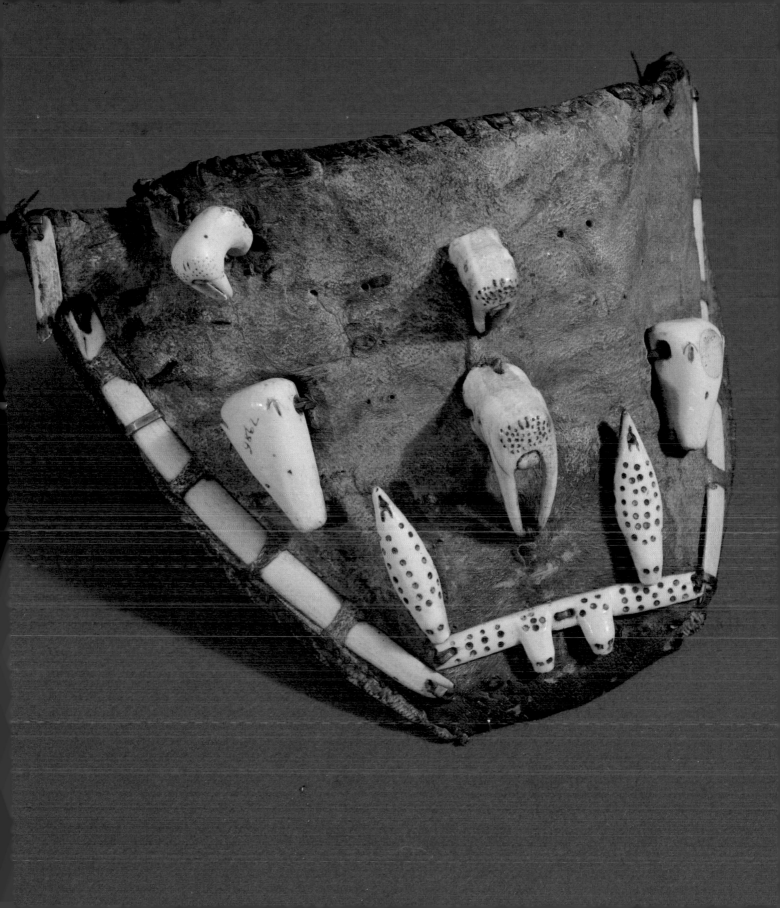

wide distribution in both the northern and southern hemispheres. Outside equatorial waters, like many other baleen whales, it spends its summers in the colder waters, migrating towards the warmer subtropical waters for the winter and to breed. It seems to prefer coastal waters and banks. The migrating population is apparently divided into groups according to sexual maturity. Immature males, under 15 years old, lead the way, followed by groups of paired males with females, and finally come the immature females also under 15 years of age, together with more young males and the females with their offspring. Recent studies have shown that large herds of humpbacks follow similar migration paths each year.

The swimming activities of these whales have earned them a reputation as comic acrobats. They not infrequently jump right out of the water and fall backwards waving their long flippers. They even perform the odd somersault. American whalers described their aquabatics as 'rolling, finning, breaching, scooping and lobtailing'. They dive vertically and show their flukes. Frequent short breaths on the surface are followed by a deep dive of up to 20 minutes. The blast is rather spread out and reaches just over 2 m. in height. Maximum speeds of 6 knots are possible for short periods but they usually cruise at 3 knots. Humpbacks form small groups of up to 4 individuals within a larger looser herd which is well spread out and which probably keep in touch by sound.

They mainly feed on krill. The occasional fish is taken. Such objects as large fish and birds which have been found in their stomachs are probably gustatory accidents rather than a predetermined act of ingestion.

As might be expected from this athletic swimmer courtship is accompanied by a good deal of frivolous activity. Much leaping, diving and jumping precedes mating which occurs in subtropical waters in the spring. Gestation lasts for 11 months after which the female gives birth to a one tonne baby, measuring over 4.5 m. long. It is suckled for about 11 months. The reproductive rate is high; copulation appears to occur soon after birth so that females are almost continually pregnant.

These delightful creatures have been hunted almost to extinction. In spite of international pro-

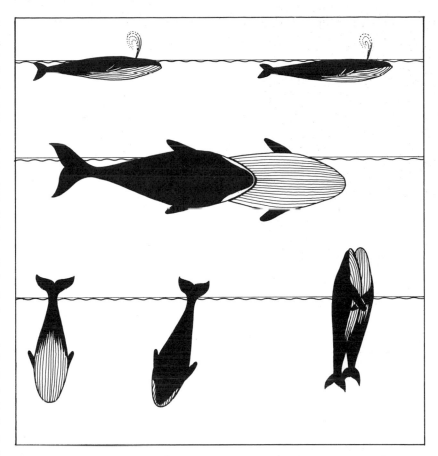

tection which is difficult to enforce and appears to be ignored in many cases, the numbers continue to decline. There are probably fewer than 10,000 humpback whales left.

## DELPHINIDAE

The classification of the genera and species in this family is constantly changing. The classification here is a modern one, but it is unlikely to remain static.

This family contains many of the better-known dolphins, including the common dolphin, *Delphinus delphis*. They are streamlined animals, active and fast moving. Their delight in jumping out of the water is a pleasure to watch and, because of their affinity to man and his vessels, they are often well-known to mariners. They usually live in large groups, and the family is distributed throughout many oceans. Their reputation is not of recent standing as they feature in man's early mythology.

Humpback whales mating. The sequence ends in copulation, here in a vertical position.

*Left* A 5 year old California sea lion, *Zalophus californianus*, is undergoing training as part of the US Navy Sealab project. It will carry messages to divers at 180 m. and will learn to respond to beckoning vibrations from them. They take 150 seconds and suffer no decompression problems. Photographed in action at the Navy Marine Bioscience Facility, Point Mugu, California.

Their speed and swimming agility enables them to catch fish which is the principal constituent of their diet.

The first 2 cervical vertebrae are fused. They have a well-defined beak and there are 40 teeth in each jaw. All are less than 4.5 m. long. There is a conspicuous notch in the tail fluke. See *Cephalorhynchus, Delphinus, Lagenorhynchus, Lagenodelphis, Lissodelphis, Sotalia, Sousa, Stenella, Steno, Tursiops.*

### *Cephalorhynchus albifrons*  True
DELPHINIDAE  WHITE-HEADED DOLPHIN

Named in 1899, it is probably that it is simply a colour variant of *C. hectori.* Little is known about the genus.

The body is 1.2 m. in length, with a low rounded dorsal fin. The head is small without distinction between the head and back. The forehead or melon is white. The body is pale grey or white. This dolphin is rarely seen. Distribution is thought to be restricted to the shallow coastal waters around New Zealand.

### *Cephalorhynchus commersoni*  Lacepede
DELPHINIDAE  COMMERSON'S DOLPHIN,
PIEBALD PORPOISE

A small species about which little is known. The forehead or melon is small so the shape of the head is flat.

Commerson's dolphin, named in 1804, reaches about 1.2 m. in length and rarely exceeds 45 kg. body weight. The beak is not distinguished from the forehead. The fin, placed slightly posterior to the mid point of the back, has a long base, and is low with a rounded tip.

The colour patterns, like those of other members of the genus, are distinctive, clearly delineated patches of black and white. One black patch includes the head and both jaws and runs back to include the flipper, leaving a white throat. The second includes the posterior and the flukes and runs forward dorsally to include the dorsal fin. A small black patch also covers the genital opening and the anus.

Virtually nothing is known of the behaviour or reproductive patterns of this species. It appears to form very small social groups.

It seems to prefer inshore waters off the coast of the southern tip of South America, in the Strait of Magellan, Falkland Islands and Tierra del Fuego.

### *Cephalorhynchus eutropia*  Gray
DELPHINIDAE  WHITE-BELLIED DOLPHIN,
BLACK DOLPHIN

Named in 1849, it is a very rare animal. Its colour pattern could place it as a variant of *C. commersoni.* It is described as having a black back extending well down the sides leaving a white belly.

It has only been found in the waters close to the southern tip of South America.

### *Cephalorhynchus heavisidei*  Gray
DELPHINIDAE  HEAVISIDE'S DOLPHIN

This species, closely related to *C. commersoni*, was first described in 1828.

It is slightly more chunky in appearance than *C. commersoni*, with a long-based, low triangular fin. The flippers are small and narrow with pointed tips. The body is mainly black but the abdomen is white with sweeping extensions up on to the sides above the flippers and below the fin, providing a distinctive pattern. Its length rarely exceeds 1.2 m.

Very little is known about this animal which has been revealed to science by a handful of specimens. It is thought to eat squid and cuttlefish.

### *Cephalorhynchus hectori*  Van Beneden
DELPHINIDAE  HECTOR'S DOLPHIN

There is confusion between this species, first described by Van Beneden in 1882, and *C. albifrons* described by True in 1899.

Hector's dolphin grows to 1.5 m. in length. It has a black back and sides, including the upper jaw and flukes, and a white belly with the colour change clearly defined. The black of the body extends at the flipper under the animal to join with a similar extension from the other side. The beak is long and merges with the head. The fin is low, broad based and triangular.

They surface slowly, breaking surface only with the head and fin and have only occasionally been seen to jump. Slow swimmers with an unusual undulating motion, they rarely dive for longer than 2 or 3 minutes. They are normally seen in very small groups, but do sometimes form large herds of several hundred.

Hector's dolphins are, apparently, exclusive to the shallow coastal waters around New Zealand where they undertake a migration northwards in the summer months.

Young, with identical markings to their parents, are born in summer.

### Delphinus bairdi Dall DELPHINIDAE
PACIFIC DOLPHIN, BAIRD'S DOLPHIN, BLACK-WHITE DOLPHIN

Like other members of the genus, the pacific dolphin has a large triangular dorsal fin, on which the colour pales in the middle. There is a distinctive physical change from forehead to the long, narrow, well-defined beak. This species grows to about 2.1 m. in length and is somewhat more bulky than the common dolphin, *D. delphis*. The body is distinctly marked in a black and white pattern with a narrow strip of black running from the angle of the jaw to the flipper, widening as it goes.

They inhabit the northern Pacific, often approaching close to the coastal waters. They are fast moving animals and can therefore feed on fish. They are commonly found in small mixed groups. The species was named in 1873.

### Delphinus capensis Gray
DELPHINIDAE CAPE DOLPHIN

The Cape dolphin very closely resembles the common dolphin, *D. delphis*. The colours are darker, however, and there is only a single line from the eye to the anus. It was named in 1828.

This species inhabits the warm waters of the Atlantic and Indian oceans. The total world population is considered to be quite small, certainly far fewer than that of the common dolphin. Little is known of its natural history.

### Delphinus delphis Linnaeus
DELPHINIDAE COMMON DOLPHIN

Man has a long association with the cetaceans and in particular with the common dolphin. By an accident of distribution it has lived close to the centre of western civilization for thousands of years. Although it is impossible to identify with any certainty the species depicted on rocks in Norway dating from 2000 years B.C., there can be little doubt that many pictures of the smaller cetaceans recorded in the art and decoration of the middle European civilizations are of the common dolphin. In addition they have become inextricably entwined with mythology and legend. Arion's rescue by dolphins is a famous tale from the Greek legends. Returning by ship to his home in Corinth from Italy with the spoils of his profession he became the victim of a plot hatched by jealous sailors. Just before he was to meet his doom he made a request to play a final tune on his lyre. As he played he leapt into the sea. A dolphin, which, the legend claims, was listening to his music, carried him to shore and safety.

The theme of humans or humanized gods riding on dolphins is a recurring one throughout the history of art and mythology. Pliny recorded the story of a small boy who was rescued and carried to safety on the back of a dolphin. A statue of the event was sculptured by Raphael in 1500 A.D. Another tale records the relationship between a boy and a dolphin. When the boy, who used to ride the dolphin around the bay of Naples died, the dolphin missed him so much that he too died. The famous celtic silver-plated copper bowl – the Gundestoup cauldron which was found in 1891 buried in a peat bog in Denmark, carries, on one of its inner plates, the horned god Cernunnos as 'Lord of the Animals'. Close by him is again a boy riding a dolphin. The Romans, not to be outdone, included cupid riding on a dolphin in one of their remarkably beautiful mosaic floors in the north wing of the Roman palace at Fishbourne, near Chichester, England. It dates from the second century A.D.

First described in 1758 common dolphins grow to 2.1 m. in length and weigh up to 136 kg. The body has a distinctive pattern, a blue-black back, and a white abdomen with 2 eliptical patches on the side. The anterior patch is yellow and the posterior one is grey. A grey line also runs back from the eye to the anus. A black stripe leaves the mid point of the lower jaw and travels to the flippers, widening as it goes, leading into the trailing edge of the flipper. The leading edge of the flipper is white. The fluke is blue. There is a white stripe running from the blowhole towards the prominent dorsal fin. The latter, often with a white

87

central patch, is triangular, but slopes backwards at the tip. The first 2 neck bones are fused. There are up to 100 teeth in each jaw.

This delightful, playful dolphin is widely distributed. It is found in the Atlantic, where the population is estimated at more than 30,000, moving into the Mediterranean and Black seas, and along the coast of Africa, around the Cape into the Indian Ocean. It is also found in somewhat smaller numbers in the Pacific. Migrating movements south to the North African coast in summer have been observed.

Socially they live in mixed schools of up to 200 individuals. They can travel at speeds of up to 20 knots and are often seen swimming from side to side of the bow of ships. As they undertake sinuous curves they twist their bodies from side to side, as if they are keeping an eye on the surface or the sky. Common dolphins do not dive to any great depth and dives rarely last more than 3–4 minutes. When swimming at the surface they breathe only twice a minute. The depth of dive possible for a species depends in part on lung size. The bottlenosed dolphin, *Tursiops truncatus*, has a relatively bigger lung than the common dolphin and dives deeper. (See Respiration.)

Within the social group there is a well-defined dominance order. Mature males are all generally dominant over all females. Among each sex there is also a fairly well-defined social order. This has been observed in captive groups, but scars and spasmodic observations in nature suggest that similar hierarchies exist in the wild. There seems to be considerable social responsibility among a natural group. On several occasions school mates have been observed in close proximity to, and even physically assisting, injured colleagues.

They eat sardines, herring, squid and crab. Their anatomical structure and physiology, together with their social behaviour, largely dictate that they prey on schooling fish.

Much still needs to be learned about reproduction in this species. The young are born in the late summer and autumn. As in all cetaceans, a single calf is born tail first. As soon as it is born the calf is encouraged to the surface by the mother. Soon after it has orientated itself it seeks the nipple. Like most mammalian mothers the female dolphin helps the young to its goal by positioning herself to its best advantage. Soon after birth the female comes into oestrus and is mated. Maternal care is intense. The mother ensures that her offspring stays with her all the time and if it wanders quickly retrieves it sometimes with physical admonition. On several occasions the mother has been known to attend an injured or sick young with apparent devotion. Mothers have been observed supporting their young at the surface.

The common dolphin has been kept quite successfully in dolphinaria. In addition it has been used by research workers, particularly those interested in the respiratory and circulatory modifications that have evolved in marine mammals. In addition a great deal of scientific investigation has been undertaken into the sounds emitted by the common dolphin, both in captivity and in the field. As this information is built up for each species of Cetacea the importance and complexity of sound waves to the navigation and communication to the whole order is emerging.

Some taxonomists name geographically separated populations as subspecies. Thus some describe the Atlantic common dolphin, *D. delphis delphis*, the east Mediterranean common dolphin, *D. delphis ponticus*, and the Pacific common dolphin, *D. delphis bairdi*, all of which also have slight morphological variations.

### *Lagenodelphis hosei* Fraser
DELPHINIDAE  SARAWAK DOLPHIN, FRASER'S DOLPHIN

This genus and species was described in 1956. It was recorded from a single skeleton found close to the mouth of the Lutong River, on the northwestern coast of Borneo. A number of specimens have been seen and collected in fisheries in recent years, and it is believed to be worldwide in distribution in tropical and sub-tropical waters.

### *Lagenorhynchus acutus* Gray
DELPHINIDAE  ATLANTIC WHITE-SIDED DOLPHIN

The species, named in 1828, grows up to 3 m. in length. It has a dark back, tail and flippers. The belly is white. A large elongated patch of pale grey or white extends from the dorsal fin to the tail. The animal is thickset, particularly in the front of the body. The dorsal fin is large, triangular and bends backwards. The tail has a pronounced keel both above and below. The fluke is notched. This dolphin has 30–40 teeth on each side of both upper and lower jaws.

It is found in fairly large numbers in the northern Atlantic mainly north of the Gulf Stream. Occurring up to Greenland, Scandinavia, northern parts of the British Isles including the Orkney and Shetland islands, and off the coast of New York. World populations are thought to be in the region of 50,000–60,000.

These fast swimming dolphins rarely jump from the water. They break surface with their head and dorsal fin, making a conspicuous bow wave as they travel at over 15 knots. Small social groups of up to 30 individuals are common but they often join together to form huge herds of over a thousand. They eat fish.

Mating occurs in the late spring and early summer, and the 1.2 m. long offspring is born after a gestation of 10 months.

### Lagenorhynchus albirostris  Gray
DELPHINIDAE   WHITE-BEAKED DOLPHIN
This species was named in 1846. It gets its common name from its white beak. Growing up to 3 m. in length it can weigh 295 kg. Its body is perhaps more streamlined than other members of the genus. The head is very short but the beak is differentiated. This is typical of the genus. The dorsal fin is large and placed midway along the back, leaning well back to produce a markedly concave posterior edge; it has a rounded point. The flippers have a broad base but rapidly narrow to a fine rounded tip. The flukes are medium in size and have a notch. The back is dark, as are the fin, flippers and flukes. There are grey side patches, however, which sweep backwards from the head to pass well on to the tail. The belly and throat are white.

White-beaked dolphins are found in the North Atlantic off the coast of northern Norway to the east, and Newfoundland and Cape Cod to the west. Around the British coasts they are more commonly found in the North Sea than the Atlantic.

*Lagenorhynchus* species are fast swimmers and can approach 20 knots when extended. They form large herds of up to 2,000 individuals. They feed on squid, fish, and crustacea.

The poor evidence that does exist suggests that mating occurs in August and September, and gestation lasts about 10 months, the young being born in summer.

### Lagenorhynchus australis  Peale
DELPHINIDAE   PEALE'S PORPOISE
This animal, named in 1848, has the typical short beak of the genus and the deep anterior body tapering markedly towards the tail. It reaches 2 m. in length. The dorsal part of the body is black, the belly white, and there are varied patterns of white and grey along the side. The jaws and eyes are black and this marking is continuous with the dorsal black. A black line runs from the corner of the mouth to the black flippers. The dorsal fin is large, triangular and upright. The notched flukes are black. A white elongated patch runs from the flipper to the tail.

Not a well-known species, it has only been observed in the waters around the southern tip of South America. Indeed such confusion exists in the genus that, as in the genus *Stenella*, taxonomists fail to agree on the number of species.

### Lagenorhynchus cruciger  Quoy and Gaimard  DELPHINIDAE   CRUCIGER'S
WHITE-SIDED DOLPHIN, HOURGLASS DOLPHIN
Cruciger's white-sided dolphin was named in 1824. It reaches 1.8 m. in length and weighs over 250 kg. The back is black, this colour extending forward onto both jaws and back to the flukes. A further black patch runs from the eyes backwards to include the flippers, widens at the dorsal fin and joins the dark of the back at the tail. The side is pale grey or white, as is the belly.

The species is restricted to south Pacific and antarctic waters. No more information about this species appears to be available.

### Lagenorhynchus fitzroyi  Waterhouse
DELPHINIDAE   FITZROY'S DOLPHIN
The species was named in 1836. The confusion which surrounds it is truly enormous. Some suggest that it is the same species as *L. crusiger*, while others

consider it to be identical with *L. obscurus*, *L. australis* and *L. superciliosus*. The differences are mainly restricted to colour pattern variations. In the specimen described by Waterhouse the white belly and sides were patterned with two backward pointing epliptoid patches extending below the dorsal fin. The upper patch almost joined a forward projection from the tail.

The first specimen of this species was collected during Charles Darwin's famous *Beagle* expedition. It was drawn by Captain Fitzroy after whom it was named.

### *Lagenorhynchus obliquidens*   Gill
DELPHINIDAE   PACIFIC WHITE-SIDED DOLPHIN, PACIFIC WHITE-STRIPED DOLPHIN

This dolphin was named in 1865. Like other members of the genus, it has a short but well-defined beak. The dorsal fin is large, centrally placed and upright. Flippers tend to medium size with a broad base. The body is deep anteriorly, narrowing considerably towards the medium-sized flukes. The body patterns are variable and rather unusual. The back is black, the sides grey and the belly white. The grey side is, however, broken by variable patterns of black patches or extensions from the back. The white belly is delineated by a black line. The dorsal fin also has variable white patches. This species grows to about 2.4 m. in length and weighs 135 kg.

Population estimates suggest it is quite abundant: 60,000–70,000 strong. It lives in cold waters of the north Pacific, is common around the coastal waters of Japan, and the western seaboard of North America.

A very gregarious species. Occasionally small social groups of 10–20 are seen, but it is more common to count herds in hundreds or thousands. Generally they are seen only by their dorsal fins, which show as they surface to breathe. Adults jump rarely. They attain speeds of up to 20 knots. There appears to be a migration to northern waters in the spring for the summer and a return south to warmer waters in the autumn. They eat squid and small fish.

Mating takes place soon after the birth of the young in April to July. Young animals are up to 90 cm. long when born and can weigh over 11 kg.

This species is well known to mariners as it often approaches boats and swims alongside them. It has been kept in captivity and taught to perform simple tricks.

### *Lagenorhynchus obscurus*   Gray
DELPHINIDAE   DUSKY DOLPHIN

Another first by that intrepid nineteenth-century taxonomist Gray, who named this as a separate species in 1828. However, some scientific opinion believes it to be a single species together with *L. fitzroyi*, *L. australis*, and *L. superciliosus*. The body is said to resemble closely *L. acutus* and *L. obliquidens*. The differences from the latter two species are very slight and may be due to individual variation.

A description of one specimen, supposed to be *L. obscurus*, reports that it has a black back, flippers and flukes. A thin line runs from the eye to the flipper. Two elongated projections of dark colour pass back on to the light sides, one below the dorsal fin and one slightly anterior to it.

They are found in temperate waters of the southern hemisphere where they appear to eat mainly squid and swim in groups of up to 100.

They are believed to migrate to warmer waters close to New Zealand and southern Africa in winter and return to the antarctic waters in summer. The young are born during the winter.

They are frequently seen by sailors as they often swim alongside boats. A few have been kept in captivity.

There can be little doubt that further study is needed to clarify a very confused situation in this genus which could be described as a taxonomist's nightmare.

### *Lagenorhynchus superciliosus*   Gamot and Lesson   DELPHINIDAE

This little-known species was named in 1826 from a single skeleton found at the Cape of Good Hope. Presumably taxonomists would like more proof than that for confirmation of a species.

### *Lagenorhynchus thicolea*   Gray
DELPHINIDAE
GRAY'S WHITE-SIDED DOLPHIN

Gray described this species in 1849 from a single skull found on the west coast of North America.

### Lagenorhynchus wilsoni    Lillie
DELPHINIDAE    WILSON'S HOURGLASS
DOLPHIN

This species, named in 1915, is closely related to
*L. cruciger*. It has, however, a larger body. It comes
from the Pacific Ocean. The common name was
inspired by the hourglass shape to the markings on
the side of the body. Again there is some confusion
in the minds of taxonomists and a great deal of
confusion in the minds of others as to the reliability
of specific classification.

### Lissodelphis borealis    Peale
DELPHINIDAE    NORTHERN RIGHT
WHALE DOLPHIN

This species was named in 1848. The body of this
slender dolphin is 2 m. long and all black except
for white areas along the abdomen. It has small
narrow pointed flippers which have a black outer
surface. The skull is slender and the beak short and
pointed. Each jaw supports about 80 teeth. The
first 2 cervical vertebrae are fused. Like all members of the genus it has no dorsal fin. The flukes are
small.

It is a relatively abundant species in the deep
waters of the northern Pacific as far south as
California to which area it is restricted. It feeds
on fish and squid.

Large herds of several hundred are normal.
They can swim at over 15 knots. Little is known
about migratory habits although it seems possible
that they respond to seasonal changes, moving
north in summer and south in winter. They appear
to associate often with other species of dolphin to
form mixed herds. Very little is known about their
reproductive behaviour.

### Lissodelphis peroni    Lacépède
DELPHINIDAE

SOUTHERN RIGHT WHALE DOLPHIN

This species was named in 1804 and resembles its
northern cousin *L. borealis*. Its body is somewhat
less streamlined and although it has a black back, a
large area of white extends well up the sides and
includes the flippers. The head is black apart from
the throat. It grows to 1.8 m.

This species is restricted to the Antarctic Ocean
It is not a well-studied species and has rarely been
seen. It normally swims in small groups but on
occasions herds of up to 1000 have been reported.

### Sotalia and Sousa    Gray    DELPHINIDAE
RIDGEBACK DOLPHINS

In 1866 Gray designated the genus *Sotalia*. Because
of geographical separation and structural
differences it has been separated recently into 2
genera, *Sotalia* and *Sousa*. These species are known
as river dolphins and inhabit large rivers and river
estuaries of S. America. Their range is restricted to
tropical and subtropical regions. *Sousa* species are
found in Africa and Asia while *Sotalia* species occur
only in South America.

All have long, very slender snouts, and long
slender bodies. Members of the genus *Sousa* have a
small dorsal fin which sits on top of a sometimes
very long ridge on the back.

Although they are quiet slow-moving dolphins,
which rarely jump or play, they are still well
known to mariners who commonly come across
them in the river estuaries.

### Sotalia brasiliensis    Van Beneden
DELPHINIDAE    BRAZILIAN DOLPHIN

Named as a separate species in 1875, it so closely
resembles *S. fluviatilis*, *S. pallida* and *S. tucuxi* that it
is hard to believe they are all separate species.

It is said to be abundant and readily seen in the
Bay of Rio de Janeiro but in spite of this no detailed
studies of the species have been made.

### Sotalia fluviatilis    Gervais and DeVille
DELPHINIDAE    BUFFEO NEGRO,
PIRAYAGUARA, TUCUXI, AMAZON DOLPHIN

This delightful little river or ridgebacked dolphin
was described in 1853. It is one of the smallest
members of the Cetacea being less than a metre
long when adult. The back and sides are a grey
brown while the under parts are a pale yellow or
white. The fin is broad based with a backward
slope. The flippers are large and spade like.

They are found several thousands of kilometres
upstream in the Amazon, often in association with
*Inia geoffrensis*, which accounts for their similar
common local names, in spite of belonging to
different families. They feed on fish and freshwater
crustacea. The population is small.

### Sotalia guianensis · Van Beneden
### DELPHINIDAE
GUIANA DOLPHIN

This species was first named in 1864. The nineteenth-century taxonomists were often over enthusiastic, giving each freshly discovered specimen a different name. It seems probable that this is the same species as the other *Sotalia* species mentioned. In other words there may only be one species of *Sotalia* not 5.

It usually grows to 1.5 m. and weighs around 50 kg.

The justification for separate classification is based on slight variations in the dental formulae and different distribution. This species is found in the rivers draining to the north-east coast of South America.

### Sotalia pallida · Gervais · DELPHINIDAE
BUFFEO BLANCO

Named in 1855. It is considered by some to be the same as *S. fluviatilis*. Separatists say these have a shorter beak and a longer body, with paler colours.

### Sotalia tucuxi · Gray · DELPHINIDAE

Named as a separate species in 1856, it seems probable that the specimen was a colour variant, or an animal of a different age, from a previously named specimen, and that it can be placed with *S. fluviatilis* and *S. pallida* as a single species.

### Sousa borneensis · Lydecker
### DELPHINIDAE · BORNEAN WHITE DOLPHIN

Named in 1901. The Bornean white dolphin is considered by some authorities to be the same species as *S. chinensis*. Certainly they are structurally very similar. The body is all white with black eyes. It grows to about 1.8 m. and weighs up to 70 kg.

This species is usually thought to be restricted to the coasts of Malaya, the Gulf of Siam and the coast of Borneo. There are suggestions however that its range may be more extensive.

Like other members of the genus it swims slowly, surfacing quietly, and breathes every few seconds. Pairs have been observed swimming together but they are thought to form small loose groups of up to 15 individuals. They eat fish, molluscs and crustacea. Little is known of their general behaviour.

### Sousa chinensis · Osbeck · DELPHINIDAE
CHINESE WHITE DOLPHIN, INDO-PACIFIC
HUMPBACKED DOLPHIN

First named in 1765, this is a lovely ivory white dolphin. The abdominal skin is sometimes tinged pink and the flippers are also pale pink. The eyes are jet black. There is a short broad-based dorsal fin. It grows to about 1.8 m. and weighs up to 70 kg.

The Chinese white dolphin is found in the South China Sea and along the coasts of Vietnam, where its rather shy behaviour ensures that it is seldom seen. It has therefore been little studied.

### Sousa lentininosa · Owen · DELPHINIDAE
SPECKLED DOLPHIN, FRECKLED DOLPHIN,
BOLLA GADIM

Named in 1866, this animal has a steel blue body with medium sized patches of mauve or pinkish yellow. The ventral part of the body is pale grey. The small dorsal fin sits on a ridge about one quarter the length of the body. The flippers are broad based with rounded, almost square-cut ends. The species grows to a length of about 1.8 m.

It is found around the coast of southern India and Sri Lanka. Its social behaviour is typical of the genus. It forms small loose groups of up to 20 members.

### Sousa plumbea · Cuvier · DELPHINIDAE
PLUMBEOUS DOLPHIN, LEAD-COLOURED
DOLPHIN

This delightful creature, first named in 1829, grows to 2.7 m. As the name suggests, the body is a dull grey colour but shades to an almost white ventral surface. It is slim, tapering rapidly in the last quarter to the flukes. The snout is long and thin, the flippers markedly triangular with rounded points. The tiny triangular dorsal fin sits atop the dorsal ridge which covers the middle third of the back.

They are distributed in the Indian Ocean commonly close to the Indian and Sri Lankan coast.

They swim silently and slowly, breaking surface gently to breathe. They seldom jump from the water and dives rarely exceed 2 minutes in length. They form loose groups of up to 20 individuals, and feed on fish.

*Above right* Walruses, *Odobenus rosmarus*, inhabit open waters in the Arctic Ocean. They ride the ice floes when migrating.

*Below* They are polygamous and tend to live in mixed herds on isolated rocky shores, islands and ice flows.

### *Sousa teuszi* Kükenthal DELPHINIDAE

WEST AFRICAN MANY-TOOTHED DOLPHIN, CAMEROON RIVER DOLPHIN, ATLANTIC HUMPBACKED DOLPHIN

Very little is known about this species which was described in 1892 from descriptions of a single damaged specimen. More recently a few stranded animals have been found on the west coast of Africa. It is somewhat larger than many other *Sousa* species, being up to 2.1 m. in length and weighing up to 90 kg.

Distribution is, as far as is known, restricted to the coast and river estuaries of West Africa.

### *Stenella attenuata* Gray

DELPHINIDAE SLENDER-BEAKED PORPOISE, WHITE-DOTTED DOLPHIN, NARROW-SNOUTED DOLPHIN

There is a good deal of taxonomic confusion in this genus. Some of the lesser known species described from just a few individuals may be wrongly classified as separate species. This one was named in 1846.

*S. attenuata* is described from about 10 specimens. They grow to just over 1.8 m. in length. It has, like other members of the genus, a largish dorsal fin which slopes backwards, placed midway along the back. The flukes are relatively small. Flippers, flukes and fin are all black. The back is metallic blue, and a dark area sweeps in an arc from the head to the posterior boundary of the fin. The sides and belly are grey and scattered with white and grey spots, and the beak is black except for a spot of white at the tip. There are about 90 teeth in each jaw.

The distribution is not well known. The very few specimens collected would suggest that the total population is small and widely distributed in the Atlantic and Pacific oceans.

Very little is known about the social behaviour or reproductive habits.

### *Stenella coeruleoalba* Meyer

DELPHINIDAE BLUE-WHITE DOLPHIN, STRIPED DOLPHIN

Named in 1833. The body is streamlined. The back, including the dorsal part of the head and the fluke, is a rich metallic blue. The triangular dorsal fin is tall and tilted backwards. A dark line runs back from the beak to the eye, then continues backwards dividing into two, the lower line fading while the upper passes to the anus. Above the line there is a varying patch of grey or white. Below the line the abdomen is white. A second line, grey in colour, runs from the eye to the flipper. The flippers, broad-based and pointed, are blue. The first 2 vertebrae are fused.

A widely distributed species in the Atlantic and Pacific oceans; populations also exist in the Mediterranean Sea. They appear to have a wide temperature range inhabiting regions from sub-polar seas to the tropics, but seem particularly abundant in the Pacific where several hundred thousand are thought to live.

They are found in very large herds, particularly in the Pacific, where groups of several thousand individuals have been observed. Apparently they form separate herds based on sex and age; they are thought to live for 25–35 years. Their principal food is reported to be squid, and many bear the marks of squid suckers around the head.

Studies have revealed that young are born at several periods throughout the year. Suckling lasts for about 9 months. They reach maturity at about 4 years of age.

Japanese hunt the species for meat and oil, chasing them with boats into shallow waters. The annual catch is conservatively said to be in excess of 20,000. Claims that this has no effect on population size must be regarded as a public relations exercise by commercial interests.

### *Stenella frontalis* Cuvier

DELPHINIDAE BRIDLED DOLPHIN, ATLANTIC SPOTTED DOLPHIN

This short-beaked dolphin, named in 1829, grows up to 2 m. in length. The back is dark grey or black, gradually shading to a white or very pale grey abdomen. The eyes are surrounded by black and from them, forward, runs a black line to meet on the forehead a similar line from the other eye. From the corner of the mouth a dark, gradually widening line passes to the rather large black flipper. The upper jaw is black. The dorsal fin and flukes are black. Small black dots decorate the abdomen. The head and anterior back are without dots but the posterior part of the back is covered with pale dots.

The species seems fairly well distributed although numbers appear small. It inhabits the temperate and subtropical waters of the Atlantic ocean. They are social animals and form groups. Their main food is thought to be squid although fish are probably also taken.

### *Stenella graffmani*  Lönnberg
### DELPHINIDAE  GRAFFMAN'S PORPOISE
A rare, dark-bodied species with white spots along its dorsal region. It is restricted to the tropical waters of the eastern Pacific. It was named in 1934. The lack of information about it puts its validity as a separate species in some doubt.

### *Stenella longirostris*  DELPHINIDAE
LONG-BEAKED PORPOISE, LONG-SNOUTED DOLPHIN, SPINNER DOLPHIN
The body of this splendid species is grey dorsally, shading to a pale grey or white belly. It is scattered with pale grey dots or small irregular patches. It attains adult lengths of over 1.8 m. The change from dark to pale grey makes a distinct curved line along the body. The upper jaw is black. A dark line runs from the eye to a point above the base of the beak. A paler diverging line runs back from the eye to the flipper which is dark grey on both surfaces, broad based and rather small. The dark dorsal fin is triangular with a backward sweep. The fluke is also dark on both surfaces.

Long-snouted dolphins are probably worldwide in tropical and sub-tropical seas: in the Indian Ocean and around Australia. They have been seen in the northern hemisphere in the Western North Atlantic south to Florida and throughout the Gulf of Mexico.

### *Stenella malayana*  Lesson
### DELPHINIDAE  MALAYAN PORPOISE
A little-known species named in 1826. It grows up to 1.8 m. in length and is a fine, agile swimmer. Its well-shaped body is an overall grey, somewhat darker dorsally. Each jaw contains 40 teeth.

This species, as far as reports have shown, is restricted to the coastal waters and islands of the Malay Peninsula.

### *Stenella microps*  Gray  DELPHINIDAE
SMALL-HEADED PORPOISE
Described in 1871 from one individual caught off the Mexican coast. Apart from very limited information about structure it remains a mystery. It is said to jump out of the water, spinning on its long axis as it goes. Such behaviour is possible, as it has been observed in other species of the genus.

### *Stenella plagiodon*  Cope  DELPHINIDAE
ATLANTIC SPOTTED DOLPHIN
A fine animal with a high well-shaped dorsal fin in the centre of the back. The body is metallic blue above, and shades to a pale grey belly. The body is scattered with pale grey spots on the blue, and blue spots on the white.

This is quite a rare species, restricted to the Atlantic coasts of America.

### *Stenella styx*  Gray  DELPHINIDAE
GRAY'S PORPOISE
Closely related to, indeed perhaps a subspecies or race of, *Stenella coeruleoalba*, distinguished from it by the patterning around the eye. A dark line leaves the corner of the eye, and almost at once divides into two. The upper line passes backwards to the anus, sending off a short rapidly fading branch one third of the way back. The lower line passes to the flipper. A dark line, parallel to the lower line described, runs from the eye to the flipper.

Gray's porpoises are distributed in both hemispheres, in the Atlantic from far north by Greenland to the West Indies, and mainly in the north in the Pacific.

### *Steno bredanensis*  Lesson
### DELPHINIDAE  ROUGH-TOOTHED DOLPHIN
A very beautifully shaped animal, almost a perfect curve from the tip of its snout to the flukes. It has a grey back and sides covered with small light grey patches, and a pale sometimes pink belly marked with dark grey spots. The flippers are narrow and long. It grows to 2.4 m. in length. The significant structures which give it the common name are the rough surfaces of its conical teeth. It was first named in 1828.

It is a little known species which seems to inhabit deep waters; occasionally seen playing in the waves created by ships. It appears to have a wide distribution in the subtropical and temperate waters of the Atlantic, Pacific and Indian oceans. Observations and strandings have been recorded on the coasts of Europe, South-east Asia, Hawaii, Africa, America and Australia.

### *Tursiops abusalem*   DELPHINIDAE
Although this was separately named by Ruppell in 1842, it is probable that *T. abusalam* is identical to *T. aduncas*, which is the form of *Tursiops* found in the Red Sea.

### *Tursiops aduncas*   Ehrenberg DELPHINIDAE
First named in 1833. Many scientists believe this species to be identical with *T. abusalem*. It is said to occur in the Indian Ocean and around the coast of Australia.

A streamlined species which reaches 3 m. in length and has a backward sloping dorsal fin. The flippers are placed well towards the head. The rather short beak is well differentiated from the head, which has a well developed melon. The back is dark grey, shading to a pale grey belly.

### *Tursiops gephyreus*   Lahille DELPHINIDAE
Described first in 1908. There are said to be skeletal variations which distinguish it from other *Tursiops* species, but as such dubious evidence exists one must await taxonomical clarification.

### *Tursiops gillii*   Dall   DELPHINIDAE
GILL'S BOTTLENOSED DOLPHIN, COWFISH, EASTERN PACIFIC BOTTLENOSED DOLPHIN
Some taxonomists consider this to be a subspecies of *T. truncatus* and it is certainly very similar in structure. It was first named as a separate species in 1873. Like *T. truncatus* it has a short beak, is grey-blue in colour with a black line running forward from the eye. The teeth vary slightly from those of *T. truncatus*, *T. gillii* having a few more. It also closely resembles *T. nuuanu* but is separated again because of more teeth, and because it has 2 extra pairs of ribs. Within the species there are local variations.

Gill's bottlenosed dolphins are restricted to the Pacific Ocean, and like other members of the genus, they form groups and are very sociable. Herds of up to several hundred have been seen and they commonly play around a moving ship, jumping and rolling as they swim. They feed mainly on fish. It is estimated that they live for at least 25 years.

### *Tursiops nuuanu*   Andrews DELPHINIDAE
PACIFIC BOTTLENOSED DOLPHIN
Again confusion. This species, named in 1911, is very closely related to *T. gillii*, and physical characteristics which are said to distinguish them are minor.

It is found in the Pacific Ocean close to the coast of Central America. Like most members of the genus, it rarely leaves the continental shelves. Its habits are similar to those of *T. gillii*.

### *Tursiops parvimanus*   Reinhardt DELPHINIDAE
Named in 1888, it closely resembles *T. aduncas*, indeed it has been suggested they are the same species. The original description noted differences in the number of bones of one phalanx.

### *Tursiops truncatus*   DELPHINIDAE
BOTTLENOSED DOLPHIN
As a result of oceanaria and dolphinaria, films and articles, the members of this genus, and in particular *T. truncatus*, have become very well known to the general public. Their apparent intelligence has attained a world-wide fame. Their popularity was reflected in a television series where the star is a bottlenosed dolphin.

The reason for the popularity of a species living in what to man is an alien medium is their playful and sociable behaviour. Mariners from earliest times have experienced the thrill of being escorted by groups of these creatures which jump and dive around the ship, apparently in the pure delight of living. Some individuals seem genuinely fond of men and there are many stories of them swimming into bays to join in the frolics of bathers. Dolphins, probably individuals of this species, make regular trips with boats.

Dolphins are well known to assist sick or injured members of their herd, helping them to the surface to breathe and staying close to them for comfort and protection. Whilst scientists are reluctant to attribute higher emotions to creatures other than man, such behaviour may be considered an extension of normal maternal concern.

Naval scientists have long studied cetaceans, and in particular members of this genus, in an attempt to perfect the shape of ships' hulls and submarines. They have also been interested in the sound echo or sonar apparatus used by cetaceans. (See Echolocation and Warfare.)

They have also been tempted to adapt these creatures' willingness to be trained to military purposes. By attaching magnetic bombs to their bodies and training them to swim towards enemy ships on 'suicide missions' they hope to overcome the difficulties of penetrating enemy sea defences.

In spite of their popularity and years of association with man, the taxonomists still disagree about the classification of the genus. Some prefer to place *T. gillii* as a subspecies of *T. truncatus*. *T. gillii* differs from *T. nuuanu* by an extra few pairs of ribs and a wrinkle in the eyelid. Many scientists are convinced that *T. abusalam*, and *T. aduncas* are the same species. Again there is considerable doubt about the taxonomy of *T. gephyreus*, which many assume to be identical with *T. truncatus*. Time will perhaps resolve the confusion.

## ESCHRICHTIIDAE

This family consists of a single species. It has no dorsal fin but a series of small fleshy elevations along the posterior third of the midline. There are a few skin depressions, running as lines along the throat. The head is about one-fifth the length of the body. Its 150 baleen plates on either side are short, fat, and pale yellow. The cervical vertebrae are unfused. See *Eschrichtius*.

### Eschrichtius gibbosus (E. glaucus)
Erxleber   ESCHRICHTIIDAE
CALIFORNIA GREY WHALE, GREY WHALE
Named in 1777, California grey whales reach over 13 m. in length and weigh over 20 tonnes. They have no dorsal fin but a series of humps along the dorsal midline of the tail. Their dark bluish grey colour is disfigured by scars, presumably obtained from constant scratching against rocks in an attempt to alleviate the irritation of skin parasites. On the throat are 1–4 longitudinal furrows. The flukes are of medium size. Approximately 150 pale yellow short thick baleen plates are situated on each side of the mouth. For a whale this species is quite hairy, tactile bristles adorning both jaws and the blow holes. The small oval eyes are placed just behind the corners of the mouth. There are 2 blowholes and the spray emitted forms a V shape. Each flipper has only 4 fingers to support it.

This whale favours the coastal regions of the North Pacific. It also migrates seasonally keeping to the coasts. There are 2 populations, one migrating along the coast of North America from Alaska as far south as Central America into subtropical waters, and a second along the Pacific coast of Asia as far south as Korea. The southward migrations occur along the western Pacific in November and December and are breeding migrations. Pregnant females are the first to appear off the Korean coast in November and stay during December until the middle of January. Males and the remaining females arrive in December and are gone again by January. For the journey north groups of whales move to deeper offshore waters and travel during March, April and May. Similar breeding migrations occur along the Pacific coast of North America. The pregnant females give birth after a one-year gestation period in the warmer southern waters and there suckle their young. They mate again soon after giving birth.

Californian grey whales are thought to feed during the migration northwards. Throughout the southward swim starvation is the order of the day. As well as the inevitable copepods, they have been found to consume small fish and sea cucumbers.

These fine animals swim in large groups of several hundred. The females with calves form distinct groups. Rather slow moving – 2-4 knots – they have been seen virtually standing upright in the water, like the well-known dolphinarium trick, presumably to look around. They have an additional escape speed of 8 knots for short periods. Several rapid breaths are taken at the surface between short shallow dives and these are followed by the usual deep dive lasting up to 20 minutes. The deep dive is signalled to observers, since, for this dive alone, the fluke comes right out of the water, and the body turns vertically downward.

The affinity of this species for coastal waters proved their undoing. Such proximity led to extensive hunting, particularly off the coast of America and Korea. They are now protected. Numbers are reduced to a few thousand, and are only very slowly increasing.

## GLOBICEPHALIDAE

A family first suggested by Gray in 1866. It has been customary however to ignore Gray's suggestion and include the genera in the family Delphinidae. This is somewhat surprising for there are marked differences from Delphinidae, and one would have expected the taxonomists' preoccupation with pigeon-holing to have supported Gray's lead. Members of this family have fewer teeth than Delphinidae, fewer vertebrae, no beak and, in contrast, more than 3 of the cervical vertebrae are fused. Nishiwaki has suggested that Gray's classification of this family should be upheld. See *Feresa, Globicephala, Orcinus, Peponocephala, Pseudorca.*

### *Feresa attenuata*  Gray
GLOBICEPHALIDAE SLENDER BLACKFISH, PYGMY KILLER WHALE, SLENDER PILOT WHALE
First named in 1871, this whale is black with only areas of white on the abdomen which may extend on to the chin and around lips. It reaches up to 2.5 m. in length and weighs over 160 kg. The dorsal fin is tall and moderately wide based. The flippers are long and narrow with a slightly irregular trailing edge. In profile the head is blunted. There are up to 25 teeth in each jaw. The first 3 cervical vertebrae are fused.

They are distributed in the tropical and subtropical waters of the Atlantic and Pacific oceans, and are most commonly seen in Japanese waters.

They form in groups of up to 50 individuals. Very little is known of this apparently rare species. It was not seen alive until 1963, when 14 animals were captured. Little is known of its behaviour. It looks rather like the false killer whale, *Pseudorca crassidens*, which explains one common name.

### *Globicephala macrorhynchus*  Gray
GLOBICEPHALIDAE  SHORT-FINNED BLACKFISH, SHORT-FINNED PILOT WHALE
First named in 1846, this has a rather similar body shape to *G. scammoni*. The forehead or melon is rather more pronounced and the dorsal fin is shorter based, lower and more pointed. The flippers are broader based, shorter and wider with a sharp backwardly pointing tip. The body is mainly black but with a pale grey belly and a white patch between the flippers. It grows to 6 m. in length and weighs up to 4 tonnes.

It is confined to the Pacific and Indian oceans preferring somewhat warmer areas than *G. scammoni*. Little information about the species has been recorded.

### *Globicephala melaena*  Traill
GLOBICEPHALIDAE  PILOT WHALE, ATLANTIC BLACKFISH, CALLING WHALE, BAG-FINNED PILOT WHALE
Pilot whales were first named in 1809. They have a flattened body with a long rather narrow tail, and grow to a length of 6 m. The melon has a marked dome; there is no distinct beak. The dorsal fin is broad based and moderately tall with a backward slope. The flippers are long, very narrow and sharply pointed. The body is mainly a very dark grey to black but with a paler abdomen.

A school of pilot whales, *Globicephala melaena*, in the open sea, showing the species' distinctive dorsal fin.

Distributed throughout the North Atlantic Ocean, they sometimes venture into rivers. Occasionally, whole herds are found stranded. Why this happens is something of a mystery. All members of the genus have, however, a strong attachment to their herds, keeping in close accoustical contact by using vibrations (see Echolocation). It is thought by some workers that when one is stranded, the others follow or go to assist and themselves become victims to disaster. They eat fish and squid.

The name 'pilot' was given to this animal by fishermen who, believing that the whale was always to be found near herring shoals, used it to guide their boats.

### *Globicephala scammoni* Cope
### GLOBICEPHALIDAE BLACKFISH, PACIFIC PILOT WHALE

A delightful, all black with light belly markings, blunt-headed animal first named in 1869. Blackfish have a rather flattened body which grows up to 4 m. in length. The large rather low dorsal fin has a wide base, and is situated one third of the way along the body. The body narrows considerably over the posterior third and is terminated by large flukes. The flippers are very long and narrow with sharp pointed ends. There are about 20 teeth in each jaw.

Pacific pilot whales, as the name suggests, are found in the Pacific. They are cropped by Japanese whalers for meat and oil.

Small groups of up to 15 animals are common but occasionally large herds of hundreds are formed. They are slow swimmers but have adapted to deep diving for long periods. It is thought that they can stay under water for well over one hour. Communication, as with all whales, depends to a large degree on sound signals. The species seems to have a strong attachment to the herd. On many occasions these animals have been stranded in large numbers, and some suggest it is probably as a result of attempting to escape the predatory attentions of killer whales, *Orcinus orca*. They commonly feed on both fish and squid.

### *Orcinus orca* Linnaeus
### GLOBICEPHALIDAE KILLER WHALE

First named in 1758, they are now well known to the frequenters of dolphinaria where humans often ride on their backs around the parkland pools. They are receptive to training and will perform all the well-known displays.

This whale is distinctive, with a beautifully streamlined body characteristically marked with black and white. The black back and sides are clearly separated from the white belly. An extension of the white underparts passes up onto the side

Killer whales, *Orcinus orca*, in the Sea of Cortez, Mexico, showing the prominent dorsal fin of the species.

two-thirds of the way along the body. A white patch occurs just above and posterior to the eye. The tall, up to 1.8 m., prominent dorsal fin is a special feature of the species. The story that this knife-shaped weapon is used to slash open its prey is pure legend. The flippers are large, almost rounded, and spade shaped; the flukes are of moderate size. Male killer whales may grow to over 9 m. in length and weigh something over 8 tonnes. The females are somewhat smaller. There is no beak, merely a demarkation of the lips. The dorsal profile of the body shows a perfect convex curve from lip to fluke, broken only by the dorsal fin.

The mouth of the killer is specialized. It has a very large gape, and about 12 strong conical teeth. They are sharp and point backwards and inwards. The jaws close to form an efficient interlocking machine for gripping and tearing. The first 4 cervical vertebrae are fused.

Man has had long associations with the terrible killer whale. Its bones have been discovered in prehistoric middens, and cave carvings thought to represent it have been found in France. We know that the Romans know this species from the writings of Pliny. It was indeed the Romans who first named it *orca*, or sea devil.

Killer whales are widely distributed throughout the oceans of the world, but are commonest in the eastern Pacific and the Antarctic. Quite unlike other cetaceans, they are not confined by any distributional boundaries and individuals travel freely through the oceans and hemispheres, although generally keeping to cooler waters. As a result of this lack of geographical separation, different subspecies related to areas have not developed.

These streamlined whales are capable of speeds of up to 30 knots. Their power and aggression is reflected by their behaviour. They jump out of the water and sometimes, using powerful tail movements, momentarily stand upright to survey the scene. Whilst out of the water they make no attempt to keep themselves from view. After several short breaths they take a long dive which can last up to 30 minutes.

Killers have voracious appetites and are not particularly fussy about their diet. Although they prefer other cetaceans, pinnipeds, and penguins, they will take fish and squid. Prey may be swallowed whole, or if too large, first torn into large pieces. Even the dreaded shark is no match for the killer whale which is only too happy to put it on the menu if one appears. The stomach contents of one killer contained the remains of over 30 seals in addition to fish and a few dolphins, while another was found to contain 13 porpoises and 14 seals.

Killers usually travel in small groups of from 6 to 50 individuals. These groups consist of a mature male – sometimes more than one – females, adolescents and young. There may sometimes be single sex groups but the significance of these is unknown. These packs appear to hunt as an organized team rather like a pack of wolves or African hunting dogs. Observers have seen them chase larger whales into an area of sea enclosed by land, place sentries at the entrance to prevent escape, and then attack, seemingly at a given signal.

These animals arouse such fear that even larger cetaceans seem to become paralyzed and float belly up unable to resist attack. Their presence is enough, on occasions, to cause panic and mass strandings of their victims, when the latter dash headlong to the shallows in an attempt to escape. They are said, by some observers, to play with their victims like cats, circling them and throwing them out of the water.

Like other cetaceans they are very dependent both on sound waves and hearing for navigation, orientation and communication.

Calves are usually born in the autumn although there is such flexibility that some authorities doubt that a special breeding season exists. It is reported that in New Zealand females and newborn calves swim along the coasts of the North Island in October and November. The female produces her offspring after a gestation period of 16 months.

There appears to be a strong social responsibility towards members of the group, mothers naturally being protective of their young. In addition, members of the group seem to protect and assist injured colleagues (see Behaviour).

In spite of their ferocity, killer whales have rarely, if ever, attacked man. Occasionally, due to curiosity, they have upturned a boat but have left the struggling humans in peace. Since they are afraid of shallow water they are no danger to swimmers, unlike sharks.

This is a species about which conservationists quite rightly have concern. It is hunted in small numbers, notably by the Japanese.

Since the first killer whale was captured alive for exhibition in the early 1960s they have become popular exhibits in dolphinaria. They consume something over 45 kg. of fish each day. They appear to take to captivity reasonably well and can be persuaded to perform remarkable feats, seeming to have a real bond with their trainers.

In addition to their place in the marine circus, these animals have been subjected to scientific study.

### *Peponocephala electra*  Gray
### GLOBICEPHALIDAE
LITTLE KILLER WHALE, MANY-TOOTHED BLACKFISH, BROAD-BEAKED DOLPHIN, MELON-HEADED WHALE

First named in 1846, this species grows to 2.7 m. in length and weighs over 180 kg. It has more teeth than the false killer, *Pseudorca crassidens*, and the slender blackfish, *Feresa attenuata*, but otherwise closely resembles them in shape. The body is very dark grey, lightening towards the belly.

The little killer prefers the warm waters of the Pacific and Atlantic oceans where it lives in small social groups of up to 20 individuals. Generally a rather slow-swimming animal although it can reach speeds in excess of 12 knots.

The original study of this species by Gray put it in the genus *Lagenorhynchus*. However, further research by Nakajima, Nishiwaki and Norris as recently as the early 1960s caused the original classification to be revised, and it is now placed in a separate genus.

### *Pseudorca crassidens*  Owen
### GLOBICEPHALIDAE
FALSE KILLER WHALE

Named in 1846, this whale has a black body, grows to 6 m. in length and weighs over 2 tonnes. With its blunt head it more closely resembles the blackfish whales than the killer, *Orcinus orca*. The dorsal fin is triangular and pointed, but is small and situated midway along the back. The flippers are small, well forward, narrow, and pointed. The flukes are of moderate size. It was probably the relatively large gape, the size of teeth and its aggressive character that recalled the killer to Owen who first discovered it. It has 20 strong teeth in each jaw.

It is widely distributed in temperate and tropical seas and is most common in the Indian Ocean.

In general they gather in small groups of up to 10 individuals. It is probable however that these small groups link together into rather larger, loose herds which keep in contact using sound communication. Certainly large, closely associated herds do form, possibly for breeding.

Observations suggest that calves are born all through the year which rather negates the idea mentioned above that the animal congregates for breeding at special times of the year. False killers feed on fish and squid.

### GRAMPIDAE
A family containing only one species, *Grampus griseus*. In most classifications it is placed in the family *Delphinidae* but is separated in the recent classification of Nishiwaki because there are 6 fused neck vertebrae, and there are no teeth in the upper jaw. See *Grampus*.

### *Grampus griseus*  G. Cuvier
### GRAMPIDAE  RISSO'S DOLPHIN
Named in 1812, this dolphin grows to well over 3.7 m. in length and weighs up to 680 kg. The body has a dark grey back shading gradually to a pale grey or white belly. The grey pales with age. The fin, flukes and flippers are black. The body, often covered with scratches, is deep and massive in the anterior two thirds, but tapers markedly in the posterior third. There is a square-ended appearance to the head when viewed in profile, as a result of a large and bulging forehead. The fin is tall, narrow, pointed and slopes slightly backwards. It is situated just posterior to the halfway point along the body. The flippers are broad based and long. There are no teeth in the upper jaw and no more than 12 in the lower jaw. The first 6 cervical vertebrae are fused.

Risso's dolphins may be found in all temperate to tropical waters, and have been stranded quite frequently off the coasts of the British Isles and America.

The difference in outline between the false killer, *Pseudorca crassidens*, and the killer, *Orcinus orca*, (below) can be clearly seen. The false killer lacks the killer's distinctive white patch, situated just above and behind the eye.

They are fairly rapid swimmers and will jump out of the water. They usually stay under water for only a few minutes but this can be extended up to half an hour. They tend to live in small groups of about 10 individuals but larger herds of up to 100 have been observed. They migrate towards the poles in summer, returning closer to the equator in winter.

Little is known of their reproductive behaviour but they are thought to give birth to calves in early spring in both northern and southern hemispheres.

They have been successfully kept and bred in captivity, and have been trained to perform tricks for public display. These dolphins have been known to make regular trips with boats. One of the most famous, named Pelorus Jack, piloted the ferry from Wellington to Nelson, New Zealand, through Pelorus Sound each day for 30 years.

## KOGIIDAE

This family, the pygmy sperm whales, contains 2 species – *Kogia breviceps* and *K. simus*. Some scientists prefer to consider them as a sub-family of the sperm whale family, Physeteridae. They have, however, marked physical differences from the sperm whale, *Physeter catodon*, so it is common to separate them.

The lower jaw of the pygmy whale is short like that of its larger relation. The head however is relatively much smaller, being only one sixth as long as the body. Like the sperm whale, they have functional teeth only in the lower jaw. They have, however, a very definite dorsal fin relatively far back, and all of the neck bones are fused together. See *Kogia*.

### *Kogia breviceps* Blainville KOGIIDAE
PYGMY SPERM WHALE, LESSER CACHALOT

These whales, named in 1838, are very shy indeed and much of our knowledge of them comes from studies of stranded individuals. They have a short lower jaw, like a bottom-feeding shark, and a broad head, which is unusual for any toothed whale. The blowhole is single and situated between the eyes, slightly to the side of the midline. The large, pointed, 5-fingered flippers are light grey all over. The size of the flippers adds to the animal's stability and manoeuvrability during locomotion. They grow to well over 3.7 m. in length and weigh at least 680 kg.

This species is widely distributed in the tropical, subtropical and temperate waters of both the northern and southern hemispheres, where it is thought to associate closely with its generic cousin. Unfortunate individuals have been stranded on the coasts of Asia, America, Europe and islands of the Pacific. World populations are unknown. From sighting records they appear to be more common in the northern hemisphere.

There is an old wives' tale abroad which suggests that senile sick pygmy whales commit suicide by beaching themselves rather than face a watery grave or submit to the carnivorous tendencies of the oceans' scavengers. Such an explanation is unlikely to be true. Most probably old or sick whales move into shallow waters, where a sandy bottom on which to rest is available, close to the air they need to breathe periodically, stranding then being accidental with tide changes. Certainly many stranded animals prove to be old or diseased.

Little is known of the behaviour of these retiring creatures. They are said to swim at 3 knots and to jump vertically out of the water, falling back with a belly-flop splash. Bursts of great speed keep them well clear of inquisitive humans. They do not appear to form large groups or herds but to live in restricted family units of one or two.

Mainly squid eaters, they also take larger crustacea including crabs.

Reproductive information is very scarce. What little is known comes from the few stranded pregnant females examined. Two foetuses from animals stranded on coasts in Europe in December measured 20 cm. and 23 cm.

Their shy nature, speed and small size protect them from man's merciless attack. A few are taken by small coastal stations particularly in Japan.

### *Kogia simus* Owen KOGIIDAE
OWEN'S PYGMY WHALE, DWARF SPERM WHALE

Very closely related to *K. breviceps* this species, named in 1866, is often found in similar areas and in close association with this species. It is somewhat shorter and has a prominent dorsal fin a little further forward, at the middle of the back. The head, too, is a little smaller.

The justification for classifying it as a separate species is based on small structural differences of the body and variations in the skull. In reality the genus has been little studied.

## MONODONTIDAE

A small family which has 2 genera, each with one species, both found in arctic waters. Throat grooves are entirely absent, there is no beak, and the dorsal fin is either absent or very rudimentary. The notch of the tail flukes is well defined. All of the cervical vertebrae are separate. See *Delphinapterus*, *Monodon*.

### *Delphinapterus leucas*   Pallas
MONODONTIDAE
BELUGA OR WHITE WHALE,
SEA CANARY

This species was first described in 1776, and the variety of common names is interesting. Beluga is rather unfortunate since it is also used in some parts of the world for the common dolphin, *Delphinus delphis*, and for the sturgeon, *Acipenser* sp. White whale is purely descriptive, and the name sea canary comes from the noise it makes, which resembles the bird. Superficially this species closely resembles a tuskless narwhal.

When young this whale is a dark bluish grey with darker speckling. During the first few years of life the colour gradually fades until the adult white colouring emerges. It grows to 4.5 m. The head is rounded with no beak, and has a large bulbous forehead. There are 8 to 11 teeth on each side of the upper jaw and 8 to 9 in each lower jaw. The eyes are set back from the corner of the mouth and are small. The blowhole is in the midline above the eyes. A small hump in the centre of the back substitutes for a dorsal fin. The flippers are large and paddle shaped, the flukes are wide with a well-defined notch.

Belugas inhabit the Arctic Ocean where they feed mainly on large fish but also take a variety of invertebrates, including squid and crabs. The body colour of these whales makes them easily visible from the air. They are known to migrate from the Arctic seas south in both the Atlantic and Pacific oceans. They have moved along the St Lawrence as far as Quebec. In addition they appear fairly abundant around the North Sea and along the coasts of Scandinavia. Occasionally individuals get further south.

Attaining speeds of around 6 knots, they keep low in the water, showing little of their head or back when at the surface. Their canary song can be heard when they near the surface. Socially they form small groups of up to 12 individuals, but they congregate during the migrations into large herds numbering several hundred.

Belugas have a 14-month gestation. They mate in the northern spring, April-May, and give birth to dark-coloured off-spring in midsummer – June or July. The young are 1.2–1.5 m. in length at birth and are suckled for 9 months. Some squid and large crustacea form part of the beluga's food but stomach contents suggest that their main food is fish.

They have been hunted in the past for their skins and for oil. Norwegian whalers accounted for several hundred each year until recently when numbers began to decline, and Canadian whalers still take some but catches are regulated. More recently the vogue of sea aquaria and dolphinaria have been instrumental in further reducing the numbers. Current estimations of numbers, based on aerial surveys, suggests there is a world population of between 8,000 to 15,000.

### *Monodon monoceros*   Linnaeus
MONODONTIDAE   NARWHAL, MONODON,
UNICORN WHALE

This species was named in 1758. Narwhals are scientifically interesting, but they have added fascination because they are intimately associated with mythology. Their horn or spike, which is in fact an elongated, twisted tooth, was and still is prized for its magical and aphrodisiac properties, but it is for its connection with the unicorn that it is best known. The relationship between a sea mammal and a mythological member of the horse family is at first difficult to understand. The origins of the unicorn tales are obscure, but may have originated in part from the Arabian oryx, an antelope which, if viewed in profile, appears to have one straight horn. The narwhal's tooth, with its characteristic twist, was presented to the gullible as proof of the existence of the mythical beast by

A narwhal with an Eskimo whaler in a kayak featured on the title page of *The Naturalists Library* vol. VI, 1839.

they can survive as long as breathing holes are available. Odd individuals have been stranded on British coasts as far south as Essex.

They feed on fish and squid but also take crustaceans.

Socially they form small mixed-sex groups of up to 10 animals. Reproductive behaviour is largely unknown, although they probably give birth in the spring.

This species was originally hunted for oil and its tusk with a hand harpoon. After being hit, it dives rapidly over 200 m. but soon returns to the surface where it falls an easy victim to its pursuers. Some hunting still takes place, but with the decline in interest in the properties of its horn its pursuit is more spasmodic.

The purpose of the strange tooth development remains a mystery. Several suggestions have been made – that it is a weapon for fighting other males during the breeding season, or a tool for digging up prey in the bottom mud or for breaking ice to provide a breathing hole. All are speculative and no observations have been made.

## ORCAELIDAE

This family has been recently created by Nishi-waki. It includes the one species *Orcaella brevirostris*, previously classified in the Delphinidae. See *Orcaella*.

### *Orcaella brevirostris*  Owen
ORCAELIDAE    IRRAWADDY DOLPHIN

This delightful dolphin somewhat resembles in shape the beluga or white whale *Delphinapterus leucas*. It was first described in 1866. It has a pronounced forehead or melon and no beak, giving it a blunt appearance; the large eyes are placed behind and above the corners of the mouth. The blowhole is to one side of the midline. A small round-ended fin placed just posterior to the half-way mark leans backwards. The flippers are large with a markedly convex trailing edge. The body is a dark grey or black, gradually paling to a light grey belly. It attains a length of over 2 m.

This species is found in coastal waters and river estuaries of South-east Asia. It is particularly common in the Irrawaddy, Brahmaputra and Ganges rivers, but has been seen close to the shores of

unscrupulous traders who thereby made a great deal of money.

The narwhal grows to a maximum length of 5.5 m. and can weigh over one tonne. It is a creamy brown when adult, but starts life a bluish grey. There are a few lumps along the back, substitutes for the dorsal fin. The teeth of the narwhal are unique. In the male the left tooth on the upper jaw grows forward twisting as it grows until it reaches a maximum of 3 m. in length. In the female the teeth do not erupt. Occasionally in the male both upper teeth grow forward. Apart from the 'horn' or tusk the narwhal closely resembles its family relation the white whale, *Delphinapterus leucas*.

Narwhals are distributed in the Arctic Ocean. They follow the ice moving north in spring and summer and return further south in winter. Occasionally some are trapped below the ice where

Singapore, Java, the Malay peninsula, and even the northern seas of Australia. No reliable estimations of the world populations are available.

They form small groups which swim slowly, breaking surface gently to breath, exposing their characteristically shaped head and their back. The fluke is rarely exposed. They seldom stay under water for longer than 2 minutes. They feed exclusively on bony fish.

In former times these dolphins were attributed with special powers over the local fish populations. Native fishermen believed they assisted them in their fishing activities. It was customary therefore for the natives to protect them from harm.

## PHOCOENIDAE

This family contains 3 genera which are referred to by some as the true porpoises. They are small, without distinct beaks, and live in cold coastal waters; they sometimes ascend rivers. The head curves up from the tip of the mouth to the blowhole without interruption. Both jaws are of equal length. The teeth are interesting in being flat and spade-like. Five cervical vertebrae at least are fused. No grooves are present on the skin of the throat. The flukes are notched.
See *Neophocoena, Phocoena, Phocoenoides.*

### *Neophocoena phocoenoides*　G. Cuvier
PHOCOENIDAE　INDIAN PORPOISE,
FINLESS BLACK PORPOISE, FINLESS PORPOISE
First named in 1829, this deep-bodied creature is, as the name suggests, black. Variation, however, does occur and shades of dark grey are common. Unusually for the family, it has no dorsal fin although it does have a dorsal ridge. It grows to 1.5 m. in length and weighs up to 45 kg. It has large flippers with pointed ends. The flukes are large for the family with a distinct, fairly deep notch.

Indian porpoises are widely distributed in coastal regions between the west coast of the Indian continent and Japan, including Singapore, Java and the East China Sea. They have been reported several hundred miles up the Yangtze river. Hunting is restricted to spasmodic activities by natives.

Slow swimmers, but very active, swimming close to the surface with frequent sudden changes of direction. They rarely jump out of the water, or dive for longer than one minute. Their favourite habitat of rather cloudy estuary water makes them difficult subjects to study, and estimates of their population meaningless. They eat fish and squid.

Little is known of their reproductive activities, but they are thought to give birth in September and October.

### *Phocoena dioptrica*　Lahille
PHOCOENIDAE　SPECTACLED PORPOISE
A small but distinctive species, first named in 1912. It has a markedly different body shape from the common porpoise, *P. phocoena*, with a narrower fore-end, widening to a maximum midway along the body and tapering gently again towards the flukes. The blunt-nosed head is small with a distinctive eye surrounded by a black circle, situated just below the sharp boundary between the black dorsal and the white ventral half of the body. The dorsal fin is wide based and low. The flukes are relatively small, and just anterior to them the black dorsal colour gives way to a small area of pale grey or white. The lips are black. The first 5 cervical vertebrae are fused. A grey line from just behind the corner of the mouth runs backwards onto the leading edge of the otherwise white flipper. The spectacled porpoise grows to a length of 1.5 m.

This species does not appear to be common and little is known of its life history. It is found along the eastern coast of the southern half of South America and the associated islands. It is hunted by natives but not on a commercial basis.

### *Phocoena phocoena*　Linnaeus
PHOCOENIDAE　COMMON PORPOISE,
HARBOUR PORPOISE
This popular sea mammal, which was first named in 1758, must be known to many who frequent coastal waters in small boats or even those who enjoy walking by the sea.

It has a blunt rounded head and distinctive beak, a deep body tapering to a fine narrow tail end. Common porpoises grow to 1.8 m. and weigh around 70 kg. The dorsal fin is a regular triangle with a broad base and low apex. The body is a dull blue-grey on the back which gradually fades to a pale grey belly. All the cervical vertebrae except the last, the seventh, are fused. The 200 or so teeth are small and blade-like. The blowhole is crescent shaped.

Widely distributed in the Atlantic and Pacific oceans, it ventures as far north as Iceland and as far south as the southern tip of Africa. It also inhabits the inland waters of the Mediterranean and Black seas. Pacific specimens are common off the coast of America and are often observed in Japanese waters. It prefers temperate, subarctic, and subtropical waters and is rarely seen in tropical seas. Abundant in the North Atlantic, where it is found as far south as North Carolina, this is without doubt the most common species around the coasts of the British Isles, often swimming well up into rivers.

It is a playful gregarious creature which forms mixed groups of up to 100. Swimming at moderate speeds it often jumps right out of the water and rarely stays under for more than a few minutes at a time. It is well known for its habit of accompanying small boats and playing among the bow waves. It feeds on flatfish, cod, herring, squid and crustaceans.

Mating takes place in the summer. Observations of courtship behaviour have been made on captive animals. Sexually mature pairs swim close to each other, touching frequently. The male touches and rubs the sides and dorsal fin of the female with his tail. Occasionally he swims under her abdomen. The male frequently presents his abdomen to the female. Both nudge the other's side with the head. These activities are accompanied by sounds which apparently relate only to courtship behaviour. Parturition occurs in the spring and early summer after a gestation period of 10–11 months. The young, sometimes twins, weighs about 5 kg. when born and is nearly half as long as the mother. Lactation lasts for about a year. As with many other cetaceans, there is a close relationship between mother and young. There is a record of one female which followed the boat carrying her captured offspring for over an hour. The young was then released and they swam away together.

This species has been kept in captivity with success and it has been used for research. Detailed investigations on its sound signals have proved very informative. When first placed in strange surroundings they emit a characteristic cry. A quite different sound is associated with social dominance. An individual known to be dominant from its success in aggressive encounters over another emitted specific sounds before moving in to chase the subservient colleague away from a proffered fish. Later work showed that these sounds were made only by the more dominant members of a social hierarchy. These sounds are characteristic of the species and can be used in identification when they are out of view.

Reference may be sometimes seen to *Phocoena vomerina* Gill which was named in 1865. This is certainly identical with *P. phocoena*. *P. phocoena relicta* Abel is considered by some authorities to be a subspecies. It was named in 1905 and inhabits the Black Sea.

### *Phocoena sinus*   Norris and McFarland
PHOCOENIDAE   GULF OF CALIFORNIA HARBOUR PORPOISE, COCHITO

This species was first named for science on the basis of a single skull as recently as 1958. Two subsequently discovered skulls add little more evidence or justification for such a classification. It is said, however, that fishermen in the Gulf of California are familiar with the animal, although it is retiring and difficult to observe.

### *Phocoena spinipinnis*   Burmeister
PHOCOENIDAE   BURMEISTER'S PORPOISE, BLACK PORPOISE

A rare black porpoise first named in 1865. It has a small head with a flat line from the top of the mouth to the blowhole. The fin is two-thirds of the way along the body, triangular and sharply pointed. This porpoise grows to 1.5 m. in length and weighs up to 64 kg. It inhabits cold inshore waters along the east and west coasts of South America, from the La Plata River around Cape Horn and as far north as Peru.

A very rare animal, about which little is known.

### *Phocoenoides dalli dalli*   True
PHOCOENIDAE   DALL'S PORPOISE

Dall's porpoise was first named in 1885. It inhabits the North Pacific in temperate and subarctic

A sperm whale stranded at Gairdner River, Western Australia.

waters up to the Bering Sea and the coast of Alaska, and as far south as Japan and the coast of California.

It reaches over 1.8 m. in length and weighs up to 136 kg. It is thick set and deep bodied with small eyes, small flippers and small flukes. The mouth slopes upwards towards each corner. There is a very distinctive reversed saddle of white on the belly, the flaps of which are well up the animal's side.

Throughout its range there are thought to be over 60,000 individuals. They feed on fish and squid.

Their social groupings vary. In some areas, notably the southern part of their range, the herds are numbered in tens, but in the northern sub-arctic waters herds of several hundred appear to be common. They can dive for several minutes. Fast swimmers, over 14 knots, they rarely jump but are seen easily by the flurry of water caused by the dorsal fin. They are often seen playing around ships. They probably migrate north in summer and south in winter. The young are born in May and June.

### *Phocoenoides dalli truei*   Andrews
PHOCOENIDAE   TRUE'S PORPOISE
Named in 1911 this subspecies closely resembles Dall's porpoise. Although in both subspecies the white saddle of the abdomen varies, it tends to cover a greater area in True's porpoise. They are separated into subspecies because of adult body size, dental formula and small skeletal variations.

Found in the north-western extremity of the Pacific, True's porpoise is playful and a fast swimmer. Groups of up to 300 individuals are often seen. They feed on fish and squid.

Little is known of the reproductive cycle but they probably give birth during the early summer months.

### PHYSETERIDAE
This family contains only one species, the popular and well-known sperm whale. Its huge head and short, relatively diminutive lower jaw provides the child's story writer, the cartoonist and the toy maker with unmistakable features for symbolic representation. See *Physeter*.

### *Physeter catodon*   Linnaeus
PHYSETERIDAE   SPERM WHALE,
CACHALOT
The general shape of these magnificent marine beasts must be well known to most people. The producers of cartoons and cuddly toys use the characteristic outline when wishing to portray whales.

First named in 1758. The largest males grow to over 18 m. in length and weigh in excess of 61 tonnes. Females are somewhat smaller. The large flat-topped, blunt-ended head achieves its unique shape from the skeletal structure of the skull. In effect bones grow out from the skull to form a box which contains an oily substance (see Spermaceti). Not much is known about this substance although it has been suggested that it is an important pressure stabilizer when the animal dives deeply. This enormous head constitutes one-third the length of the body. The S-shaped blowhole, situated well forward to the left of midline, produces a characteristic blast. Most whales blast vertically but in this species it is diverted forwards at an angle. This obviously aids recognition at sea during whaling operations. The lower jaw is much shorter than the upper and is very narrow. Teeth, conical in shape, usually occur only in the lower jaw; the upper jaw has a series of holes into which these teeth fit. The upper jaw has teeth but they only rarely erupt. Some animals have a twisted lower jaw which, although presumably interfering with eating, does not prevent survival.

The body of the sperm whale is dark grey-blue or black, fading to a pale abdomen. They tend to become paler with age. Albino animals have also been observed. The flippers seem almost pathetically small for the animal, and have a blunt end and a convex trailing edge. There is no dorsal fin, merely a series of bumps along the dorsal midline of the tail. The flukes are large and notched. The first cervical vertebra is free to articulate, but the posterior 6 are fused. The skin of the sperm whale is smooth and hairless. These animals are thought to live to about 75 years.

Sperm whales are widely distributed in the oceans of the world. Because they are large, relatively easy to see and of commercial importance, a good deal is known of their distribution, population numbers and migrations. Female sperm whales do not venture from warm waters, rarely migrating out of the 40° latitudes. Males, however, commonly travel as far north and south as the 70° latitudes. They have been recorded in the Bering Sea. Males form groups consisting of old animals which, some think, have lost their prowess with females, and young immature males. There is apparently no mingling of northern and southern hemisphere populations. The world population is unknown but is probably in excess of 150,000.

After a period at the surface during which breaths are taken every few minutes interspersed with short shallow dives, a long deep dive lasting over an hour occurs.

Several types of social group are formed. The breeding unit consists of up to 8 individuals consisting of a male with several mature females and their offspring. Males defend their harem and fight off the challenges of younger males for as long as possible. When they finally succumb to a younger male they join one of the bachelor groups mentioned previously. The social interaction of these groups and the actual migrations to the females in breeding seasons are largely unknown. Group care and group responsibility is a feature of sperm whale behaviour, as it is in other cetacean species. Wounded animals are protected and assisted by the group, who circle the endangered animal, helping it to the surface and attempting, by frequent splashing with their tails, to avert threats of their predators, all too often man.

Aggressive behaviour towards tormentors is a feature of their behaviour well known to whalers. Many men have met a sudden watery grave when an enraged and wounded sperm whale has turned on its pursuers. They charge and butt ships, upturn them, lash them with their huge flukes and crush them with their mouths – a mouth large enough to swallow a man.

Play seems to be a feature of a sperm whale's life. They are often observed slapping their flukes on the surface, jumping half out of the water and sometimes fully out, falling back with a tremendous splash.

Sperm whales eat fish, including large sharks, squid and octopus. There are often large sucker marks left on the head of whales as a result of a battle with a giant squid.

Males return to warmer waters, and to the females, for the breeding season. In the northern hemisphere the season is in April and May; in the south it is in November and December. Gestation lasts about 16 months after which a calf, some 3.5–4.5 m. long, is born. Lactation is thought to last some 10–12 months when the offspring will be about 7.5 m. long. Estimates suggest that whales begin to mature sexually at 10 years of age, long before they are fully grown.

The Australian fur seal, *Arctocephalus doriferus*. This profile can be compared with that of the northern fur seal (see p. 123). The shape of the head distinguishes the northern from the southern species.

Whaling has seriously reduced world populations. In modern times small social groups of no more than 10 are seen. In earlier days large herds were common. At its peak the whaling industry took an annual toll of over 30,000 sperm whales. Today the population is so small that there is serious concern for their survival. A total embargo is unenforceable and far too many are still slaughtered in spite of an international moratorium. These majestic creatures were hunted for meat and blubber and, in addition, for 2 valuable products, spermaceti (see Spermaceti) in the head and ambergris (see Ambergris) in the intestine. Both substances were primarily used in the cosmetic industry as stabilizers before modern techniques largely negated their function. Sadly they are still considered better than synthetic chemicals and the price remains high.

## PLATANISTIDAE

This is an interesting family which lives only in large warm freshwater rivers and lakes. The beak is long and well defined. A long-based low dorsal fin is present. The structure of these animals is thought to resemble more primitive cetaceans. This is interesting since it provides an added chapter in the story of their evolutionary return to water from land living ancestors. Their cervical vertebrae are separate and relatively large. They are often called river or freshwater dolphins and are therefore strictly out of place in this book.

All except one species live well up the river away from the mouth. See *Inia, Platanista, Pontoporia, Lipotes.*

### *Inia geoffrensis* Blainville
PLATANISTIDAE AMAZON DOLPHIN, PINK PORPOISE, BOUTU, BOTO, BUFEO

This species, which was named in 1817, has a darkish grey body which fades with age to a pale grey on the back, and a pink belly. It will grow to 3 m. and can weigh over 115 kg. With its well defined long beak and domed forehead, it presents a distinctive profile. It has a mobile neck, unusual in the Cetacea, which allows it to twist through 45° from its central axis. It has 24 to 30 teeth on each side of the upper and lower jaws. The dorsal fin is long and low, and the flippers are very large. Its

*Above* Sperm whale hunting from small boats in the mid-19th century.

eyes are minute, and the large cheeks would seem to prevent downward vision. It has stereoscopic vision and can see upwards, and as a result swims upside-down at the bottom to get its food. The dorsally placed blowhole is a long slit.

This species is restricted to tributaries of the Amazon and Orinoco rivers where it lives some 2,400 km. from the sea.

It has mostly been observed living alone but a certain percentage live in pairs or groups of up to 6 individuals. Though usually a lethargic swimmer – 2 knots, it is capable of speeds of up to 10 knots, presumably essential for hunting, at which it seems to be very efficient. Much of its time is spent resting on its flippers at the bottom. Each dive lasts for less than 2 minutes. It then rises almost horizontally, with noisy blows which reach 2 m. in height.

Females show considerable maternal care (see Behaviour) and have been known to follow for long distances boats which carry their captured young. The close relationship between mother and young is reflected by the fact that the calf remains with her until it is nearly full grown.

Adults have been known to 'heave to' (see Behaviour) shoal mates which are injured or in danger. On one occasion it was reported that several individuals swam in attendance on an injured colleague for several hours.

South American Indians believe that Amazon dolphins come ashore at certain ceremonies, take

*Opposite* The New Zealand fur seal, *Arctocephalus forsteri*, raises its head in aggression.

part in the celebrations, and then father human children before returning to the water. Native superstition among some tribes prevents the slaughter of these animals.

One particular animal is said to have taken a fancy to a local group of fishermen and assisted the men in herding the fish towards the nets. It spent hours at this occupation and apparently responded to the calls and whistles of the fishermen in the boat.

These animals have been kept in captivity with reasonable success. Like all members of the Cetacea observed in captivity, they enjoy body contact with other members of the species. This may take the form of gentle stroking with head or flippers, or quite violent banging with heads, and even gentle mouthing.

This species has also been used in research programmes designed to investigate the development of echolocation. It seems as if this more primitive species has yet to develop this sense, unlike the more advanced bottlenosed dolphin, *Tursiops truncatus*, which apparently emits sound from a very few days of age.

### *Lipotes vexillifer*  Miller
PLATANISTIDAE   CHINESE LAKE DOLPHIN, WHITE FLAG DOLPHIN, CHINESE RIVER DOLPHIN, PEI C'HI

This animal, named in 1918, grows to over 2.4 m. and weighs a maximum of 90 kg. It has a blue-black body, which shades to a pale grey belly. The beak is very long and curved upwards. There is a small dome to the forehead. The flippers are large and triangular with rounded corners. A small dorsal fin is situated half way along the back. The flukes are large. A rectangular blowhole is situated to the left of mid-line just behind the forehead. There are about 70 teeth in each jaw. The eyes are very small indeed and the animal may, like the river dolphin, *Platanista gangetica*, be blind.

It lives only in the Tung Ting Lake in China, which is situated 960 km. up the Yangtze river; it eats fish and freshwater crustaceans.

The species is usually found in small groups of 3 and 4 individuals, but during the dry season, when the water level drops, they herd together in larger colonies in the deeper parts of the lake. When spring brings rain again, they move into the small rivers surrounding the lake to breed.

Local superstition has so far protected this species. Such folklore is better than unenforceable legislation when attempting conservation.

### *Platanista gangetica*  Roxburgh
PLATANISTIDAE
GANGES RIVER DOLPHIN, BLIND DOLPHIN, SUSU

This species was named in 1801. The dark grey or dark brown body shades to a pale grey or pale brown belly. The animal grows to a maximum of 2.4 m. and weighs well over 45 kg. The beak is long and well defined. The flippers are very large, spade-like appendages. It has a wide, notched fluke and 2 ridges running along the back, and one from the anus to the tail to assist stability. The eyes are extremely small and are said to be structurally degenerate causing the animal to be blind. The large rather elongated cervical vertebrae allow flexibility and the neck can be differentiated externally.

They inhabit the Ganges, Brahmaputra and Indus rivers where they live on fish, freshwater crustacea and other invertebrates, possibly sifting the mud with their beaks to find them.

When they surface to breathe they partially, or occasionally totally, leave the water before diving again. Small groups of 4 or 5 individuals form a social group. Gestation is believed to be about 8 months in length.

They are sporadically hunted by the local population for food.

### *Pontoporia blainvillei*  Genrais and d'Orbigny  PLATANISTIDAE
LA PLATA RIVER DOLPHIN, FRANCISCANA

This is a little known species which was named in 1844. It has a pale grey-brown body. The beak is very long relative to the total body length of about 1.8 m. The neck is well defined and because of the long separate neckbones is mobile. A relatively tall dorsal fin is present with a long base. The flippers are large and triangular. They have over 100 teeth in each jaw. Unlike their close relative the Ganges River dolphin, *Platanista gangetica*, the eyesight is quite efficient. They feed on small invertebrates and fish.

Found only in La Plata River and in coastal brackish waters close to its mouth. Migratory movements have not been studied but there is some suggestion that during the winter they travel northwards along the coast. Population estimates do not exist.

## ZIPHIIDAE
This family contains five genera of medium-sized whales growing up to 12 m.

The jaws are elongated into what in many species resembles a duck's beak and the lower jaw extends to the tip of the snout or beyond. The single blowhole is somewhat posterior from the anterior point of the jaw. They have long slender flippers and large wide flukes with a shallow or completely absent notch. Characteristically they have two V-shaped grooves on the throat. A dorsal fin is present but is situated well towards the tail. See *Berardius, Hyperoodon, Mesoplodon, Tasmacetus, Ziphius*.

A group of Amazon dolphins, *Inia geoffrensis*, showing their elongated snout and mobile neck.

**Berardius arnouxi**  Duvernoy
ZIPHIIDAE  SOUTHERN BEAKED WHALE,
ARNOUX WHALE

There are close similarities between this species and its generic cousin *B. bairdi*. It is, however, somewhat smaller with a relatively large head and flippers, and a wider fluke. Its dark blue-grey back becomes mottled on the side and finally lightens to a pale grey underneath. It was named in 1851.

The southern beaked whale has the 2 pairs of teeth characteristic of the genus; these are apparently used in fights during the breeding season by both males and females, because the skins of mature animals are generally scarred.

It is found only in the southern hemisphere. One concentration centres around Australia and New Zealand while a second is found in the waters off the coast of South America, including the Falkland Islands. Some observers have reported migrations to warmer water in the summer for breeding and calving.

Little is known about the behaviour of southern beaked whales but they appear to live in very small groups. No large herds have ever been recorded. The scant information available about this species is the result of studies made on stranded specimens.

**Berardius bairdi**  Stejneger
ZIPHIIDAE  BAIRD'S BEAKED WHALE

This attractive whale, named in 1883, reaches 10–11 m. and sometimes more in length and weighs over 12 tonnes. It has a long beak, and the V-shaped throat grooves, characteristic of the family, are well defined. It has rather small narrow flippers and a medium-sized fluke. The grey body colour extends over most of the animal although there is a tendency for the abdomen to become paler. A small triangular dorsal fin is situated well back, fairly close to the tail. There are just 2 pairs of teeth in the lower jaw and none in the upper. The first 3 neck bones are fused together.

This whale is restricted to the northern hemisphere. It is found in the western Pacific around the Kuril Islands and as far north as the Sea of Okhotsk. Some also spend part of the year around the Aleutian islands, in the Bering Sea, off the coast of Alaska and as far south as California.

The migration of these whales is unusual. They spend the summer months in the warmer waters, around Japan, and winter in the cooler waters around the Aleutian Islands. They first appear as quite large herds off the Japanese coast in May, and move northwards to disperse in August. Several hundred are taken annually by the Japanese coastal whaling industry as they migrate northwards. It appears from what figures are available that the population is able to replace the present amount of cropping. However complacency and conservation are not happy bedfellows, so a careful watch must be maintained.

Following the pattern of larger species, Baird's whales make several shallow dives with frequent breaths, followed by a deep dive of some 15–20 minutes. They are thought to swim at about 3 knots but undoubtedly short bursts of greater speed are possible.

Baird's whale is a social animal and lives in herds, possibly made up of individuals of different ages and maturity. Sometimes one male appears to be leading a group of females. They appear to breed in the warmer waters during the spring. Gestation probably takes about 10–11 months. They feed mainly on squid, but a number of fish, crustacea and other invertebrates have been found in their stomachs.

**Hyperoodon ampullatus**  Forster
ZIPHIIDAE  BOTTLENOSED WHALE,
NORTHERN BOTTLENOSED WHALE

This species, named in 1770, grows to around 9 m. in length and weighs up to 10 tonnes. It gets its common name from the shape of the jaws. The large, rather bulbous, head grows with age and in males is particularly noticeable. The back is dark grey shading through to a pale grey abdomen. Above the small eyes, behind the head, opens the single blowhole. The flippers are of medium size. A small dorsal fin is placed about two-thirds of the way down the body and is angled backwards, with a concave posterior edge. This whale usually has only one pair of teeth which occur in the lower jaw.

The bottlenosed whale is found only in the northern hemisphere where the majority inhabit arctic waters, but the range extends south in the Atlantic to Newfoundland and Europe, and in the Pacific to the Bering and Okhotsk seas. During the

This 6 m. specimen of the bottlenosed whale, *Hyperoodon ampullatus*, was killed when fouled by a ship in the River Tees on 14 August 1958.

winters they probably migrate to the warmer, temperate waters returning to the arctic for summer. Information about the world population is scanty.

As this whale swims at the surface, making about 3 knots, it rides well out of the water, with its head and back exposed. It takes a series of short breaths at the surface before diving deep for up to half an hour. They are carnivorous and enjoy a variety of animal food including squid.

Socially, apart from the breeding season, they form small herds of up to 12 animals usually separated into male groups and females with young. Details of reproduction behaviour remain largely unknown. Quite a bit of fighting between males occurs during the breeding season. Calves are born, after a gestation period probably lasting up to a year, in the spring. The young may be 3 m. in length.

Hunting activities in the nineteenth century undoubtedly seriously reduced the population of this species. Apart from valuable amounts of blubber, their store of spermaceti was highly prized.

### *Hyperoodon planifrons*   Flower
### ZIPHIIDAE

SOUTHERN BOTTLENOSED WHALE

This species closely resembles its generic relative from the northern hemisphere. The dorsal fin is further towards the tail; the forehead bulge is even more pronounced, and the flukes are slightly larger. It has blue back shading to a pale blue-grey belly. It was named in 1882.

Like the northern bottlenosed, it swims at 3 knots and takes several breaths at the surface before a deep dive of up to half an hour. The blast is low and wide.

They are only found in the southern hemisphere where they inhabit the antarctic waters in summer, migrating to warmer seas for the winter. Several strandings have occurred around the coasts of Australia and New Zeland. Population figures are fragmentary and unreliable. Strandings suggest the species is very rare but reported sightings indicate larger numbers.

Small groups of up to 10 are usual. Separate male groups and females with calves are formed.

Various foods are taken but there is a preference for squid if stomach contents of stranded specimens are a reliable indication.

Little is known on reproductive behaviour.

### *Mesoplodon bidens*   Sowerby
ZIPHIIDAE   SOWERBY'S BEAKED WHALE

Named in 1804, this rare beaked whale is not unlike Cuvier's beaked whale, *Ziphius cavirostris*, and the bottlenosed whale, *Hyperoodon ampullatus*. It has, however, a very slender streamlined body, less deep in the middle than many of the genus. The beak is elongated but is continuous with the small head. This species grows up to 4.6 m. in length, is black all over but may have white patches on the belly. The single tooth on each lower jaw is large and flat, and is positioned midway along the mouth; in the male it is visible because it protrudes.

Since no recorded sighting or strandings have been made outside the Atlantic Ocean, it is assumed they are restricted to that ocean.

Information about social behaviour and reproduction is very limited. The young are thought to be born in the spring. Its feeding habits are unknown.

### *Mesoplodon bowdoini*   Andrews
ZIPHIIDAE   BOWDOINI'S BEAKED WHALE, ANDREW'S WHALE

Found only in the South Pacific, this species, named in 1908, is given separate status from the sabre-toothed whale, *M. stejnegeri*, which is found only in the north of that ocean. This species is known only from 6 strandings – which were often originally 'wrongly' attributed to the sabre-toothed whale, so there is strong reason to doubt its validity as a separate species.

### *Mesoplodon carlhubbsi*   Moore
ZIPHIIDAE   HUBB'S BEAKED WHALE

A beaked whale found only in the North Pacific. Information is sparse, as in many other beaked whales, and in this case gleaned from 5 stranded animals only. The flippers are small and elongated. A small dorsal fin is situated two-thirds of the way along the dark grey body. Present information suggests that these animals reach some 5 m. in length. It was named in 1963.

### *Mesoplodon densirostris*   Blaïnville
ZIPHIIDAE   BLAINVILLE'S BEAKED WHALE

This species was named in 1817. Its spindle-shaped body reaches 4.5 m. in length and is rather compressed laterally. The dorsal fin is large and is situated three-quarters of the way along the body. As in many members of the genus, the flippers are small and narrow. The overall body colour is black with a dark grey abdomen. An outgrowth on either side of the lower jaw, midway along its length, houses the roots of the simple pair of teeth. These are well developed in the male and rather distinctive.

In spite of the few strandings, less than 20, and even fewer living observations, the species seems to be widely distributed. Reports come from the Indian Ocean, the coasts of Africa and Spain and the eastern seaboard of America; it does not appear to inhabit the northern Pacific.

### *Mesoplodon gervaisi (M. europeus)*   Gervais
ZIPHIIDAE   GULF STREAM BEAKED WHALE, GERVAIS' BEAKED WHALE

Gulf Stream beaked whales are known from only a few specimens. The species was named in 1866. They closely resemble True's beaked whale, *M. mirus*, and Sowerby's whale *M. bidens*. They reach 7.3 m. in length and can weigh 2.7 tonnes. They have small heads. The body is compressed laterally and the flippers are small and very narrow. The fluke is small and the dorsal fin is situated well back along the body.

The Gulf Stream beaked whale gets its name from the distribution known to date which is in the Atlantic, along the east coast, from New York to the islands of the West Indies, and across to the English Channel.

**Mesoplodon ginkgodens**   Nishiwaki and Kamiya   ZIPHIIDAE
JAPANESE BEAKED WHALE, GINKGO WHALE, GINKGO-TOOTHED BEAKED WHALE

This streamlined whale, named in 1958, reaches 5 m. in length. The body colour is dark grey or black from the back and well down the sides, shading to grey on the abdomen. The beak is long but gradually merges with the head. On the lower jaw there is a flap of skin which contacts the upper jaw. The dorsal fin is small and situated about two-thirds of the way along the body. The flippers are small and narrow. The flukes are large with no notch.

This species is found in the North Pacific in the seas off Japan. It apparently eats mainly fish. It is known from only 3 specimens caught by Japanese fishermen. Such scant information about this species, which is difficult to distinguish from close relatives, must make us have serious reservations about the validity of their specific status.

**Mesoplodon grayi**   von Haast
ZIPHIIDAE   NEW ZEALAND SCAMPERDOWN WHALE, GRAY'S BEAKED WHALE

Named in 1876, the scamperdown has the typical spindle body shape of the genus. The body colour shades from a greyish green to a pale browny green on the abdomen. The dorsal fin, two-thirds of the way along the body, is sharply pointed and triangular. The ventral V shaped grooves are very well defined.

It has only been found in the southern hemisphere although one individual was claimed on the coast of Europe. It is most commonly reported from Australia and New Zealand and the coast of South America.

From one stranding of a herd of 28 scamperdown whales in New Zealand, it is assumed that it forms social groups.

**Mesoplodon hectori**   Gray   ZIPHIIDAE
HECTOR'S BEAKED WHALE

Described from 3 immature skulls and an adult found in Tasmania. There is a pair of teeth in the lower jaw just away from the tip. Knowledge of this whale's natural history is scant. It was named in 1871.

**Mesoplodon layardi**   Gray
ZIPHIIDAE   STRAP-TOOTHED WHALE

The name of this little-known beaked whale comes from the 2 flat teeth in the lower jaw which grow outside and over the upper jaw to resemble a white strap. Information about it has been gathered from less than 50 stranded animals. It grows to 6 m. in length, has a small, streamlined head, and a laterally compressed body. It is dark grey along the back, shading through slate grey, to an off-white belly. The fluke has no notch.

It is thought to swim in small groups at about 4 knots and give birth to young in the spring. To date it has only been found in the southern hemisphere. Virtually nothing is known of its life history. It was named in 1865.

**Mesoplodon mirus**   True   ZIPHIIDAE
TRUE'S BEAKED WHALE

A little-known whale with a small streamlined head and short jaws. They are rarely seen, even more rarely caught, and strandings are very infrequent. The back is very dark grey or black, shading to paler grey sides and a reddish grey abdomen, which is flecked with black. They grow up to 5.5 m. The body is slender and the sides are compressed. The fin is behind the mid point of the back. The flippers are small, far forward and vertically positioned. They closely resemble Cuvier's beaked whale, *Ziphius cavirostris*.

The distribution is not known. Named in 1913, it has only been found in the North Atlantic.

**Mesoplodon pacificus**   Longman
ZIPHIIDAE   LONGMAN'S BEAKED WHALE

This whale personifies our lack of knowledge about the whole genus, species of which are rarely seen and rarely caught. It was described in 1926 from a single skull found in Australia. More recently Dr Maria Azzoroli described a second skull found in 1955. Some sightings have been claimed but the species awaits further investigation.

**Mesoplodon stejnegeri**   True
ZIPHIIDAE   STEJNEGER'S BEAKED WHALE, SABRE-TOOTHED WHALE

Named in 1885, this is another species of the genus found only in the northern Pacific. The body is all black. It has one pair of teeth in the lower jaw placed some way back from the tip. They are triangular and very much larger in males than in females. It grows to 5 m. in length and has a spindle shaped body. It is known from a few specimens stranded on the coasts of the Pacific Ocean.

This rarely sighted animal is said to swim in small groups of up to 4 individuals.

***Tasmacetus shepherdi***   Oliver
ZIPHIIDAE   TASMAN BEAKED WHALE,
SHEPHERDS BEAKED WHALE
Named in 1937, this species has rarely been seen. It reaches 8 m. in length and is dark brown or black with a pale belly. The jaws are rather short for the family. Both upper and lower jaws are well endowed with teeth, there being 19 teeth on each side of the upper jaw and 26 on each side of the lower. The body is very rotund. Few specimens have been examined and these were all found in waters around New Zealand.

***Ziphius cavirostris***   Cuvier
ZIPHIIDAE   CUVIER'S BEAKED WHALE
This streamlined whale was named in 1823. The head is small but wide and merges smoothly into the body. The blowhole is near the anterior tip of the jaw. This whale grows up to 7.6 m. in length and can weigh up to 5 tonnes. The male has a pair of teeth at the point of the lower jaw; in the female these do not erupt. Body colour seems to be quite variable, from dark grey-blue to brown on the back, shading to pale grey on the abdomen. Occasionally, however, there is an individual which is quite pale on its back. The dorsal fin is small and placed well back towards the tail.

Cuvier's beaked whales are probably widely distributed in all tropical, subtropical, and temperate waters. They have never been sighted in the polar seas. They are known to migrate northwards close to Japan from May to September. If stranded numbers are anything to go by, they are quite common.

Acceleration from a cruising speed of 3 knots to 10 knots is possible when danger threatens. They swim at the surface with their back exposed. Small groups of up to 10 individuals are the usual social formation.

Undoubtedly squid is their favourite food but a variety of invertebrates and fish are also consumed.

Little is known about reproduction in this species except that fighting seems to accompany it, if the body scars are any indication. Young are about 2.4 m. long when born and are thought to arrive at all times of the year.

They are hunted for oil and meat by Japanese shore stations.

*Right* Otariid females give birth soon after arrival on land. A female South African fur seal, *Arctocephalus pusillus*, nurses her pup, while her mate lies in the background.

*Over left* Amongst the sea lion and fur seals, only the female cares for the young. A Kerguelen fur seal, *Arctocephalus tropicalis* suckles her pup on South Georgia Island.

*Over right* A bull northern fur seal, *Callorhinus ursinus*. Both sea lions and fur seals have a layer of coarse hair, but only the fur seals possess a distinct, fine underfur. It is this property which makes the pelt commercially desirable.

# Pinnipedia:
## *Seals, Sea Lions and Walruses*

California sea lions, *Zalophus californianus* are gregarious all year round, both in the wild and in captivity.

## Introduction

Unlike the Sirenia and the Cetacea, seals, walruses and sea lions are well known, being common in zoos and circuses and possible to see when taking a gentle walk along certain coasts of Britain and North America.

Although some taxonomists, particularly in the past, have placed pinnipeds as a suborder of the Carnivora, it is now usual to consider them as a separate order in their own right.

Pinnipeds – literally fin- or feather-footed – are well adapted to an aquatic life. The body is streamlined and without projections which would cause resistance in water. The head is smooth and rounded without, or with only small, ears. The forelimbs are modified to flat paddle-like flippers and the hindlimbs, which have sacrificed to varying degrees their ability to assist movement on land, are also flat and flippered. The body has a very thick layer of subcutaneous fat which helps to reduce heat loss, and there are complex functional or physiological mechanisms to reduce heat loss in the flippers and to allow prolonged activity under water where breathing is impossible. In addition the ear and nostril openings are closed by specially developed muscles during dives.

The distribution of pinnipeds is wide indeed. They are found in all the seas of the world including inland seas and there is even one freshwater species in Lake Baikal, the large freshwater lake in Siberia. They are however most common both in species and in numbers of individuals, in the arctic and antarctic areas, preferring also a coastal habitat to the open ocean. In water is where pinnipeds spend most of their time and where they are best suited structurally for movement. There they are graceful, fast and confident; on land they generally become sluggish and ungainly.

In general pinnipeds live in groups of various sizes. It is common for them to congregate on land for breeding. During this time they fast, and as a consequence use up their body fat.

The 32 species of pinnipeds are divided into 2 superfamilies, the Otarioidea and Phocoidea. The former includes the fur seals, walruses and sea lions, and the latter the true seals. They are distinguished by detailed variations in the skeleton, particularly in the skull. Fortunately, however, they are simple to differentiate externally by their different methods of locomotion on land. The Otarioidea are able to bring their hindflippers forward to give support to the body and assist in poor but clear quadrupedal progression. The contact surfaces of both fore and hind flippers are naked, covered merely in dark-pigmented skin. The Phocoidea, however, have hind flippers pointing backward with opposed soles covered in fur and they are quite unable to bring them forward to assist in terrestrial movement.

### Otarioidea

The significant feature of this superfamily is their ability to turn the hindlimbs forward to assist in walking on land. In addition they have naked black skin palms on both fore and hind limbs. The fore limbs are long and are the main means of movement in water and on land. There are claws on the middle 3 digits. The mammary glands have 4 teats. The males are much larger than the females. The superfamily is divided into 2 families, Otariidae and Odobenidae.

### *Otariidae*

This family contains the sea lions and the fur seals. They have streamlined slender bodies and are easily distinguished by the presence of the small external ears. The long fore limbs have 5 rudimentary claws. The tail is small and flattened but free. Males are considerably larger than the females and they form polygamous groups, with a single male protecting several females during the breeding season.

The family is subdivided into 2 subfamilies. The Otariinae, the sea lions, have a blunt snout with a short coat consisting of little underfur protected by the coarser guard hairs. The first digit of the front flipper is longer than the second. The Arctocephalinae, or fur seals, have a somewhat more pointed head and the long guard hairs of the coat protect the thick underfur which is of such commercial value. The first and second digits of the fore limb are the same length. (See *Arctocephalus, Callorhinus, Eumetopias, Neophoca, Otaria, Phocartos, Zalophus*).

### Odobenidae

This family contains the single species *Odobenus rosmarus*, the walrus.

### Phocoidea

This superfamily includes the true or earless seals which are widely distributed throughout the oceans of the world. There is only the one family, namely Phocidae.

### Phocidae

The true or earless seals all belong to this one family. They are widely distributed throughout the world and are contained in 13 genera.

Both males and females are of similar size. They have no external ear but the ear canals, like the nostrils, can be firmly closed when under water by the action of the surrounding musculature. The fore limbs are relatively short and are used primarily for manipulation rather than swimming, which is mainly accomplished by the movement of the hind part of the body. True seals cannot bring their hind flippers forward to assist in movement on land, and as a result are rather slow and laborious travellers out of water. The flippers have

World distribution map of Pinnipedia. The phocids: the antarctic monachines and arctic phocines are pack-ice breeders, as are the predominantly arctic odobeniids. The otariids are sub-polar, and are land breeders.

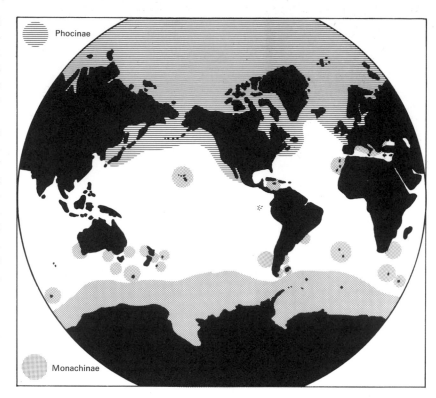

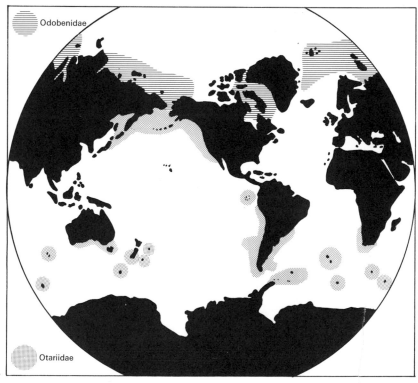

An Australian fur sea, pup, *Arctocephalus doriferus*, showing the external ears characteristic of the superfamily Otarioidea.

*Top right* A sea lion bull has external ears and the ability to turn the hindlimbs forward to assist movement on land.

*Below right* The common seal, *Phoca vitulina*. Its hindlimbs provide the main means of propulsion through water.

hair on all surfaces and claws on all digits. The coat, usually spotted, is composed of stiff hairs.

Seals are very good swimmers, well adapted to the aquatic medium in which they spend so much of their time. They can dive quite deeply, and although they normally breathe regularly every 20 seconds can stay under for several minutes at a time. Poor though they may be on land, they like to haul themselves out of the water and will spend hours basking in the warm sun. If danger threatens they can, over short distances, move deceptively fast. While groups lie asleep or idle on land, one member is designated to guard the others and will raise the alarm if they are threatened.

In polar regions, where ice covers the water, they make breathing holes and keep them open all winter, allowing for both breathing and exit.

Seals have a very varied set of vocalizations. They have particularly good sight but can also smell and hear reasonably well. Sensitive vibrissae on the lower lip are used for touch.

Most species are monogamous. Seal mothers are excellent and will clutch their offspring to them and escape in the water if they feel in danger.

Apart from the inevitable predation by man, wild life's universal enemy, they fall victim to killer whales and polar bears.

Many species have been successfully kept in captivity and become extremely tame, responding favourably to their keeper and even performing simple tricks. (See *Cystophora, Erignathus, Halichoerus, Histriophoca, Hydrurga, Lobodon, Leptonychotes, Mirounga, Monachus, Ommatophoca, Pagophilus, Phoca* and *Pusa*.)

## AGEING
Scientific studies on populations require that a reasonably accurate estimate of the age of an individual can be made.

The commonest method used in pinnipeds is the study of growth-layers found in the roots of the canine teeth. The root continues to grow after eruption, laying down dentine on the inner surface. In some species the deposits are laid down all through life but in others the process ceases in later life.

Some seals have annual growth rings visible on the claws. These are very useful, particularly in younger animals, but as the claws become worn and their length covered in rings, the number lost is unknown and their value lessens.

## ANAESTHESIA
There are fewer problems associated with anaesthetizing pinnipeds than found with the Cetacea. Pinnipeds are given an inducing dose of barbiturate and can then be connected to the anaesthetic machine. Under anaesthesia body temperature can drop and this must be carefully controlled. Following anaesthesia the animal must be carefully watched during the recovery period and should only be allowed to swim when fully recovered.

## ANATOMY
The pinniped body is constructed to cope with its aquatic environment. The principal modifications are related to the external shape, the respiratory system, the cardiovascular system, and the method of locomotion.

The pinniped is fusiform in shape, and protuberances are reduced to minimize water resistance. The respiratory and cardiovascular systems, dealt with fully under separate headings, have been modified to enable the animal to dive for long periods. Since it spends much of its life, and finds its food, in water, it is a fast and agile swimmer (see Locomotion). The pinniped, unlike the cetacean, has not completely deserted its terrestial origins, and though ungainly on land, is capable of suprising speed when the need arises. (See Cardiovascular System, Digestive System, Muscular System, Nervous System, Senses, Skeletal System, Skin, Urogenital System.)

## BEHAVIOUR
Unlike the Cetacea, most pinnipeds come onto land to breed. At these times scientific observations on their social and sexual relationships can be made with relative ease – our knowledge of their behaviour between haul-out periods is as scanty as it is of cetaceans in general. Considerable variation in social behaviour between species has been observed; the main features are detailed under the species descriptions. Some species spend much of their life in organized social groups while others are more solitary between the breeding seasons. Males of species which form harems, whatever their normal relationship with others of their sex, must become territorial and aggressive. Their breeding behaviour is related to the seasonal increase in the weight of the testes. Harems are formed only in those species which mate on land. Males arrive at the breeding grounds first, and establish a territory with much fighting, although this rarely results in serious damage or death. With the arrival of the females, fighting intensifies and great efforts are made by the males to collect and keep their harems; these vary considerably in size and some contain only 2 females while more successful males command the attentions of up to 50 females.

In migrating species, females often arrive just before their pups are born. They are taken into a harem and protected by the male. Copulation occurs at varying times after parturition; in some

*Right* Bull elephant seals, *Mirounga leonina*, fighting to establish breeding territory.

*Below* Female elephant seals are kept huddled together by the bull, who keeps guard over his harem and wards off rivals.

species females come into oestrus soon after giving birth while in others it is delayed until the pup is weaned. The interesting phenomenon of delayed implantation occurs in the Pinnipedia. The fertilized egg develops to the blastocyst stage when it stops growing and is not implanted onto the wall of the womb. After a period of time, which differs in length according to the species, development starts again and the egg is implanted. This process means that the pup can be born on land when the female is due to mate again without having developed to an excessive birth weight.

In species which form harems, males are considerably larger than the females. Species which mate in water do not form harems and there is little difference in size between the sexes.

Birth of young pinnipeds takes place with a minimum of assistance from the mother who seems almost indifferent to the procedure and makes no attempt to break the umbilical cord. It usually severs as a result of the movements of both participants. When the birth is complete, the mother attends her pup with varying degrees of devotion, depending on the species, and an intense maternal relationship is established. The mother appears to recognize her own offspring by its vocal sounds and smell. In some species, the walrus, *Odobenus rosmarus*, for example, the mother takes care of and suckles her pup for a long period. In others, notably the fur seals, her maternal ministrations may be very limited indeed, lactation being complete in 2 weeks.

*Above* A grey seal pup, *Halichoerus grypus*. The dense white coat protects the newborn in the transition from the warmth inside the mother and the freezing temperatures outside. It is replaced in a month by the thinner adult coat more suited for life in water.

*Right* A captive sea lion mother allows her young to ride on her back.

In general the male takes little interest in the pups, being far too intent on the defence of his territory and the protection of the harem.

As soon as the pup is born it begins to seek out the nipple. The first attempts are usually vague and poorly directed but when it finds its goal the milk is squirted into its mouth. One of the most interesting features of pinniped lactation is the long periods, up to 2 weeks, which the pup can spend without nourishment of any kind while the mother is away hunting. In spite of this, pinniped pups gain weight at a remarkable rate due to the very high fat content of the milk. The stomachs of most pups contain stones and it has been argued that these in some way reduce the hunger pains during the periods of starvation. However, since most adults also ingest stones and sand, the explanation seems unlikely.

The age of pups when they take to the water varies greatly from the birth day to several weeks afterwards depending on the species. It seems to happen without the mother's involvement.

Pinnipeds are carnivorous and consume a wide variety of animal food, from small shrimps and crabs to penguins. The leopard seal preys largely on penguins and has a voracious appetite.

The physical limitations of pinniped pups make play a difficult undertaking on land. In spite of this, while their mothers are absent, they do indulge with their fellows in rather cumbersome activities. By nature inquisitive, they investigate their environment and mouth strange objects. It is not, however, until they take to the water that the mammalian need for play can be fully seen. They soon gain the confidence and agility which enables them to play.

A little is known of the migrating habits of the Pinnipedia. Some species migrate many thousands of miles each year, while others do no more than move around an island chain. The purpose of migration is only poorly understood and it may have evolved as a result of changes in environment. For example, while a species may be faithful to the breeding sites of its ancestors, each generation having learnt from its predecessor their physical attributes, these would have to be shifted in order to follow any changes in the availability or type of food. It is sometimes suggested that continental drift has also been a factor in the origins of migration. However, it is certainly not easy to explain migration in terms of contemporary function in all cases, and it seems as if it may have its origins in history.

The ability of pinnipeds to learn tricks is well known to circus enthusiasts although, until very recently, there has been little attempt to study this facility scientifically. One study found that they compared favourably with cats and primates, and were considerably more intelligent than rodents. It is to be anticipated that with the interest now being taken in marine animals by the United States Navy, more information on the mental capacity of these creatures will be forthcoming.

## CAPTIVITY

Seals and sea lions have been kept in captivity for many years. The grey seal, *Halichoerus grypus*, has been kept for over 40 years, the South African fur seal, *Arctocephalus pusillus*, for over 20 years, the ringed seal, *Pusa hispida*, for over 40 years and the California sea lion, *Zalophus californianus*, for over 30 years. They are normally caught on land which is easier, and less dangerous to the animal. Several people quietly get between the animals and the sea. Then by slowly moving towards them they are driven further inland, where cages are placed in readiness. Ageing adults and very young animals are released and the others are placed in cages. Care must be taken in handling. Small animals can be lifted while larger ones can often be driven into cages directly. Animals up to 3 years are best able to adapt to captivity.

Another method is to draw a net at sea and then drive the animals off the shore into it. However there is the danger that the animals may become entangled in the net and drown before assistance is given, or damage themselves by struggling.

In zoos pinnipeds are kept in large enclosures consisting mostly of ornamental pools with rocky islands on which to haul out and sunbathe. Many zoological parks keep their pinnipeds in fresh water with apparently little ill effect although others prefer to ensure salt water baths occasionally. Damage to the eyes (corneal opacity) has been blamed on the sole use of fresh water but no definite evidence is available. The absence of

A female Hooker's sea lion, *Neophoca hookeri*. This species is very mobile on land, and will wander inland to distances of 10 km.

salt in the water should also be remembered when considering essential minerals in the diet.

Cleanliness is essential in the pinniped pool. Good zoological collections have either a filtration system or allow for frequent cleaning.

Captive pinnipeds are fed on a diet of fish; the California sea lion, *Zalophus californianus*, will consume between 4 and 14 kg. of fish daily. It has been found that some fish contain a substance which destroys thiamin – one of the B vitamins. Animals fed exclusively on fish containing this thiaminase may well show symptoms of thiamin deficiency. It is essential therefore to offer a variety of fish, including species which do not contain thiaminase, and to supplement the diet with thiamin. Mackerel, *Scomber scombrus*, for example, are thiaminase free.

A good indicator of adaptation to, or acceptance of, captivity is the willingness to breed, and certainly the California sea lions oblige. Other captive otariids which have bred include Steller's sea lion, some of which have lived for over 15 years in captivity. The South American sea lion, *Otaria flavescens*, first exhibited by the Zoological Society of London in 1866, has been bred in several zoos. A few specimens of the northern fur seal, *Callorhinus ursinus*, have been maintained successfully for several years, as have the South African fur seal, *Arctocephalus pusillus*. The South American fur seal, *A. australis*, Guadalupe fur seal, *A. philipii*, and the Australian fur seal, *A. doriferus*, have also appeared in zoos and seem to adapt well.

The story of captive walruses is far from satisfactory. The earliest records of walruses kept in captivity is one in London early in the seventeenth century and another in Europe some years later. In the middle of the nineteenth century 2 specimens were purchased by the Zoological Society of London but they lived for only 2 years. As recently as the 1960s a young animal was presented to the Society but died within a few months.

The Zoological garden in Copenhagen has been more successful. There one female lived for nearly 12 years and a second for over 7 years. In America one male lived for nearly 4 years in the New York Zoological Park. Several others in various American zoos have survived for periods counted in months rather than years although one of a pair secured by the New York Zoological Society in 1956 have adapted successfully.

Of the phocids the harbour or common seal, *Phoca vitulina*, is most commonly kept although it is an animal which is not a favourite among zoo directors for exhibition. Sadly attempts to acclimatize them are rarely successful although some have survived in captivity for over 14 years. Ringed seals, *Pusa hispida*, harp seals, *Pagophilus groenlandicus*, and grey seals, *Halichoerus grypus*, have all been kept with varying degrees of success, particularly by European zoos. Baikal seals, *Pusa sibirica*, have been exhibited with limited success at the Zoological Society of London.

Monk seals, genus *Monachus*, have been only infrequently exhibited and although some have survived for several years, an early death seems more usual.

The ferocious leopard seal, *Hydrurga leptonyx*, has rarely been kept in zoos.

One of the most exciting sights of the pinniped world is the elephant seal, genus *Mirounga*. Diminished in stature by captivity but still presenting a never-to-be-forgotten sight, they tower above their keeper as he plies them with vast quantities of fish. Experience of them dates from the late nineteenth century when several young animals were sent to San Francisco, and some to the Philadelphia Zoological Garden in 1883. All died rapidly. In Europe the southern species, *M. leonina*, has been exhibited on and off since the early twentieth century and several have survived for a number of years. In America the northern elephant seal, *M. angustirostris*, is more common but again has survived for a few years only.

Sea lions have long been a feature of the circus ring where their natural aptitude for catching and balancing things on their noses is exploited with enthusiasm. The pleasure they give must always be marred by the thought of their backstage living conditions. They have little chance of a good swim and the best they can hope for is a wash down or dip in a human-sized tub. Some compensation for captivity!

An unusual circus animal was one elephant seal named Goliath who, having spent 2 years in captivity in Europe, was sold to a circus in the late 1920s and spent several years in the ring. In nature

a splendid beast adapted to its environment – in the circus merely a freak.

There is no doubt that given suitable conditions many pinnipeds adapt to captivity. Sadly they have a low exhibition priority in most zoos and their enclosures are not always entirely suitable, nor is their management always of the best. Providing adequate funds are available to provide for their needs, so long as the veterinary, scientific and technical controls are catered for, and so long as the zoological park in which they are exhibited has educational, scientific and conservation functions in addition to pure entertainment, then captivity may be justified. There is little justification for the confinement of pinnipeds for music hall, vaudeville and circus shows.

## CARDIOVASCULAR SYSTEM

The structure and function of pinniped hearts are very similar indeed to the ordinary mammalian pattern. The arterial system is likewise unmodified. It is in the venous system that most of the adaptations have occurred.

The amount of blood relative to the size of the body is much increased. This is an adaptation which assists diving. A similar adaptation is found in the Cetacea. The extra blood acts to increase the store of oxygen and to hasten its transport within the body.

The venous system has considerable modifications which relate to the diving behaviour of the order. The jugular veins, so important in land mammals, have been much reduced. Most of

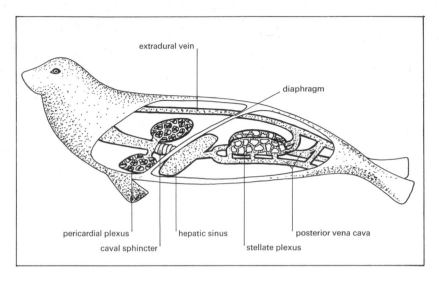

Venous system in a seal.

the blood from the head passes into 2 hypo-condylar veins which unite to form a sinus within the spinal canal. From this sinus, vessels pass dorsally on either side of the cervical verte-brae to form a very large vein – the extradural vein. This large single vessel runs along above the spinal cord the length of the body as far as the sacrum where it divides into two. Its importance to the vascular modification can be judged by its very large size and because of its frequent connec-tions with all other parts of the venous system. It almost certainly acts as a rapid transporter of blood since it has no valvular structure.

Blood from the kidneys is drained into the stel-late plexus which covers the kidneys. From here it passes through one of 3 vessels to the branch of the posterior vena cava adjacent to it. Among other connections the stellate plexus also connects with the extradural vein. The 2 branches of the vena cava also collect blood from the hindquarters of the body. The 2 branches join to form a single vessel halfway along the body and this in turn passes into the hepatic sinus which is situated im-mediately posterior to the diaphragm. The hepatic sinus is formed from the hepatic veins. Blood from the hepatic sinus is carried to the heart. The hepatic sinus can hold large quantities of blood and seems to have a significant function in the Pinnipedia's adaptation to aquatic life. Surround-ing the vessel carrying the blood from the hepatic sinus to the heart is the muscular caval sphincter.

This sphincter controls the flow of blood to the heart. In some species it is a specific bundle of muscles, in others it is less well developed, being formed of strands of diaphragm muscle.

From the extradural vein, branches leave in the anterior abdomen to form the right and left azygos veins. In the chest they become the intercostal veins and the left azygos is reduced, its blood pass-ing into the right azygos vein from where it drains into the anterior vena cava. (See also Diving.)

## CLASSIFICATION

Classification is man made and therefore liable to human error. Its purpose is to establish the re-lationship between living species based on their evolutionary history. Therefore groups of species very closely related with many similar features are placed together in genera. Groups of genera are placed in families which show broadly similar fea-tures while the orders consists of families con-sidered to have originated from common or closely related ancestors in bygone eras. These show some-times quite widely dissimilar features although broadly are definitely related.

The evolutionary history of the order Pin-nipedia is still uncertain (see Evolution). It is how-ever divided into 2 super families, the Phocoidea and the Otarioidea. The former contains one family Phocidae and the latter 2 families Otariidae and Odobenidae.

## CONSERVATION

The story of man's abuse of his natural heritage is horrific, and perhaps nowhere more so than in his treatment of sea mammals for short term com-mercial gain. The greed with which eighteenth and nineteenth century sealers attacked the hith-erto almost unmolested populations of pinnipeds is sickening. Nowhere in the history of sealing can one find any compassion for these delightful crea-tures, and the scientific world, itself intent on the collecting of dead specimens to line museum walls, seemed hardly to have raised a voice in protest.

The story of exploitation of a species is all too common. Once a new species was discovered the sealers fell on it, killing vast numbers annually until, usually within a few years, the species was so decimated that its commercial exploitation became unprofitable and it was left in peace. Some species never recovered, their numbers having dropped below the minimum level necessary. Others began to show signs of a healthy population after a few years. If the signs became too healthy, again the sealers turned in their direction, fortunately rather late in the day, as governments had often, by this time, passed protective legislation and the killing was controlled or prevented altogether. For example, in 1810 the southern elephant seal drew the attention of sealers when their activities had so reduced the fur seals as to make them unprofitable. By the 1890s it was no longer a commercial proposition to exploit them and they were left in peace. By 1910 they had recovered sufficiently for the greed to gleam in the sealers' eyes again. Protective legislation, however, now controls their slaughter. Only bulls may be killed and then sufficient numbers must be left in each breeding area for reproductive necessity.

Today with an added awareness of the need to control commercial sealing in the interests of conservation most species that need protection have it, though it may now be too late to save the Carib-

bean Monk seal, now believed extinct. The law prevents little; it is the enforcement that counts and where commercial greed is involved this is extremely difficult.

## DIGESTIVE SYSTEM

The digestive system of pinnipeds is very simple as befits a carnivorous animal which does not need to break down cellulose. Pinnipeds, depending on species, restrict their intake to fish, squid, octopus, penguin, the young of other seals, and carrion.

The mouth contains a set of efficient teeth (see Teeth) with which to secure the prey. From the mouth leads the long very dilatable oesophagus which is able to accommodate quite large items, often swallowed whole. The stomach is a simple single curved chamber; it is glandular and receives quantities of digestive juices and hydrochloric acid, which start the digestive process. The duodenum follows the stomach from which it is separated by the pyloric sphincter. The duodenum indistinctly joins the rest of the long small intestine. At the junction between the large and small intestines is a small, sometimes hardly visible, caecum. The large intestine shows the usual enlargement, is short, and passes into the rectum which terminates at the anus.

Rather strangely the contents of pinniped stomachs usually include a number of stones, some of them quite large; in some cases hundreds of small stones have been found. The purpose of these stones remains a mystery. Several ingenious but unlikely suggestions have been voiced, one being that the stones grind up parasitic worms commonly found in the stomach. The motivation for swallowing is said to be the irritation caused by the worms, but as worms in the stomach do not cause irritation, the theory holds no weight. A more recent suggestion proposes that the stones are swallowed for stabilization and/or ballast. This theory currently commands much popular support but in view of the anatomical modifications made by evolution in allowing mammals to reconquer an aquatic environment, including structural changes such as the repositioning of lungs, it seems unlikely that stabilization or ballast would rely on each individual swallowing sufficient stones; instinctive behaviour does not command such

Seals are driven to the killing place; Bering Strait.

finesse. It may be argued that the animal can meter the quantity of stone in some way, and thus learn how many to swallow, but it seems improbable.

During the annual life cycle pinnipeds undergo periods of fasting, and one ingenious theory, with little scientific evidence in support, suggests that the stones provide some bulk on which the stomach contracts to prevent or alleviate hunger pains. From the behaviourist's point of view an animal with motivation enough to swallow stones would be more likely to ignore its reproductive responsibilities and go off to feed.

The presence of stones in the forestomach of the Cetacea, it has been suggested (see Digestive System, Cetacea) acts as a grinding mechanism for food reminiscent of the grit used by birds. Clearly if this holds true for Cetacea and birds, why not for pinnipeds? Experimental work with birds, however, shows that grit is not essential for digestion.

Young pups still being suckled by their mother are known to have stones in their stomach. Again, since they are often suckled at infrequent intervals, it has been suggested that stones alleviate hunger pains. A more acceptable explanation is that, as a result of normal exploratory behaviour, the pups mouth stones and accidentally swallow them. Clinical experience with dogs reveals that those individuals which play with stones not infrequently have several stones in their stomach. It seems most likely that the habit of playing with stones learnt as a seal pup continues into adult life, and with a system of deglutition so well designed for swallowing large objects a few stones inevitably find their way to the stomach.

The liver, always associated with the alimentary canal, normally has several lobes clustered around the hepatic sinus. Pinnipeds have a gall bladder. Three hepatic ducts join to form a common bile duct. The bile duct in turn joins with the pancreatic duct to form a common entry to the duodenum. Pinnipeds have a large, highly functional pancreas.

## DISEASE

Much that has been said in general terms about the Cetacea (see Cetacea: Disease) applies equally to the pinnipeds and will not be repeated.

In some ways the pinnipeds present fewer problems as they can be quite happily maintained out of water for long periods if treatment requirements dictate. They are however more mobile out of water and are more difficult to handle.

Clinical diagnostic techniques present few problems outside of the normal difficulties with which most veterinary surgeons are trained to cope. Urine and faecal collection is much simpler; the animal needs only to be placed in a wire bottomed cage through which the material passes to be collected in a tray beneath. A technique has been worked out for collecting blood of the Phocidae from the extradural veins.

## DISTRIBUTION

With very few exceptions the pinnipeds are creatures of cold water and are rarely found in water warmer than 20°C. Monk seals, being one exception, are found in temperatures of up to 25°C, and the elusive, perhaps even extinct Caribbean monk seal, *Monachus tropicalis*, in water as warm as 30°C.

The truly polar species live in water close to freezing. These include the ringed seal *Pusa hispida*, the bearded seal *Erignathus barbatus*, the walrus *Odobenus rosmarus*, the leopard seal *Hydrurga leptonyx*, the Weddell seal *Leptonychotes weddelli*, the crabeater seal *Lobodon carcinophagus*, and the Ross seal *Ommatophoca rossi*. The grey seal *Halichoerus grypus*, the common or harbour seal *Phoca vitulina*, and the harp seal *Pagophilus groenlandicus* are associated with the Labrador Current and their distribution is curtailed by the warm Gulf Stream. In the North Atlantic the Gulf Stream is cooled by arctic waters before it reaches the coasts of the British Isles and Scandinavia so that the grey, common and harp seals are able to colonize these areas.

The cool Oya Shio Current in the Western Pacific flows south along the coast of Japan and governs the distribution of the common seal, the Pribilof or northern fur seal *Callorhinus ursinus*, and the California sea lion *Zalophus californianus*.

The reason why pinnipeds are associated mainly with cold water is not fully understood. It may be due to the adaptive mechanisms of the pinniped physiology, or possibly cold water provides a greater supply of food.

A herd of some 70 seals resting on a sandbank off Great Yarmouth, Norfolk.

## DIVING

One of the fundamental necessities for members of this order is an ability to dive deeply in order to catch their prey. To what depths they can descend is unknown and figures used often depend on very scanty circumstantial evidence. For example seals sometimes are caught in fishing nets and the maximum depth achieved by the net is often recorded as the depth to which the seal naturally descended. Such an assumption is nonsense. The animal could have been trapped at higher levels as the net went down or came up. Net trappings are therefore almost valueless. The greatest depth to which seals have descended naturally, and been recorded by man, is 60 m. Experimentally this has been increased to 92 m. Net trappings record depths of over 180 m. Presumably implanted pressure meters and telemetry could be used for this with relative ease. Seals can remain submerged for up to half an hour but normal dives rarely exceed a few minutes.

The important body mechanisms for diving relate to the respiratory and cardiovascular systems. Prior to diving the animal expires most of the air contained in the lungs. The residual volume is trapped by a system of valves present in the bronchi. From experimental work with those Cetacea which do not breathe out before diving, it has been shown that air remaining in the lung during a dive is not used; so little potential oxygen is lost by expiration. There are real advantages, however, in emptying the lungs. The problem of caisson sickness or 'bends' in human divers has been referred to in the section on cetacean diving. (The 'bends' are caused by breathing air under pressure during the diving as a result of which nitrogen is forced into solution in the blood. If the diver surfaces too quickly the gas leaves solution to form bubbles of the gas causing severe pain in joints and real danger of a fatal gas embolism.) By removing most of the air from the lungs, very little nitrogen can be dissolved in the blood and the bends will not develop when the animal surfaces rapidly.

One important factor which the pinniped body possesses to allow it to dive is a considerable increase in blood. The volume of blood to body weight is greater than that found in land mammals.

Alterations in heart rate are also activated by pinnipeds during the diving and recovery cycle. As soon as the dive begins the heart rate drops from its normal resting rate to less than 10 beats every minute. The slowing down depends on the depth and speed of dive. After some time the heart rate rises slightly. On completion of the dive the heart rate rises to above the normal rate for a few minutes in order to resaturate the tissues with oxygen. It then returns to the resting rate.

The primary concern of the body during a dive is to maintain adequate supplies of oxygen to the essential organs and, in particular, to the brain. To achieve this the blood supply to less essential organs is restricted. Blood supply to the muscles is stopped, and the muscle then has to make do with locally available oxygen stored in the adequate supplies of myoglobin. There is evidence that one special modification to the aquatic environment is the muscles' ability to work in the absence of oxygen (anaerobically). Cetacean and pinnipedian tissue also seems to be less sensitive to carbon dioxide than other mammals'.

The section of the vascular system through which flow is maintained is also modified during the dive. It is thought that the blood leaving the brain, now containing little oxygen, is prevented from circulating back to the heart by activation of the caval sphincter (see Cardiovascular System). It is stored in the hepatic sinus. Stores of oxygenated blood continue to be pumped into the system to maintain the supply to the essential organs. When these are depleted the caval sphincter opens releasing the venous blood to the heart. Physiological mechanisms demand that the seal returns to the surface and as it does so the heart rate increases to hasten the reoxygenation of the tissues. (See also Cardiovascular System, Respiratory System.)

## DRINKING

The obvious question which arises in animals which spend their lives in and around sea water is, 'Do they drink it? If not, where do they get their fluid replacement?' The answer is that we do not know in the case of pinnipeds. They have not been seen drinking sea water but that would not be an easy observation to make. They certainly will and do drink fresh water in preference to sea water in the unusual environmental conditions that exist during captive travel. On some experimental diets in captivity they also drink fresh water. In the wild however it may be that they obtain sufficient moisture from their food.

The drinking behaviour of captives is of interest. When offered a bucket of water they drink by immersing the snout like a cow or a horse and not by lapping like land carnivores.

## EVOLUTION

The origins of the pinnipeds are as elusive as they are interesting. There is considerable controversy among the experts. Turning to the traditional fossil evidence offers little assistance. The earliest fossils which are indisputably pinniped originate from Miocene deposits. These remains are already well advanced along the evolutionary pathway to modern pinnipeds. Undoubtedly the pinniped line or lines originated much earlier.

Available evidence is confusing and several interpretations are possible. Some investigators believe that all pinnipeds originate from a single branch of the primitive carnivore stock. Others believe that there were 2 quite separate branches originating later, one from the early bears (Ursine) and the other from the primitive otters (Lutrine).

One of the difficulties arises because the relationship between the 3 major families – Phocidae, Odobenidae and Otariidae – remains unclear. Were it possible to establish one as more primitive than the others and identify clear lines from that group to the others, a single origin would be confirmed and some of the major problems of pinniped evolution would be solved. The Odobenidae are considered by many authorities to be intermediate between the otariids and the phocids. Others believe the Odobenidae share a more recent ancestor with the otariids. Unfortunately the fossil records are rather scanty. Some consider the fossils support one theory, others believe they indicate the alternative.

Evidence from the distribution of the fossil record is interesting but resolves little. The information can be marshalled to agree with either a single origin or double origin theory. Those supporting a single origin have suggested that pinnipeds all began their line in the north Atlantic.

From this a branch, which was to become the ancestral otariids, migrated to the north Pacific through the Bering Sea. From these primitive otariids developed the modern otariids and the odobenids, the latter later migrating back to the Atlantic where the first odobenid fossil, *Prorosmarus*, was found, associated with deposits of the Upper Miocene age, over 12 million years ago.

Those who subscribe to the double origin theory, however, believe the otariids and their offshoot, the odobenids, originated separately from bear-like ancestors in the northern Pacific, the odobenids later migrating back to the Atlantic while the otariids extended their range to the south. The phocids, they believe, originated from primitive otter-like ancestors, possibly in fresh water complexes in Tertiary Asia and migrated later to the Atlantic where fossils relating to the Miocene age, 25 million years ago, have been found.

It can be seen that the overriding conclusion to be drawn from the fossil evidence and its distribution is that there is insufficient evidence available to draw definite conclusions.

Studies using the more modern technique of serology shed little light on the problem. If anything they do side with the single origin theory but the evidence is not by any means conclusive.

Finally a mention of the recent use of cytogenetics in the study of evolution. By examining both the number and structure of the chromosomes in the cells of each species further evidence becomes available about the relationships between species, families and orders.

The science is relatively new and considerably more work needs to be done, but at the present this new addition to the investigative armoury suggests a single origin for the pinnipeds.

## EXPLOITATION AND USES

Pinniped bones have been found in prehistoric middens, demonstrating their use to some early human societies. Many species however inhabited areas where no man ventured and these were left in peace. Eskimos have traditionally relied on the seal for a great deal of their needs; indeed, without pinnipeds it could be claimed that their life in the frozen north would have proved impossible.

In modern times, roughly from the eighteenth century, man has exploited the seal more ruthlessly than ever before, (see Conservation). The demand for oil, skins and to a lesser degree meat led to massive slaughter of these animals in a totally uncontrolled manner. Literally millions of animals were killed for fur.

The fur seals in particular were sought for their very fine skins, and hunted nearly to extinction. When the Pribilof seal was discovered in 1786 there were, it is estimated, two and a half million animals in their range. By 1911, just 125 years later, man had reduced that population to about 200,000 individuals. Fortunately legislation, though belatedly introduced, has saved the species and the population is estimated to be about one and a half million. However they are still exploited to some extent since about 60,000 animals are taken each year for their skins under government licence.

The print *left* shows the killing of walruses for ivory by 'shooting, sticking and knocking on the head'. (Engraving by Robert Dodd, 1748–1815.)

*Far right* An Eskimo thong with ivory toggles carved in the form of seal heads and a seal. Collected from Point Barrow, Alaska.

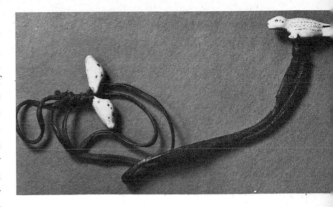

The Guadalupe fur seal was so ruthlessly hunted for its skin that by the late 1890s it was assumed to be extinct. In 1927 a small group was discovered and incredibly 2 animals were captured and taken to the San Diego Zoo. Zoos had yet to hear of conservation it seems! In spite of such stupidity the numbers continued to recover and a small breeding colony of a few hundred individuals now exists.

Fur seals have really delightful fur if one can override one's conscience enough to wear it. Other seals have less spectacular coats but the common and ringed seals, for example, are still hunted for their skins in large numbers. Apart from skins, the blubber makes fine oil not dissimilar to that of whales. It has a variety of uses; in particular that from the southern elephant seal is used to make edible oils incorporated in margarine.

Finally mention must be made of the walrus. This remarkable creature has been a target for man's greed and aggression for many years. It has for centuries been prized by Eskimos for its ivory, but they also use the whole carcass for meat, oil for lamps, and hides for ropes, dog harnesses and a wide variety of other domestic uses. Modern man did not need the meat, oil or hide. For him the shiny white gold from the mouth was prize enough. Many thousands were killed and their

bodies wasted. By the late nineteenth century some 4,500 kg. of ivory was being taken annually. Even today they enjoy only loose protection which is difficult to enforce.

Man's history of exploitation is endless and ruthless. Mindless greed motivated men to wantonly slaughter some of the most delightful creatures on earth. Only careful conservation can redress the balance.

## LOCOMOTION

Water with its great resistance presents problems for things which move even slowly through it. Therefore the Cetacea, the Pinnipedia and boats

*Left* Mrs Kleinschmidt, her husband and the 2 ton walrus she killed in the Arctic (*c.* 1926).

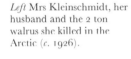

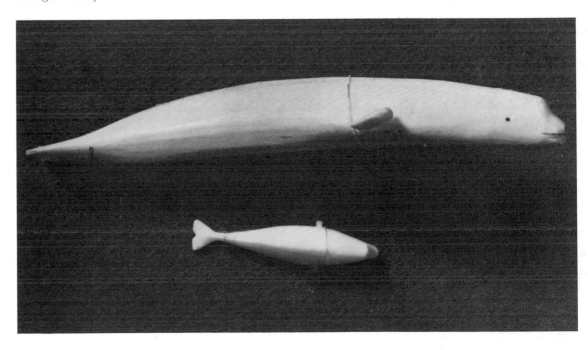

*Right* Whales carved in ivory by Eskimos. Collected from the Great Whale River, Hudson Bay.

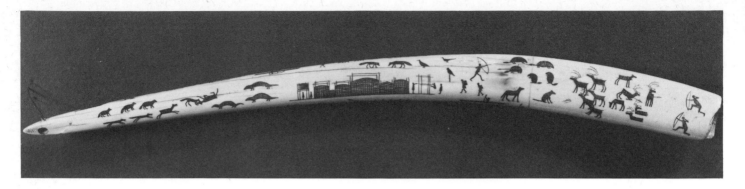

are streamlined to improve efficiency. Pinnipeds have an elongated oval or fusiform outline. Protuberances are reduced to a minimum. In most species even the external ears are absent, while in the otariids they are much reduced.

The head is rounded and smooth and in many species the neck is short. The greater part of the fore flipper is retained in the general body mass. The hind flippers in Phocidae and Otariidae are shaped and positioned to form a continuous contour, and the tail fits well between them. The walrus goes one stage further and has a web joining the hind flippers which completely incorporates the tail.

The various groups of pinnipeds adopt different methods of locomotion. The sea lions, fur seals and walrus all belong to the superfamily Otarioidea. Their fore limbs are long and paddle shaped and these are used as the main propulsive force in water. The hind limbs can be turned forwards and used to walk or run on land. The surfaces of all flippers are either naked or at best sparsely covered with short hair. The neck is long and able to turn in water in order to search for food. Modifications have been made to the fore flipper to improve its propulsive efficiency. Since it is the surface area pushing through the water which provides locomotion, evolution has increased this by webbing the feet and extending the flipper beyond the bony digits. Strengthening fibrous bands also give the edge of the flipper rigidity. While swimming the hind flippers are positioned with soles together, forming a single functional rudder. The hind flippers are also provided with extra surface area by cartilaginous extensions to the digits and webbing. When moving on land the fore flippers are

placed sole downwards on the ground, the longitudinal axis of the flipper at right angles to the body. When moving slowly the flippers are placed alternately, but when running they are brought forward together. The structure of the walrus is slightly different. The flipper is somewhat smaller in surface area and added power is provided by the lateral movements of the hind end of the body. In this it is somewhere between the true seal on the one hand and the fur seal and sea lion on the other.

The phocids have short fore flippers, an indication of their reduced locomotory function. The hind limbs cannot be twisted forwards, being specially modified for their primary function of locomotion. Phocid propulsive power comes from the hind part of the body, the flippers merely add manoeuvrability. Mechanically a long neck, as seen in the otariids, would hamper movement and it is therefore reduced in length. On land the phocids are, to say the least, at a physical disadvantage. Species differ in their ability to move out of water. Many adopt the 'inch worm' technique. They anchor the front end of the body at the sternum and draw the hindquarters forward; then, anchoring the pelvic region, they extend the body forward. Some species make use of their flippers, others do not. One interesting variation is found in the crabeater seal, *Lobodon carcinophagus*, which moves on land very effectively by using the same lateral movements of the hind part of the body as it does in water.

On land pinnipeds are at best ungainly but in the water, the medium to which they are so well adapted, they are supreme. Underwater films alone can present them in a way which does them justice.

*Above* A 32 cm.-long walrus tusk engraved with hunting scenes by Western Eskimos. Collected in 1896 from St Michael.

*Right* A sea lion swimming underwater, showing the hindlimbs positioned together to form a rudder, while the forelimbs provide propulsion.

## LONGEVITY

Below are listed the potential average ages of some pinnipeds based on currently available information.

|  | years |
|---|---|
| S. African fur seal, *Arctocephalus pusillus* | 20–25 |
| Pribilof fur sea, *Callorhinus ursinus* | 25 |
| Steller's sea lion, *Eumetopias jubatus* | 15–20 |
| Grey seal, *Halichoerus grypus* | 35 |
| Walrus, *Odobenus rosmarus* | 20–30 |
| S. American sea lion, *Otaria flavescens* | 20 |
| Greenland seal, *Pagophilus groenlandicus* | 25–30 |
| Harbour seal, *Phoca vitulina* | 20 |
| Ringed seal, *Pusa hispida* | 45 |
| California sea lion, *Zalophus californianus* | 20–25 |

## METABOLISM

Pinnipeds show a higher metabolic rate than would be expected by comparison with land mammals of similar size. For explanation see Cetacea: Metabolism.

## MOULTING

The skin is the first line of defence against the environment. It is also constantly being repaired and is a dynamic organ, which has to adapt to changing environmental conditions. At the beginning of the phocid breeding season the sebaceous (oil) glands become more active and the blood supply increases. A cornified layer develops which consists of cells without nuclei. This layer is shed in large patches in some species, and may come away with the old hairs still attached.

Fur seals moult losing single hairs at a time, and only some of the underfur hairs are lost each year; most of the long guard hairs, however, are moulted. Similarly sea lions are believed to lose hairs separately, not like the phocids in sheets.

## MUSCULAR SYSTEM

The muscular system is based on the typical mammalian pattern. Differences result from functional changes of emphasis. Otariids, for example, have appropriate musculature for the movement of the head which accompanies their long neck and method of locomotion. To attach the muscles there are strong transverse processes or powerful neural spines to the cervical vertebrae. In phocids the processes and neural spines are smaller and less strong, reflecting the less exaggerated head movement.

Otariid locomotion is associated more with flipper movement. This again is reflected in the size and strength of the neural spines of the thoricic vertebrae. Phocid locomotion depends on hind body movement, and to this end the transverse processes of appropriate vertebrae are enlarged to take the attachment of the large muscles.

## MYTHOLOGY

Seals have been associated for many centuries with man's history, but they do not feature as frequently as the cetaceans. They occur in the mythology of some coastal peoples but perhaps their most important contribution is to the mythology of the Eskimos. This is not at all surprising since the economy of the Eskimo is intimately bound up with these creatures. Even today Eskimo art uses the seal in many of its themes, reproducing them in some very fine pieces carved from stone and bone.

Older scientific drawings are less important for imparting factual information than for their artistic merit. It is all too apparent that the artists were working from verbal rather than visual sightings. Seaweed-shaped tails, flamboyant flippers and almost human faces were commonly attributed to these gentle aquatic creatures.

## NERVOUS SYSTEM

The central nervous system of the pinnipeds is basically similar to other mammals. The brain is, however, more spherical and has a greater number of convolutions than is found in land carnivores. The superficial cortical structure apart, the anatomical configuration is practically indistinguishable from that of land mammals.

The olfactory structure varies somewhat with the families; otariids have more development than the phocids. The auditory apparatus is also very important and this is reflected in the complexity and size of the structures. The trigeminal sensory development, which is concerned with the snout region, is important in all pinnipeds but is particularly so in the *Phoca* species.

The cerebellum, which controls movement coordination and balance, is relatively more important in pinnipeds compared with other carnivores.

On the whole, the pinniped brain differs little from the land carnivores when compared to the highly specialized nervous system of the cetacea.

**REPRODUCTION** see Behaviour

## RESPIRATORY APPARATUS

The nostrils of pinnipeds are at the end of the snout. They closely resemble the pattern of land carnivores. A most obvious modification in their position occurs in the subfamily Cystophorinae which includes the hooded and elephant seals. Here the nostrils are situated at the end of the nasal prolongation, and the nostrils point ventrally. While under water the nostrils are firmly closed. Such is the completeness of this adaptation that active muscular action is required to open the nostrils when out of water. When relaxed they are closed. Some families have hair covering at least part of the nostrils, presumably for heat conservation, although in others they are naked.

From the nostrils air passes through the nasal cavity, which is filled with a complex turbinate bone which markedly increases the surface for reception of olfactory (smell) agents.

The larynx of pinnipeds closely resembles that of the carnivores, showing little of the considerable modification which has evolved in the cetacean larynx. There is a small epiglottis composed of cartilage. Just at the entrance to the larynx are paired lateral saccules. Some pinnipeds have an unusual pharyngeal feature – walls which are very elastic and capable of forming large pouches.

The trachea, leading from the larynx to the lungs, is supported by cartilaginous rings. In some species they completely encircle the trachea, in others the rings are not complete and in others, notably those which swallow penguins whole, the rings have been reduced to very small, almost fragments of cartilage.

The trachea divides into 2 bronchi which lead to the 2 lungs. In some species the branching occurs just before the lungs while in others it occurs closer to the larynx and the 2 long bronchi continue posteriorly, lying close together until they enter the lungs. In the phocids the bi-lobed lungs are symmetrical; the otariids follow the normal carnivore pattern of a much larger right lung.

The lungs are placed dorsally in the chest to help buoyancy. The diaphragm is slightly modified in position, being more oblique than in land carnivores. It has the normal attachment from the xiphisternum but curves backwards to the second lumbar vertebra.

An important modification of the bronchi exists, rather similar to that found in the Cetacea. This is a series of valves which effectively sections the bronchi during a dive into airtight compartments. These may assist in preventing lung collapse or function to prevent the solution of gaseous nitrogen in the blood under pressure. (See Diving.)

## SENSES
### Sight

Seals feed on animals living in water and probably rely on sight to catch them though there is some evidence for echolocation. There are special mechanisms to enable them to see both in water and in air. The cornea has the same refractive index as water and the function of the cornea therefore is lost. To accommodate this loss the lens is spherical. In water the iris opens wide, making a wide pupil, to allow in as much light as possible. On land the pupil becomes a slit in most species. The walrus pupil on land takes the form of a horizontal slit, and in the bearded seal it is diagonal.

In spite of the importance of sight, blind animals exist in nature and it seems that other senses can be developed to compensate.

### Hearing

This is almost certainly of tremendous importance for communication between members of a herd at all levels, on land or in water. On land it is also used by bulls for territorial control, and by mother seals which probably identify the individual calls of their young before confirming it with smell.

The ear structure is similar to that of other mammals. Since the meatus is closed when the animal is in water it is likely that sounds are transmitted along the wall of the meatus as in the cetaceans.

### Smell

Smell, judging by the size of the olfactory lobes of the brain, is relatively unimportant. Mothers, however, probably make positive identification of their offspring on the breeding grounds by smell. It also seems likely that smell is used as a sexual signal during the breeding season.

## Taste
Anatomical examination confirms the behavioural observation that taste is not of great importance. Seals swallow their prey whole and no chewing takes place. As in the dog, taste therefore is of limited value.

## Touch
Most evidence of the pinnipeds' sense of touch comes from behavioural observations. Some species lie together in close contact, others do not. Some species are alerted by touch, others remain indifferent. No controlled investigations appear to have been made on this sense. The sensitive vibrissae or whiskers are touch sensitive and are probably used, in dark or murky conditions, to locate and finally guide food to the mouth.

## SKELETAL SYSTEM
The skull of the pinniped is relatively large and rounded with a narrow bridge of bone between the very large orbits or eye sockets. It has a short snout. There is considerable variation between the families. Otariid skulls for example have large mastoid processes while in the phocids they are relatively small. Mandible size depends largely on the demands made upon it by the related muscles.

   The common formula for a pinniped vertebral column is cervical (C7), thoracic (T15), lumbar (L5), sacral (S3), caudal (Cd10–12). It closely resembles the basic mammalian pattern but has some modifications common to all aquatic animals. There are significant differences between phocid and otariid structure resulting from markedly different methods of movement. In the otariid, where movement of the head and fore limbs is considerable during locomotion, there are suitably structured vertebrae in the anterior part of the column with large strong neural spines and transverse processes. The phocids show smaller neural spines and transverse processes anteriorly. The phocids, which depend on lateral movements of the hind part of the body, have well-developed trans-

Two common seals, *Phoca vitulina*, *left* nuzzle each other with their sensitive whiskers.

*Right* Two young California sea lions swimming in the Sea of Cortez, Mexico. Their agility in the water makes it easy for them to catch small fish, squid and octopus.

Skulls of walrus (top) and common seal (below) both showing the teeth of carnivores.

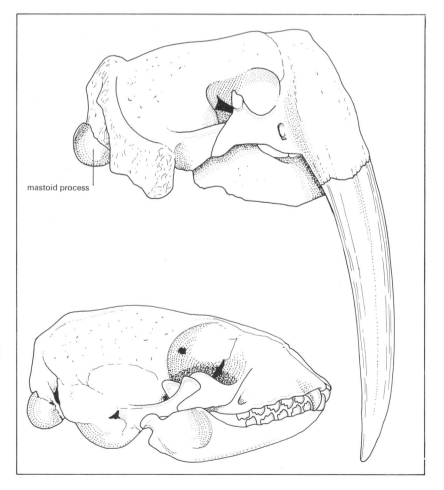

mastoid process

*Above left* The leopard seal, *Hydrurga leptonyx*, is the only seal preying regularly on birds and other pinnipeds.

*Below left* The crabeater seal, *Lobodon carcinophagus*, here on an Antarctic ice floe, may be the fastest pinniped, and can outrun a man racing with it.

The sea lion is able to bring the hindlimb forward and to flex the wrists backwards and so adopt a sitting position on land. The seal's limbs are of little assistance to locomotion on land, when they rely on hunching, rolling and sliding along.

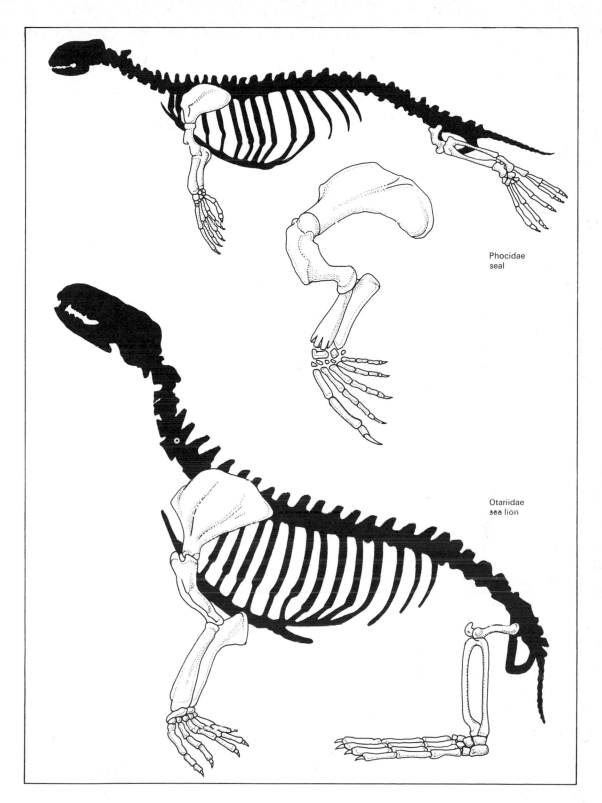

Phocidae
seal

Otariidae
sea lion

verse processes and modifications which allow the spine to move from side to side and up and down.

The fore limb consists of the same bones as that of terrestrial mammals – scapula, humerus, ulna, radius, carpus, metacarpus and phalanges. There is no clavicle in pinnipeds. Modifications of the scapula reflect the differences in locomotion. Otariid scapulas are large with well-developed areas for attachments of the muscles of the fore limbs used in locomotion. Phocid scapulas, while by no means small, have not the large surface area seen in the otariids. The walrus, as in many structural parameters, is somewhere between the two. The humerus, ulna and radius are shorter but stouter in all pinnipeds but there are adequate protuberances for muscle attachment.

The bones of the carpus, metacarpus and phalanges show modifications depending on function. Where the flippers are used to support the animal and assist locomotion on land, the fingers (phalanges) have good joint movement. In those species which use the flippers mainly for manoeuvrability in water, the bones are flatter, less mobile and some are longer.

The pelvic girdle of pinnipeds consists, as in land mammals, of the ilium, pubis and ischium. Otariids and odobenids can turn their hind legs forward and have an appropriate pelvic structure, but in the phocids the ilium has an everted anterior border giving attachment to the powerful muscles mainly associated with lateral body movement. The femur in pinnipeds is relatively much shorter than is common in land mammals. The tibia and fibia are fused at the knee joint, and the tibia curved in the phocids to give greater muscle attachment. Powerful ligaments prevent the feet turning out of a straight line with the tibia and fibula in the phocids.

## SKIN

Fur- or hair-covered skin is not perhaps an ideal coating for long periods of immersion in water. Indeed evolutionary mechanism has allowed the Cetacea to dispense with hair virtually completely.

Studies on pinniped skins have been few but it emerges that there are differences between the true seals (Phocidae) and land mammals. The surface layer consists of cells retaining a nucleus, unlike that of land mammals in which the nucleus disappears and the structure becomes cornified as the exposed surface is approached. The *stratum granulosum* is entirely absent in pinnipeds. The skin is well supplied with oily sebaceous glands which cover both the hairs and the skin with a waterproof layer. Sweat glands which secrete a strong-smelling, very thick substance are also present in large numbers. Both types of gland open into each hair canal.

The dermis below the epidermis is composed of a thin vascular upper layer and a thicker lower layer constructed mainly of fibrous connective tissue in which reside the hair follicles.

Below the dermis is the blubber layer which is of irregular thickness filling in depressions and smoothing bumps to produce a streamlined contour.

Unlike the phocids, fur seals have a thin epidermis with the normal terrestrial mammal pattern of cornified epithelium at the outer surface. The nuclei disappear as the cells near the surface.

The hairy exterior of fur seals is characteristic and demands special mention since it is this covering that attracts commercial exploitation. The hairs are arranged in groups. In each group is a single rather stiff long flattened guard hair together with a variable number of shorter, less rigid underfur hairs which arise behind it. Each hair in the group has its own follicle but all of the hairs emerge from the surface through a single aperture. The number of underfur hairs varies with the species. (See Moulting.)

## SLEEP

Most pinnipeds whether captive or wild will leave the water to sleep. Many seem to enjoy sunbathing, lazing on the rocks in idleness. In addition they are able to sleep for quite long periods on the sea bed. Harbour seals, elephant seals and sea lions have all been observed resting, eyes closed and motionless, on the bottom of tanks in captivity for up to 20 minutes. It is assumed that they were asleep. Most pinnipeds also sleep at the surface of the water. Several field observations confirm this. Such an adaptation is necessary, for many pinnipeds spend quite long periods away from land. Much more work needs to be done on the sleep patterns of these animals. It is possible that they are different when the animals are on land from when they are at sea.

## TEETH

As in most mammals the number of teeth is reduced from the maximum mammalian number 44. The typical carnivore has incisors for nibbling, long powerful canines for catching and holding prey, and pre-molars and molars for grinding and chewing. Pinniped dentition varies with species and families but in general there are incisors present, very strong canines, and behind the canines rather small teeth, the post canines, which represent pre-molars and molars.

As in most mammals (cf. Cetacea) the adult teeth are preceded by temporary dentition (milk teeth). Milk teeth are shed by the age of 6 months in the Otariidae. The usual adult otariid dental formula is $I\frac{3}{2} C\frac{1}{1} PC\frac{5/6}{5}$ (incisor, canine, post canine) although there are some variations. The teeth of otariid are fairly uniform in structure unlike the Phocidae.

Phocid milk teeth are well developed in the young embryo of approximately 3 months of age but from that time they are gradually re-absorbed. At birth a few residual points may remain but it is more usual for the pup to have lost all evidence of them. Most Phocid jaws have a full set of permanent dentition by the time the animals are one month old. It is impossible to write a dental formula for the Phocidae in general since the number of incisors is variable between the families. The post canines are very variable in shape particularly in the degree of cusping. The crabeater seal, *Lobodon carcinophagus*, has a special modification. This species feeds on krill. It swims, like some of the baleen whales, with its mouth open into the krill-infested water and sieves them from the water as it is expelled between the frilled teeth. The upper and lower teeth interlock when the mouth is closed.

The dentition of the walrus, *Odobenus rosmarus*, as might be anticipated, is unique among pinnipeds. There are 28 temporary teeth composed of incisors, canines and post canines, all of which are shed soon after birth. However they are not all replaced by permanent teeth and there is some variation in adult dentition. The obvious walrus modification is the enormous pair of tusks (canines) in the upper jaw of both sexes which modifies the anterior structure of the skull. By the time the males are adult they can have tusks well over 90 cm. in length and weighing up to 6.35 kg. In addition to the tusks are one incisor and 3 post canines on each side of the upper jaw. The lower jaw has no incisors, just a small canine and 3 post canines on each side. Some of the so-called permanent teeth are in fact shed before maturity, a rather unusual modification.

## THERMOREGULATION
(See Cetacea: Thermoregulation)

## TRAINING
The ethics and justification for training wild animals for public performance have been discussed under Cetacea: Training and will not be repeated. Identical arguments apply.

Although spasmodic attempts to train other species have been made with varying degrees of success, it is the California sea lion, *Zalophus californianus*, which for many years has been a favourite in circus rings. In particular trainers exploit the long mobile neck which is ideally suited for balancing. No performance of trained sea lions is worth the name unless it includes a group of these splendid creatures balancing large spinning balls on their noses.

It always seems a pity that these aquatic creatures are usually exhibited by trainers on land where they are to say the least inhibited, instead of being allowed to perform in water where they could acquit themselves with honours. Scientists also train sea lions to assist them in research work.

It is common for trainers to start with young animals, mainly for economic reasons. The process takes at least a year but once trained a working life of over 10 years can be anticipated. The disadvantages of youth are slower learning, greater rearing problems, and increased susceptibility to disease. Advantages include greater play potential which can be exploited by experienced trainers, greater inquisitiveness, and greater enthusiasm.

It has always been the belief of experienced trainers that young animals learn a trick faster if allowed to observe an older trained animal performing it first. For many years the scientific world remained sceptical but recent scientific investigations have added weight to these empirical beliefs.

## TRANSPORTATION

The same care and sympathy is required for handling and transporting pinnipeds as is essential for cetaceans (see Cetacea: Transportation). They are however able to remain out of water for much longer periods than the Cetacea without harm. It is important that handlers are experienced not only for the animals' protection but for their own, as pinnipeds can inflict very nasty bites. Larger pinnipeds are often placed in squeeze cages similar in principle, though different in design, to those used for the larger wild members of the cat family.

## UROGENITAL SYSTEM

The kidney of most pinnipeds is bean-shaped, like that of most land-living carnivores. The tissue, however, is divided into lobules rather like the cetacean kidney. These lobules are separated by fibrous tissue. The degree of separation varies with the species. In most species the ureters leave the inner curvature or medial surface of the kidney in the same way as in land mammals' kidneys, but in the crabeater seal, *Lobodon carcinophagus*, the ureters leave the under surface of the posterior end. In fact careful study suggests a gradation over the pinniped species, from the typical land mammal kidney to the cetacean form, presumably more perfectly adapted by evolution to the aquatic life style.

The ureters pass to the rather elongated bladder. The urethra passes from the neck of the bladder almost immediately through the poorly developed, rather small prostate gland, and on through the penis to the exterior.

The testes are found externally in the scrotal sac in the Otariidae but are situated in the inguinal region in phocids and odobenids. The inguinal position is attained before birth but the descent to the scrotum in otariids is delayed for several years after birth. The testes show seasonal activity related to the distinct breeding seasons usual in the order. The penis is retracted except during mating. The penis of the pinnipeds has a well-defined, quite large bone – the os penis – which increases in size with age.

The paired ovaries are markedly indented by fissures. These are exaggerated during the breeding season. Interestingly fissures are present in land carnivores, and are particularly well defined in the ovaries of the badger. Just prior to parturition, the ovaries become active and several follicles develop. Only one persists to ovulate at the post partum oestrus.

The two horns of the uterus join to form the body of the uterus, but in pinnipedia there is a partial or complete septum, dividing the body into two. In otariids and odobenids the septum is often complete, having two openings to the vagina. The anus and vagina open into a common recess which is controlled by a sphincter muscle. The vagina does not show folds as in the cetacea. The clitoris of most species has an os clitoris.

Otarids and odobenids, and the phocids belonging to the genera *Erignathus* and *Monachus*, have 4 quarters to the udder, 2 are just anterior to and the other 2 just behind the umbilicus. Other phocids have just the posterior pair. When not lactating each nipple is withdrawn into a pocket. The glands enlarge considerably during lactation and can produce large quantities of milk. In some species the glands fuse to form a large homogeneous mass; in others they remain discrete. The milk produced by the pinnipeds is rich in fat and protein. On it, pups grow at tremendous rates. The necessity for high quality milk is apparent if one recalls the short lactation period.

## WARFARE

While behavioural engineering has been of great interest to the Department of Defense in relation to the Cetaceans, the Pinnipeds have not escaped their attention. Using operant conditioning techniques – punishment and reward – sea lions have been trained to carry and retrieve in ways similar to those learnt by the small cetaceans (see Cetacea: Warfare).

# Dictionary of Species

## ODOBENIDAE

This family contains the single species *Odobenus rosmarus*, the walrus. It is restricted to the Arctic Ocean. The large streamlined body is covered with a thick layer of blubber and a tough outer skin. All adults have the very long upper canine teeth or tusks, the males' being the longer and heavier. There are no external ear pinnae but a fold of skin protects the auditory openings; the tail too is externally absent. The testicles, like those of the Phocidae, are internal. The flippers are naked on the lower surface but have a covering of hair on the upper surface. Each digit on the fore limbs has a small claw (see *Odobenus rosmarus*).

## *Odobenus rosmarus* Linnaeus
### ODOBENIDAE  WALRUS

The tusked and whiskered face of this delightful animal is one of the best known of the pinnipeds. It was named in 1758. A male in his prime grows to over 3.7 m. in length and can weigh well over 1,350 kg. The female, less massive, is slightly shorter, rarely exceeding 3 m. and weighs 900 kg. The heavily whiskered snout and the long tusks are unique features of this pinniped. The thick, heavily wrinkled skin is thrown into several folds as though far too large for the body. It grows in places to over 5 cm. in thickness, and it is supported by a 7.5 cm. layer of blubber. Young animals have a few scattered wisps of reddish orange hair but these disappear in older animals. The well-defined moustache of whiskers is an important tactile organ in the search for food. The tusks are mainly used to dig for food in the sea bottom, although they do have minor roles as a weapon and for manoeuvring objects including offspring. The tusks are exaggerated canines from the upper jaw. In mature males they weigh over 4.5 kg. and reach 1 m. in length. Female tusks are more slender and rarely exceed 60 cm. Permanent upper canines erupt at 4 months of age; they continue to grow throughout the animal's life. The remaining teeth, 6 incisors and 8 premolars in each jaw, and 2 molars in the upper jaw, are rather underdeveloped.

The adult walrus has an inflatable pouch on each side of its head which originates in the pharynx. It can be inflated with air from the lungs which is then trapped by muscular action at the opening which acts as a sphincter. The inflated pouch is used when the animal sleeps at sea, rather like a lifejacket, to keep the head above water. This is another feature unique to the walrus among the Pinnipedia.

There are 2 subspecies of walrus, the Atlantic walrus, *O. rosmarus rosmarus*, and the Pacific walrus, *O. rosmarus divergens*. They are differentiated by minor variations of the skull.

Today the walrus is restricted to shallow coastal waters of the Arctic although until recently it was found much further south. The present distribution of the Atlantic subspecies is around Iceland, Svalbard, Franz Josef Land, Novaya Zemlya and along the northern coast of Russia to the east, and throughout the Hudson and Baffin bays as far south as Frobisher Bay and Hudson Strait in the west. Spasmodic observations of the walrus are made around the coasts of the British Isles, even as far south as the Thames and Severn rivers. They are also seen on islands in the Gulf of St Lawrence.

The Pacific walrus is mainly found in the Bering Sea, the Bering Strait and along the Siberian coast to the Laptev Sea.

Walruses form one-sex groups. These groups tend to follow the ice, moving south in winter, and north again as the ice retreats in summer. The groups move over the same areas but separated according to sex. Estimates of the world population vary but it is placed at between 60,000–100,000.

Using their tusks, walruses stir up the sea-bed to find the molluscs that form an important part of their diet. They rarely dive deeper than 75 m. and for this reason stay close to the shallow inshore waters. Stomach contents show that the bivalve molluscs *Mya truncata* and *Saxicava arctica* are common dietary constituents but are supplemented by a variety of other invertebrates. From the lack of shells in the stomach, it is assumed that the soft fleshy parts are sucked out and the shell discarded. Very occasionally the remains of seals have been found in the walrus stomach. It is assumed this form of food is taken only when the usual food is short or as a result of aberrant eating behaviour.

The pups are born during April and May. They are 1.2 m. in length, weigh about 45 kg., and have grey coats. Mating takes place in late May. It is interesting that, unlike many other pinnipeds, the female gives birth only every 2 years. There is apparently no delayed implantation of the blastocyst, and gestation lasts about one year. In spite of polygamy there is no evidence of even loose harem formation. The young stay with their mothers for several years. Lactation itself lasts well into the second year. Naturally social animals, walruses are found in very large social groups with only rare exceptions.

Walruses have been hunted by man since earliest times. Eskimos have used their flesh for food, their blubber for fuel, their hides for leather harnesses and clothing, and the tusks' ivory for spears and works of art. Modern hunting of these exciting animals started in the seventeenth century and drastically reduced their numbers and denuded large areas of their previous range. Man's desire for ivory has meant the slaughter of thousands of these creatures.

## OTARIIDAE

Apart from the walrus, *Odobenus rosmarus*, which is easily identified, members of this family can be distinguished from the Phocidae by the presence of distinct external ear pinnae, a tail, and naked flippers. The adult males are much larger than the females in all species, and the testicles are situated externally in a scrotum. The hind limbs point forwards which allows greater movement on land; they are equipped with long, clawless outer digits while the inner 3 are short and have well developed claws. The fore limbs of otariids are relatively long, giving the animal a more upright resting position on land. Their first digit is long, becoming progressively short medially; all digits have poorly developed claws. See *Arctocephalus, Callorhinus, Eumetopias, Neophoca, Otaria, Zalophus*.

### *Arctocephalus australis* Zimmerman
OTARIIDAE   SOUTH AMERICAN FUR SEAL, FALKLAND FUR SEAL

Like all members of the genus *Artocephalus*, these seals have an under fur of rich reddish brown. The mane of the male has a grey appearance due to the

colour of the long guard hairs which are black with a white tip. There is, however, a good deal of colour variation, particularly in the female. Males reach 1.8 m. in length and weigh over 130 kg. while the smaller female barely achieves 45 kg. The species was named in 1783.

South American fur seals have a similar distribution to the Southern sea lion, *Otaria flavescens*, but tend to keep to different habitats, sea lions preferring sandy beaches and fur seals rocky coasts. They are found from Rio de Janeiro on the Atlantic coast, round the southern tip of the continent, and as far north as northern Chile. They also inhabit the Falkland Islands and some of the Galapagos group. Migrations are poorly understood. Some groups remain fairly stationary while others, for example those in the Falkland Islands, appear to move north in winter.

*Far left* A bull walrus, *Odobenus rosmarus*. On the left side of its head is a scar, probably from a fight with another bull in the mating season. The heavy bristles on the muzzle are sensory, and may act as food filters when feeding on muddy ocean floors.

*Above* South American fur seal, *Arctocephalis australis*.

Studies by taxonomists on the skull proportions have suggested various subspecies which also relate to geographical location. Those on the mainland have been designated *A. australis australis*, and those in the Galapagos Islands *A. australis galapagoensis*. Estimates of population suggest there may be over 150,000 animals altogether.

The mature bulls establish the breeding territories in November, a few weeks before the females arrive. Harems of these pregnant females are collected together and jealously guarded by the belligerent males. Rarely does a bull have more than 5 in his transient family. A few days after their arrival, the females give birth to the pups they have been carrying since the previous breeding season. These are covered in a fine, soft black fur. Mating takes place again within a further few days. Once mated the females are allowed more freedom by the bull and they take to the water again, leaving their offspring on shore, but returning to suckle them at frequent and regular intervals. It is not long before the young are encouraged to take their first dip by their mothers and they soon become proficient. By the end of January the harems have broken up. The males return to the water to recuperate. The mothers continue suckling their offspring for several months, in some cases as long as a year, by which time the young are accomplished swimmers and have left the breeding ground.

The egg, once fertilized, divides repeatedly until it has developed into a sphere of cells known as the blastocyst. At this stage it stops further divisions for some weeks and is not implanted onto the wall of the womb. After this period of arrested development the blastocyst implants and development continues. This is an adaptive mechanism essential for a breeding system which synchronizes birth and mating. It is clearly preferable to an extended gestation, without arrestation, with which the female's physiology and anatomy could not cope.

Knowledge of the diet is limited but it is probably confined to fish, crustaceans and cephalopods.

These delightful animals have been exploited for meat, oil and skins in Uruguay in recent years, where canning and processing factories were still functioning in the late 1960s.

### *Arctocephalus doriferus* Wood Jones
### OTARIIDAE AUSTRALIAN FUR SEAL
First named in 1925, this animal has been very little studied by scientists. It is usually classified as a separate species from the Tasmanian fur seal,

*Right* According to some sources, the Weddell seal, *Leptonychotes weddelli*, lives beneath the ice in Antarctic waters, breathing through cracks its teeth cut in it.

*Over left* The hair in phocids is stiff and lacks underfur; in the elephant seal the skin is almost naked. The northern elephant seal, *Mirounga angustirostris*, is a resident species with a range from British Columbia to California.

*Over right* The largest of the pinnipeds, elephant seals inhabit sub-polar waters, and in common with other land-breeders the males have large harems. Aggressive postures, such as the one displayed here by the southern elephant seal, *Mirounga leonina*, are often necessary to frighten off rivals.

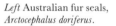

*Left* Australian fur seals, *Arctocephalus doriferus*.

*Left* Monk seals are one of the few tropical phocids. Sluggishness and an unsuspicious nature has contributed to their vulnerability. The Hawaiian monk seals, *Monachus schauinslandi*, are non migratory.

*Right* Australian fur seals, *Arctocephalus doriferus*.

*A. tasmanicus*, but since the characteristics are so slightly different, time may find them reclassified as the same species.

The Australian fur seals are found along the southern coast of Western and South Australia. They are a blackish brown colour, and males reach over 1.8 m. in length.

Males assume territorial roles around the end of October and harems are gathered as the females arrive. Parturition takes place at the end of December.

These animals are hunted in Australia for their skins. Some control is exercised by the relevant authorities.

### *Arctocephalus forsteri*   Lesson
OTARIIDAE   NEW ZEALAND FUR SEAL
Named in 1828. These are medium sized animals growing up to 2.1 m. in length and rarely exceeding 70 kg. in weight. They have a dark grey coat, shading to a fawn ventral surface.

These are stationary animals spending most of the year on the rocky coasts of New Zealand's South Island or the small islands in nearby waters. These include Chatham and Solander islands to the north and the Macquarie Islands further south. There does not appear to be any kind of migration. They leave on feeding expeditions during which they consume fish, crustacea and penguins. Penguins are skinned before being eaten in a style similar to that employed by the leopard seal, *Hydrurga leptonyx*, which shakes the body free of its integument.

Males with breeding inclinations stake their territories in November and gather together under their protective eye a group of up to 12 females. Pregnant animals give birth to grey pups soon after, during the early part of December. The males assume a protective role towards the pups of their females although they are probably not their fathers. This defensive role continues until the harem begins to disintegrate in February. The females continue to feed the pups until May or June, by which time they are well on the way to self-sufficiency.

This is one seal which has been the subject of farsighted conservation by governments for over 50 years. It is now estimated that the total population exceeds 80,000 individuals. Earlier sealing activities during the eighteenth and nineteenth centuries drastically reduced the population until the industry became uneconomic and it was left in peace.

### *Arctocephalus philippii*   Peters
OTARIIDAE   GUADALUPE FUR SEAL
A rare seal, first named in 1866. Males approach 1.8 m. in length and can weigh up to 160 kg. The fur is grey with some brown shading about the head.

Very little is known about this species, which breeds on the island of Guadalupe, off the Baja California coast, because so many were slaughtered during the nineteenth century that the species tottered perilously close to extinction. Before the massacre began the species was present in large numbers on the rocky offshore islands of the Pacific coast of both Americas from California to Chile. So relentless was the carnage that by the end of the nineteenth century the industry died from a lack of raw materials. It is of interest that the fur seal from Juan Fernandez, off the Chilean coast, was related to this species, while the fur seal from the Galapagos Islands, *A. australis*, is a different species. Sadly the population of Juan Fernandez appears to be extinct and there is no migration between Guadalupe and Juan Fernandez. Since the middle 1920s, when it was supposed that the Guadalupe fur seal was extinct, there has been a slow but definite recovery. In the early 1950s a small breeding colony was discovered and from that time the numbers have increased but remain very precarious and at only 500 individuals.

### *Arctocephalus pusillus*   Schreker
OTARIIDAE   SOUTH AFRICAN FUR SEAL
Named in 1776. Males of this species grow to 2.4 m. in length and in the peak of condition weigh 360 kg. Females, smaller with thinner and more graceful lines, rarely exceed 1.7 m. and weigh considerably less – up to 113 kg. The males have a blackish appearance as a result of their coarse black guard hairs. Females are light brownish or grey in colour.

South African fur seals inhabit the offshore islands and rocky coasts of South West Africa, from Cape Cross as far east as Bird Island by Algoa Bay. The extent of the range covers over 1,500 km. of coast. There appears to be no definite pattern of migration, but tagged animals have shown that individuals at least travel throughout the range. There are probably some 500,000 representatives populating the South West African coast.

These seals are known to hunt alone normally. Occasionally, however, several will be seen around a large shoal of fish. They hunt by sight and at the surface, rarely diving to depths of more than 36 m. Animals close to shore will return to the rocks at night but they can, and do, sleep at sea. Both bulls and cows spend at least half their time feeding. Their diet consists of large quantities of shoaling fish, although crustacea and cephalopods are consumed in small quantities.

Bulls begin to establish their breeding territories on the rocky shores during October. The females give birth to their pups towards the end of November or the beginning of December. The pups, about 75 cm. long, have fine close black curly fur. Mothers stay with their pups for the first few days of life. About a week after the birth, mating takes place, usually on land but occasionally in the water. The implantation of the blastocyst (see *A. australis*) is delayed for 6 months. When mated, mothers stay away from their offspring for short periods, starting with a few days until, by the time the pup is 2 months old, she may be away for 2 weeks. The pups gradually begin to supplement their milky diet with small crabs and other crustacea, although the lactation period often continues until the next breeding season, a year later. During March and early April the pup's black coat changes, over several weeks, to one of greeny grey. One year later, when about 18 months old, a second moult produces a suit of shining grey. Thereafter moults occur each February.

These animals are hunted for their pelts and blubber, but in recent years have shown an encouraging recovery of numbers.

### *Arctocephalus tasmanicus*  Scott and Lord
OTARIIDAE  TASMANIAN FUR SEAL
Named as a separate species in 1926, there are serious doubts about the validity of ascribing it

species status. The males grow up to 2.4 m. in length, the females up to 1.8 m., and they very closely resemble the Australian fur seal, *A. doriferus*, with which it may be synonymous.

They are found all around the coast of Tasmania, where suitable habitats exist, on the islands in the Bass Strait and along the south-eastern tip of Australia, including the coast of Victoria and New South Wales as far north as Sydney. There are probably in excess of 12,000 animals in the range.

Fish and squid are their staple diet.

Harems are gathered by the adult males who have formed temporary breeding territories in October and November. The pups are born soon after the females take up residence in November and December. The dark brown pups are suckled for 6 months.

They are protected by law but some are killed under licence.

### *Arctocephalus tropicalis*  Peters
OTARIIDAE  KERGUELEN FUR SEAL,
SUB-ANTARCTIC FUR SEAL
Named in 1875. Males grow up to 1.8 m. in length. They are dark grey dorsally with a distinctive yellow throat and chest. The dark back stops at a point on the forehead. There is a crest on the head. A chestnut brown area extends backwards from the flippers. Bulls have a long straggly-haired mane.

Kerguelen fur seals live on the rocky shores of several islands of the south Atlantic and Indian oceans. They have been observed on Tristan da Cunha, Gough Island, South Shetlands, South Orkneys, South Georgia, South Sandwich Islands, Bouvet Island, Marion Reef, Prince Edward Islands, Crozets, Kerguelen, Amsterdam and St Paul. There is a possibility that they inhabited the Islands of Macquarie south of New Zealand in the early nineteenth century, but that hunting exterminated them, the ecological gap being effectively filled by the New Zealand fur seal, *A. forsteri*. Some authorities consider that there are two subspecies, *A. tropicalis tropicalis* and *A. tropicalis gazella*, distributed north and south respectively of the Antarctic Convergence, the point where the surface temperature of the water suddenly changes due to the interference of cold antarctic waters and

the warm temperate seas. There is an estimated total of 50,000 animals in the range and this is increasing.

Their diets have not been well studied but are thought to contain fish, crustacea and cephalopods.

Breeding begins, as usual with the genus, when the bulls arrive on the breeding shores in October to establish their breeding territories. The females are collected into small groups of up to 5 individuals. The black, thick-furred pups are born towards the end of November and mating takes place about one week later. The pups form lethargic play groups, keeping well out of the way of the bulls. It is assumed that there is a delayed implantation of the blastocyst though detailed study is lacking.

Sadly this delightful creature has a high grade fur and the sealers were quick to exploit it. This they did with the usual ruthlessness. Within about 30 years, from 1790 to 1820, over one million animals were slaughtered for profit. The numbers were so small by the 1920s that the industry dissolved.

They are now belatedly protected on some of the islands.

### *Callorhinus ursinus*  Linnaeus
OTARIIDAE  PRIBILOF FUR SEAL,
NORTHERN FUR SEAL, ALASKAN FUR SEAL

Named in 1758. This is the only living member of the genus but is perhaps the best known of the fur seals, being highly prized in the fur trade for its very high quality pelt.

Males reach some 2.1 m. in length and weigh, in the peak of condition, over 270 kg. The females are shorter, measuring from nose to tail about 1.5 m. only, and are considerably less in bulk weighing less than 70 kg. The males are a dark brown with a greyish brown neck, the females grey with a paler, almost fawn belly. Both sexes have a pale patch on the chest.

The breeding grounds of this seal are restricted to the islands of the Pribilof group, notably St George and St Paul, the Medny and Bering islands of the Komandorskie group, and Robben Island off Sakhalin in the Sea of Okhotsk. During the cold winter months, however, the females and imma-

ture animals migrate south, either singly or in small groups, as far as San Diego on the Pacific coast of North America and latitude 35°N on the Japanese coast. The bulls move little, probably travelling and remaining just south of the Aleutian Islands. They return to their breeding grounds again for the summer. During the winter migration to warmer waters, between November and April, this species distributes itself widely, keeping well away from the shore. In April the journey back begins and between May and June there are congregations in the Gulf of Alaska and off the west of Kamchatka. During the summer months, June to October, all animals of breeding age will be close to the breeding grounds. The world population of Pribilof fur seals has been estimated at well over one and a half million animals. The forces of nature which control population size are many and variable. In this seal, mortality among the young is very high; probably over 70 per cent of each year's crop die within the first 3 years of life. Causes of death include parasitic worm infestation, bacterial enteritis, physical damage due to overcrowding, predation by killer whale and man, poor weather conditions and bad mothering. The parasitic worm challenge to the young must be high on islands which are seal sick. Years of breedings must have markedly increased the parasite population. Those animals which survive the rigours of infancy have a life expectancy of more than 25 years. Seals feed at sea at dusk and dawn. Their basic diet consists of squid and a variety of fish including herring, cod and occasionally salmon.

The breeding bulls take up their territories early in June. Studies have shown that many return to a preferred site each year. There, with much vocalization, fighting and posturing, they establish their rights of might, and claim territorial domination. Young males frustrated at their failure to claim a breeding area linger around the outside of the breeding grounds hoping to entice a female from her rightful master. The females arrive 2–3 weeks later and are gathered together into harems of up to 50. The male must defend his female flock alone. Hardly sleeping, taking no food, and mating, he stays at his post for over 2 months.

The pups are born a very few days after the females take up their harem responsibilities. The pups are about 60 cm. long and weigh 4.5 kg. For a few days the mother is very attentive to her offspring. She stays close by it, cleaning and caressing it, keeping it away from danger and protecting it from the attentions of the bulls or other females. After 6–7 days this mother love diminishes in intensity. Mating takes place and then the mother disappears off to sea for days at a time, returning only once a week to feed her infant charge. During her absence the pup gathers with others in small play groups. On her return the female lands at a specific spot on the coast and then begins to call. All young are prepared to feed from her but she will have none but her own. She sniffs each newcomer until she finds her pup and then permits suckling. Female seals produce very rich, high quality milk of which the pup consumes almost 4 litres at one session after its long fast. Such a system would cause severe dietary enteritis in any other young mammal, and mastitis of the mammary glands of the female. It is interesting to examine the physiological adaptation required to allow such alimentary abuses. The pup takes to the water when it is about 4 weeks old although it can swim earlier if pressed. Suckling lasts for about 4 months.

The harem breaks up in August. A few young females may linger on the breeding shores, being belatedly mated by an ardent bachelor male. Females rarely give birth to their first pup before they are five years old. Males, mature at 3–6 years, do not establish breeding territories or harems until they are well over 10–11 years of age. As in so many seals, there is arrested development of the blastocyst, implantation being delayed for 4 months.

This seal has been exploited for its pelt since earliest times. First the Russian and then American sealers relentlessly killed thousands, without a thought for conservation. All ages and sexes were slaughtered indiscriminately. As a consequence, the population was reduced from an estimated two and a half million in the 1780s to 200,000 in 1911. The government of the United States assumed responsibility for the species in 1911 and since then, with short breaks during the war periods, the numbers taken by sealers have been closely monitored.

## *Eumetopias jubatus* Schreber
### OTARIIDAE STELLER'S SEA LION, NORTHERN SEA LION

This is one of the largest of the sea lions. It was named in 1776. Males are magnificent beasts, growing to over 3 m. in length and weighing over 1 tonne. Females are about two-thirds the size of the males. The fur is an attractive yellow-brown colour. Males in maturity grow a mane of long coarse hair.

Steller's sea lion is widely distributed in the northern waters of the Pacific. It ranges from the coast of the United States, along the coast of Canada and Alaska, the Aleutian and St Lawrence Islands in the Bering Sea, to the coast of the Soviet Union, throughout the Sea of Okhotsk as far south as Hokkaido. It lives mainly on the rocky islands off the coast. During the winter adult males move to the north of their range, returning south again, when they are often seen off the coast of California, for the summer. It is thought that there is a world population of about 300,000.

Cautious animals, they take to the water at the slightest sign of danger; if already in the water they dive out of sight rapidly. They have a very varied diet of fish of all kinds and squids. They are under attack for consuming fish of commercial importance to man and large numbers have been slaughtered. Although they are found near the salmon nets and no doubt take some salmon, there is equally convincing evidence that the sea lions are after the lampreys which themselves harm the salmon. Sadly, man all too often resorts to the slaughter of a species without sufficient evidence to justify his actions, only to find that the ecological balance has been upset to his own detriment.

The mature males arrive at the breeding sites in late April or early May to claim and establish their territories. Females appear some 3–4 weeks later and are collected into harems of 10–20 by the bulls. A few days after their arrival, the calves conceived the previous year are born. Very shortly after giving birth mating takes place. The pups, born usually early in July, remain on land but are swimming by the end of July or early in August. The period of lactation is a little uncertain. It definitely continues after the herd leaves the breeding grounds and lasts at least 3 months, but

A colony of Steller's sea lions, *Eumatopias jubatus.*

may last as long as a year. The interesting reproductive phenomenon of delayed implantation occurs. After conception, the egg develops until a sphere of cells, the blastocyst, is formed and then development stops until October when it continues again; implantation to the wall of the womb occurs, and pregnancy continues uninterrupted. The mechanisms behind this delay are poorly understood but it has evolved to suit the breeding behaviour of these animals.

Northern natives in former times relied on this animal for food, clothing and fuel. Today sophisticated demands for western standards have reduced the slaughter for man but they are still killed to provide protein for animals. Rarely seen in zoos and never in the circus, they are less well known to the general public than some of their close cousins.

### *Neophoca cinerea* Peron OTARIIDAE
AUSTRALIAN SEA LION

Named in 1816. Australian sea lions are large animals; the males grow to over 3.5 m. in length and are rich, deep brown with a yellow mane of coarse hair. Females, less bulky and more streamlined, are somewhat shorter, rarely exceeding 3 m. in length. They are a lovely rich brown with pale yellow abdomens.

They are distributed along the southern coast of Australia from Houtmans Abrolhos, a group of offshore islands north of Perth, to Kangaroo Island close to Adelaide. The numbers are believed to be quite small. No migratory movements have been recorded. Most animals appear to stay within very small areas.

Gregarious, they prefer to remain in loose social groups. They are well adapted to climbing and some reports suggest that they travel some miles inland from the shore.

They live on fish and penguins.

During the breeding season, from October to December, there is a gathering on shore. Males establish their territory and gather around them a small harem of up to 6 wives. Females give birth to their pups in late November or early December and are mated a few days later.

### *Neophoca hookeri* Gray OTARIIDAE
HOOKER'S SEA LION, NEW ZEALAND SEA LION

Named in 1844. The males are dark brown in colour with a splendid dark brown mane. They grow to over 3 m. in length. The females, slighter of build and shorter, have a light brown fur.

They are restricted to some of the islands of New Zealand, being found on the Falkland Islands,

*Right* The common or harbour seal, *Phoca vitulina*, suckles her young. These animals are easily tamed.

*Left* Two bull Hooker's sea lions, *Neophoca hookeri*, fighting during the mating season.

The dugong, *Dugong dugon*, is found in tropical marine waters, where it browses on coastal vegetation.

Snares and Campbell islands. They are frequently seen on the sandy beaches, but often venture further inland among the shore scrubland. Estimates suggest a total population of over 30,000 animals. Little migration takes place.

During the early part of October the mature males arrive to establish and defend territories. The females arrive 4 weeks later and are gathered together by the bulls as they land into harems of up to 12. The females give birth to their pups towards the end of December or early in January. Soon after the birth the female is mated and is then allowed to leave the confines of the harem. She returns at frequent intervals to feed her pup. Some 4–5 weeks later the pups are all confident swimmers and the bull, now tired and hungry, since he fasted throughout the breeding season, allows the harem to disintegrate.

These animals eat fish, crustacea, and other small invertebrates, in addition to a basic diet of penguin which is often eaten at sea. Like several other species, they swallow stones, the reason for which can only be speculated upon.

The nineteenth century saw considerable slaughter of these sea lions for oil and skins. Today, however, they are fortunately not commercially viable and are largely left in peace. They are completely protected in the Auckland Islands.

### *Otaria flavescens* Shaw OTARIIDAE

SOUTHERN SEA LION, SOUTH AMERICAN SEA LION
Named in 1820. The males grow to over 2 m. in length and weigh over 300 kg. The slimmer females rarely exceed 1.8 m. in length and weigh half as much. They have dark brown bodies usually with paler necks and heads. The males have manes. There is a good deal of colour variation. This species is smaller than the northern sea lion, *Eumetopias jubatus*.

Southern sea lions are found along the rocky coasts of South America, from just south of Rio de Janeiro on the Atlantic coast to Paita in northern Peru on the Pacific coast. A large colony inhabits the Falkland Islands. Population estimates suggest that up to 800,000 animals live along the coasts of South America.

These animals are very sociable and live in large mixed groups. As the breeding season, from December to January, approaches the male selects a part of the coast as a territory and defends this against all comers. As they land at the breeding areas, females are taken into a harem belonging to one of the males. Each harem consists of up to 15 animals. The senile animals, immature males and females all cluster close to, but not inside, the breeding area. The female gives birth to her pup soon after arrival in the harem. It will be nearly 90 cm. long and dark brown or black in colour, lightening to a paler brown and eventually to a yellow-ochre by the age of one year. At this age a moult occurs which provides the pup with a brown coat. Soon after giving birth the females are mated by their bull and are then allowed to return to the water; they return periodically to suckle their young. Lactation can continue for up to a year but pups are partially weaned by 5 months. The pups left on land by their mothers form play groups between the feeding visits. They do not enter the water until encouraged by their mothers, who help them until they are confident; she allows the occasional ride on her back. The harassed male has, all through the breeding season, been defending his territory, fighting off challenges from upstart males, mating, starving, and sleeping little. At the end of the 2 months' stretch he is exhausted and hungry. When all the females are mated the harem breaks up and the male eats and sleeps to recover his former glory. Males become mature and grow manes when they are 6 years old. The more precocious females mature at 4 years of age.

Southern sea lions eat fish, squid, crustacea and occasionally penguins. Strangely they swallow small stones, over 11 kg. of which have been found in one specimen's stomach. What purpose this practice serves is unknown but it has been suggested that it relates to buoyancy problems.

These sea lions have been used from early times for meat, oil and hides. Today there is, theoretically, control over exploitation and population numbers but its effectiveness is open to question.

### *Zalophus californianus* Lesson

OTARIIDAE CALIFORNIA SEA LION
Named in 1828, this is perhaps one of the best known of all pinnipeds. Its popularity with zoo proprietors and its easy acceptance of training for

circus performances have been an important public relations exercise for the whole order.

The neatly streamlined body grows, in males, to over 2 m. in length and weighs over 270 kg. Females are slightly smaller. They have a lovely deep brown fur which, of course, is darker when wet. Males have a prominent horny crest on their heads. They live up to 20–25 years.

By far the largest population lives along the Californian coast. There are, however, populations on the Galapagos Islands and around Japan. Structurally these are very similar indeed but are given subspecies status based on the geographical separations; *Z. californianus californianus* refers to those found on the California coast, *Z. californianus wollebaeki* to those in Galapagos waters, and *Z. californianus japonicus* to the Japanese colony. They live close to shore, usually within a 15 km. limit, on the rocky coasts and wealth of small islands off the California coast. There is a poorly defined seasonal movement, the males in particular moving north in winter. The California and Galapagos colonies seem fairly secure at the present time; populations in both cases can be counted in tens of thousands. It is the Japanese subspecies which is most in danger, if not already beyond redemption, for estimates put their numbers only in the hundreds.

Strangely, very little is known about their behaviour in the wild. Social animals, they live in groups with definite dominance orders. On land while resting, guard animals give warning of danger to the rest of the group who take to the water. The bark or roar of sea lions is well known to anybody who has watched them being fed in zoos. Vocalizations are also extremely important in nature for social communication.

Breeding behaviour has been studied recently. The young of the California subspecies are born in May and June, of the Galapagos subspecies in October and November, soon after arrival at the breeding grounds. Males, already established in a territory, collect together a loosely organized harem of up to 20 females. They mate very soon after parturition. The pup begins to suckle less than 2 hours after birth and indulges in frequent meals of mother's milk at 2-hourly intervals throughout the day. Lactation continues for over 6 months. The pup will remain on land for the first 2 weeks after birth, but then readily and easily takes to the water, rapidly becoming a proficient swimmer.

California sea lions are well known in captivity, where they remain healthy if not happy for many years. They have bred successfully and reared young in many zoological gardens. A placid temperament and considerable intelligence allows them to be exploited for circus training. They easily learn to perform tricks and are particularly adept at balancing and juggling acts. Several stories of their ability to remember are on record. Animals who have once been trained, when asked to go through the routine after prolonged lapses, accomplish their tasks without error. They have also been trained to assist research programmes and for military purposes (see Training and Warfare).

## PHOCIDAE

The members of this family of pinnipeds are commonly known as true seals. They have no external ear pinnae. Naturally agile in water, their anatomical adaptation makes them clumsy on land.

Widely distributed in most seas and oceans of the world, they even enter rivers and river estuaries, and in some cases are found in land-locked lakes which once had a connection with the open water; Lake Baikal is the best known example.

Pups are born once each year when the animals of breeding age congregate on land. The female is mated soon after the birth of her pup and the gestation lasts until the next breeding season. Growth of the embryo is arrested in the early stages by a phenomenon known as delayed implantation.

Anatomically the phocids differ from the otariids and odobenids. The limbs are covered with fur; the fore limbs point forwards; the first digit is long, the others progressively shorter. The hind limbs are directed backwards, an adaptation to aquatic life which makes movement on land difficult. The outer digit is also longer than the others. Most phocids have claws. The testicles are internally situated. See *Cystophora, Erignathus, Halichoerus, Histriophoca, Hydrurga, Lobodon, Leptonychotes, Mirounga, Monachus, Ommatophoca, Pagophilus, Phoca, Pusa.*

## Cystophora cristata  Erxleben
### PHOCIDAE   HOODED SEAL, BLADDERNOSE SEAL, CRESTED SEAL

Named in 1777, this animal is an unusual and interesting member of the order. It is usually found on drifting ice in deep water and rarely seen on firm ice or terra firma.

Males and females are of very similar size but males are slightly larger reaching up to 3 m. in length and weighing close on 450 kg. The body colour is a very pale grey. Dark irregular patches cover the body. The characteristic feature of hooded seals is the inflatable hood, in reality a modification of the nasal cavity, which can be blown up at will to form a tense bladder some 45 cm. in diameter. At rest it is an unimpressive, almost ugly, wrinkled structure which covers the top of the head from the eyes to the tip of the nostrils, overhanging the mouth in a dangle of superfluity. The function of this gas-filled bladder is not known. It may be used as a threatening posture against other members of the species or in pre-sexual courting displays. It is bright red when inflated. Not content with this grotesque anatomical development, hooded seals have an inflatable balloon which extrudes at will from one of the nostrils. It is formed from the lining of the nasal septum. Details of it are not known, but it is thought that air taken into the stomach is blown into both the hood and the nasal balloon while the nostrils are closed. Again the purpose of the balloon is not understood but it is likely that it is related to the uses of the hood.

Hooded seals are found in deep water from Svalbard across to Baffin Island in the north, and from Iceland to Newfoundland in the south. It is thought there may be some 500,000 individuals alive.

Except during the breeding season, when they form family groups of bull, cow and offspring, these seals live solitary lives. Their behaviour during this period of the year remains largely unknown. Certainly some travel great distances, since individuals have been found quite far south, along the coasts of both Europe and America. Most, however, are thought to follow their arctic heritage and remain in the icy waters of the north. Feeding habits are imperfectly understood, but they are known to eat a variety of fish, crustacea, squid and octopus.

During the early spring these solitary creatures gather for the annual breeding. The main breeding areas are around Jan Mayen Island and northern parts of Newfoundland. The pups are dropped soon after the gathering has assembled in March and April. The embryonic coat is shed while the pup is still in the womb, and it is born with a fine highlighted grey covering above and a distinct pale yellow belly. During lactation the cow and the bull stay in close proximity to the pup and defend it. After two weeks, parental enthusiasm wanes and both desert the pup and return to the sea after mating. The pup stays on the ice for another 2 weeks and then takes the plunge. A congregation later forms in the Denmark Strait region where moulting takes place. When complete, the group disintegrates until the following spring.

The hooded seal pup skins are sought after for the fur trade and young seals are taken while still afloat on the ice. In addition sealers do take adults which gather for the moult. International agreement limits the hunting season but this is difficult to enforce.

## Erignathus barbatus  Erxleben
### PHOCIDAE   BEARDED SEAL

This seal was first named in 1777. Two subspecies have been defined. *E. barbatus barbatus* known as the Northern Atlantic bearded seal occurs from the Laptev Sea to the Hudson Bay. *E. barbatus nauticus*, named by Pallas in 1811 and known as the North Pacific bearded seal, occurs from the Laptev Sea eastwards to the Canadian Arctic. There are minor skull variations between the 2 subspecies.

Both males and females reach 2.5 m. in length and weigh up to 270 kg. The body is grey but with a brownish coloration on the head, which extends as a darker shading along the back. As its name suggests it has a splendid set of whiskers.

Bearded seals prefer shallow coastal waters and are found in the seas surrounding the North Pole. They hardly ever venture further south than the Gulf of St Lawrence, the northern coast of Norway and the Sea of Okhotsk. They do not normally form large herds but keep to small units or pairs.

Much of their time is spent at sea but close to shores; they rarely swim in deep waters. Estimates of the total population are obviously difficult as the species does not form large congregations. It has been placed, however, at between 120,000–180,000. Bearded seals do not migrate but are constantly on the move within their range. They are able to sleep at sea, remaining virtually submerged with only their nostrils exposed.

Food consists of a wide variety of animals which live on the sea bottom in shallow water – crustacea, molluscs and bottom-feeding fish are all taken in large quantities. Exactly how they ingest their food is unknown, but since shells are very rarely present in the stomach and the grinding teeth are well worn it seems likely that hard exteriors like shells and exoskeletons are crushed and the soft flesh sucked clear before the remnants are rejected.

Female bearded seals give birth only once every 2 years. There is no annual get-together for the breeding season; pups are simply born on shores or ice floes somewhere between March and May. The grey woolly-coated pups are large, about 1.2 m. in length and weighing up to 40 kg. Motherhood is taken seriously, the pups staying close for long periods, although the length of lactation remains unknown. The pups moult a short time after birth, losing their neonatal fur and gaining a stiff-haired coat like the adults. Exactly how or why there is only biennial breeding remains a mystery, although it seems likely that the postnatal ovulation which occurs soon after birth in many species is delayed until after the male's sexual activities have drawn to a close. The female therefore remains barren until the following April or May. After mating the egg grows to the blastocyst stage and is then arrested until August or September

Grey seal cow, *Halichoerus grypus.*

when implantation occurs and the foetus continues to develop.

Its wide distribution and diffuse social behaviour have protected this seal from extensive commercial exploitation by modern man's destructive technology. Eskimos have, however, always taken small numbers for food, fuel and hides.

### *Halichoerus grypus* Fabricius
### PHOCIDAE   GREY SEAL

The grey seal was first named in 1791. Adult males reach up to 3 m. in length and weigh up to 300 kg. They have a distinctive crest on their heads, and the neck characteristically carries 3 deep indentations. Adult females are smaller, rarely exceeding 2 m. in length or 250 kg. body weight. They are very variable in colour, often with smaller irregular patches on the body. Generally the body is a dark brown which appears black when wet.

Both sexes have paler bellies. Adult males have prominent arched noses and occasionally are found with exceptionally pronounced ears – very unusual in this family.

Grey seals are found in the Atlantic. There are 3 main breeding localities, and in spite of a good deal of intermingling, animals from each geographical group appear to return to their area of origin for breeding. Thus the populations tend to remain genetically separate. The north-western Atlantic group is based in and around the Gulf of St Lawrence. They are found as far north as Belle Island and as far south as Sable Island, inhabiting all the waters and rocky coasts in between including Newfoundland, the eastern coast of Canada, Anticosti, Prince Edward Island and Cape Breton Island.

In the eastern Atlantic an important geographically based population inhabits the rocky coasts

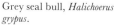
Grey seal bull, *Halichoerus grypus*.

around the British Isles. They are found in Shetland and Orkney islands, the west coast of Scotland, Wales, and Ireland, the north coast of Devon and Cornwall and the Scilly Isles. There is in addition a large breeding colony on the east coast, on the Farne Islands and more recently on the Scroby Sands off Great Yarmouth. Still further north there are colonies on the Faeroe Islands and the shores of Iceland, and eastwards along the Norwegian coasts and on into the White Sea beyond Murmansk. There is a discrete population in the Baltic Sea which breeds mainly in the northern Gulf of Bothnia.

Except during the breeding season the grey seal travels widely and, as has been said, the mixing of the various breeding colonies occurs regularly. Young animals in particular are known to travel far in their first two years of life. Estimates of the population place the world total at about 50,000, the majority being found around the British Isles, mainly in northern Scottish waters. Undoubtedly the largest and most spectacular colony is centered on North Ronaldsay which supports about 10,000 animals in all.

During the early months of the year females, followed by males, land to moult – the cows during February and March and the bulls March to late April and early May. The moult takes 10–15 days after which they return to the sea to feed and fatten for the breeding season.

Grey seals have a catholic taste in sea food; a wide variety of fish is consumed in addition to small amounts of crustacea and molluscs.

Colonies inhabiting the coastal areas of the British Isles have been the subject of quite detailed studies and in particular their breeding behaviour has been closely observed. The breeding season extends from late August to December although pups are found at all times of the year, and those outside the usual range are assumed to be offspring of young first pregnancy females. A few weeks before territorial stations are assumed by the bulls pregnant females and bulls at all stages of maturity congregate close to the beaches used for breeding. Atypically in this species it is not until the first pups are born that the bulls are stimulated to claim territories. The older, most mature bulls claim large areas well inland which gives them prime choice of the available females. However, as the season progresses and male ardour intensifies, these large plots of land become increasingly difficult to police by the older bulls and the young upstart males nibble away at the edges establishing their own patches on the circumference while the big bull barons are busy courting or mating. Territories eventually take up all available space close to the tidal edge. Females have to pass through numerous territories as they go to and from the sea. In so doing attempts are made to seduce them by the bull into whose territory they have wandered.

The female gives birth to the pup, delivery being normally a rapid affair, and the umbilical cord is fractured by a deliberate jerk of the mother's hind quarters. The placenta is passed soon afterwards to be ignored by the mother and eaten by scavenging ever-present seagulls. Failure to consume the placenta is an adaptive variation which has developed as a result of the particular circumstances of breeding – no predators. Pups are covered with a long woolly off-white coat which is shed 3 weeks after birth for a shorter bluish grey model. Pups are suckled for about 3 weeks after which the mother's maternalism is totally depleted and she speeds off to the deep, leaving her offspring to face the world alone. As soon as the first moult is complete the pup takes to the water. During suckling the weight-gain of the pups is quite astounding. They grow at a rate of over 1.4 kg. a day, doubling their weight and more during suckling. During this period the mother eats nothing and looses weight. The females are mated by the bull during the postnatal receptive period which occurs 2 weeks after the pup is born. Copulation occurs either in the water or on land with a preference for the former. The eggs develop to the blastocyst stage but implantation is delayed for 12 weeks, finally taking place in early spring.

Bulls mature at about 7 years of age and then begin their social climb for territorial status. Cows breed first when about 2 years old. However, since only pregnant females arrive at the beaches it is assumed that virgin females are mated away from the breeding areas either by young males or mature bulls prior to, or after, the season proper.

The western Atlantic and Baltic populations produce their young in early spring – February to

April – but few details are known about their behaviour.

Fortunately for the grey seal they are of little commercial value. There are, however, continual complaints by fishermen that they damage nets and eat the fish with the inevitable result that representations are made to have their population reduced. Fortunately an Act of Parliament protects seals to some extent in the United Kingdom. They are, however, culled each year, theoretically for their own good.

### *Histriophoca fasciata*   Zimmerman
PHOCIDAE   RIBBON, BANDED, HARNESS OR SADDLED SEAL

Banded seals were named in 1783 but very little is known about them.

Males and females are of similar size, rarely exceeding 1.5 m. in length and 90 kg. in weight. Their name comes from the light banding which resembles a collar around the neck, a similar band around the hindquarters of the body, and one roughly spherical band on each side of the body around the flipper.

Banded seals are restricted to the north-west coastal region of the Bering Sea, as far north as St Lawrence Island, the Sea of Okhotsk and Tatar Strait. Rough estimates of the species' numbers based on scanty evidence suggests there may be up to 80,000.

They eat fish, crustacea and squid.

Mating takes place during August. The fluffy white pup is born on the ice during March and April. The pups are suckled until the mother moults in June.

### *Hydrurga leptonyx*   Blainville
PHOCIDAE   LEOPARD SEAL

Named in 1820, the leopard seal is a sleek, lithe creature, well adapted to its predatory behaviour. Its huge mouth is designed for attacking its large prey. Females exceed males by up to 60 cm. in length, growing to over 3.7 m. and weighing up to 360 kg. The common name is derived from the spots and patches which decorate the head, neck and sides against a background of various shades of grey. Usually a dark dorsal colour shades to a pale belly. All in all theirs is a very characteristic shape which is easily recognized.

Solitary animals, they spend their time mostly around the edges of the Antarctic pack ice. Some move north to warmer seas in winter and not infrequently reach the southern shores of Australia and New Zealand. Others appear to remain at the pack ice edge all through the year. The population is roughly estimated at 100,000 to 300,000.

As indicated, its gustatory habits are catholic. It pursues fish, squid and the pups of other seal species and will eat carrion of all kinds, but its main diet consists of penguins which are caught in the water, brought to the surface and shaken violently to kill.

Very little is known about its reproductive behaviour. The fluffy pups with a dark stripe along the back and white sides flecked with black are born in December.

### *Lobodon carcinophagus*   Hombron and Jacquinot PHOCIDAE   CRABEATER SEAL, WHITE SEAL

Named in 1842, these are more numerous than the other members of the antarctic phocid seals and may be the most numerous of all pinnipeds.

Males and females are of similar size, reaching up to 2.7 m. in length and weighing over 250 kg.

A sea leopard, *Hydrurga leptonyx*, chasing a penguin, its staple food. (Drawing by Edward Wilson.)

Slender, streamlined animals, they are able to move with amazing speeds across the ice, as fast as 24 km. per hour. Dorsally the body is dark grey with a brown tint, shading to a pale, almost white belly. The sides are marked with variable patterns of brown rings. The coat colour gradually fades to become almost white in summer.

Crabeaters are social animals and congregate in herds. They frequent the area between the polar coast which the Weddell seal, *Leptonychotes weddelli*, inhabits and the edge of the pack ice populated by leopard seals, *Hydrurga leptonyx*. They follow the breakup of the ice south in summer and move farther north with the freeze in winter. Isolated individuals are found in Australian, New Zealand and South American waters.

Crabeaters feed exclusively on krill. They keep their mouth open as they swim, sucking in the food. The teeth and special bony projections of the jaws prevent the escape of krill by acting as a sieve.

Females are thought to produce their pups just before the ice breaks up in August and September, but there is little real information about this. Pups have a long, fluffy grey coat which is shed as lactation finishes and the pup takes to the water. What little scientific evidence there is suggests that mating occurs soon after the birth of the pups.

Since the ice protects these creatures from the commercial ravages of man, crabeaters have little to fear but killer whales. Many adults carry scars as evidence of skirmishes with their enemies.

### *Leptonychotes weddelli*  Lesson
PHOCIDAE   WEDDELL SEAL

Named in 1826. Both males and females reach between 2.7–3 m. in length. The females are fractionally larger than the males and can weigh as much as 450 kg. The body is black along the back, changing with ever-increasing numbers of white lines and patches along the side to a pale grey or white belly.

Weddell seals are one of 4 species in 4 separate genera often known as the antarctic seals. These are the leopard seal, *Hydrurga leptonyx*, Weddell seal, *Leptonychotes weddelli*, crabeater seal, *Lobodon carcinophagus*, and the Ross seal, *Ommatophoca rossi*. Weddell seals live near the antarctic coastline, keeping close to the land, and are not found on the pack ice. They do not migrate. Population estimations are difficult but may be around 500,000.

During the antarctic winter months these seals spend the greater part of the time actually in the water. To breathe they must ensure a supply of air which is achieved by constant attention to breathing holes. These are kept clear by breaking the ice at the edges, using their teeth. During this time the seals maintain communication by a continuous cacophony of submarine sounds. Investi-

Crabeater seals, *Lobodon carcinophagus*.

gations with hydrophones have reproduced these calls, and scientific studies have carefully analysed a variety of different components.

Weddell seals rarely venture far from the shallow coastal waters. Most of their feeding activities are localized. Young, newly weaned pups feed mainly on small crustacea, and crustacea remain a part of the seal's diet throughout its life. Adults, however, feed mainly on fish.

Female Weddell seals have a strong maternal instinct. They make very good and very protective mothers. Around the middle of August pregnant females are gathered together into breeding harems. Fluffy grey pups with a dark line along the back are born in September and October. They can weigh as much as 27 kg. and are well over 1.2 m. long. Pups take to the water before they are 6 weeks old, while they still have their fluffy coat. By the time the mother concludes suckling the pups, about 6–8 weeks, they have moulted their

*Left* Weddell seal,
*Leptonychotes weddelli.*

*Above* Female Weddell seal
and pup photographed on
Captain Scott's Polar
Expedition, 1910–13.

baby coat and are adorned with an adult covering.
As the weaning is completed the females are mated
and take to the water to restore their fat reserves,
which have been depleted during suckling. Females do not eat while they have dependent
young, but stay close to them on constant guard.

### *Mirounga angustirostris* Gill
### PHOCIDAE NORTHERN ELEPHANT SEAL

This species was almost extinct in the later years of
the nineteenth century as a result of commercial
exploitation. Indeed one small herd of less than
100 animals was all that remained of the once
large population. Given protection in 1922, it has
gradually increased until the present healthy
population of 20,000 has been attained. It was
named in 1866.

Physically the northern and southern elephant
seals are very similar. The northern elephant seal
has a much longer proboscis which hangs down
over the mouth by more than 23 cm.

Northern elephant seals are found on the islands
off the western coast of North America. The breeding grounds are restricted to San Nicolas, San
Benito, San Miguel and Guadalupe.

The mature harem bulls come to these islands in
November. Territorial rights are established, and

as the females land they are gathered into harems of 10–12 pregnant animals. Young bulls wait around the edge of the territory ready to seize the opportunity to mate with a female with lax loyalties. The females drop their young about one week after arrival at the breeding grounds. Newly born pups are covered in black woolly fur. The period of lactation is somewhat longer than for the southern elephant seal, *M. leonina*, and during the suckling period females go off to feed. Mating also occurs during lactation. Two months after birth, following a period of tremendous growth when up to 9 kg. a day can be attained, the pups have changed their black embryonic coat for a grey adult model and are independent of maternal milk. Their mothers return to the sea and the pups begin to eat any small invertebrates around. They also indulge, as do several other species of seal, in stone eating. Exactly what purpose this serves, if any, is not known. The pups are able to swim a few weeks after the end of lactation. Following the break-up of the breeding harems there is a period of feeding. This in turn is followed by a further gathering for the annual moult. The younger adults come ashore first followed by mature females and harem bulls. The moult takes about a month to complete, during which time large sheets of skin and hair are shed, probably assisted by scratching and rubbing against rocks. Feeding does not occur during the moult. The whole process is complete by the end of July.

The main exploitation in the nineteenth century was for oil. No commercial hunting is now permitted.

### *Mirounga leonina*  Linnaeus
PHOCIDAE  SOUTHERN ELEPHANT SEAL

Named in 1758, these enormous seals are the well known giants of the order. Adult males exceed 6 m. in length and weigh over 3,600 kg. Females are much smaller, rarely exceeding 3.7 m. in length, and scarcely match the males magnificence at some 1,125 kg. Males are a greyish brown with a paler belly. Females are a distinctive rich dark brown.

Male elephant seals, like hooded seals, *Cystophora cristata*, have an inflatable area on the anterior part of the head. The young male begins to show signs of its development when it is 18 months old, and it is fully formed at maturity when the bull is 8–9 years old and claims its rights as a harem master. Deflated it appears as a rather wrinkled area of skin, the nostrils of which hang down over the mouth. Inflated it is a taut, air-filled sac, proudly proffered by its magnificent owner. The enlargement arises from a development of the nasal cavity. During the breeding season it is in frequent use. It blows up into an enormous balloon which appears almost to lift the head. The purpose of the structure is unknown, but since it is so apparent in the breeding season its function must relate to reproductive behaviour. It is either an ornament of display or an adjunct to vocalization.

Southern elephant seals are found far south in the waters surrounding the antarctic ice and the associated islands. This species breeds on the Falklands, Tierra del Fuego Islands, South Shetlands and South Orkneys, South Georgia, Gough, Marion, Kerguelen, Heard, Crozets, Macquarie and Campbell Islands. Other islands are frequented by non-breeding animals as is the Antarctic land mass itself. Occasionally isolated animals are found further north, along the South American and African coasts. Population estimates suggest as many as 1 million may still inhabit the Antarctic waters.

Studies of their social behaviour have been made while they are on the breeding or moulting grounds in spring and late summer. Less is understood about their life between these beachings, but they are known to move to deep waters to feed. Food consists of fish, crustacea, squid and octopus.

At the beginning of the breeding season in September the mature males arrive at the breeding areas to establish territories. At this time their characteristic head balloon is functioning fully. Females gradually appear and after a little inspection of the available territories seem to succumb to the charms of one of the harem bosses. Groups are formed and as more females appear these gradually enlarge until the harem males are taxed by keeping 60–70 temporary wives in order.

The harem male deals with all young pretenders to his throne until he becomes so old that he succumbs. Young males hang around the edge of each harem territory awaiting an opportunity to mate

Bull southern elephant seal, *Mirounga leonina*, showing the inflated sac which is either an ornament of display or an adjunct to vocalization.

with an errant female. The female drops her black-coated calf a few days after arrival at the breeding area. It is about 1.2 m. in length and can weigh up to 40 kg. The mother fasts during the total 3-week lactation, while the pups gain some 9 kg. weight a day. Since the female is fasting she uses up considerable amounts of her blubber store. Two weeks after the birth she mates with the male and a week later returns to the sea, leaving her offspring to his fate. By this time the pups have started to moult and they wait until this is complete before they take the plunge. Pups still on land eat small crustacea and other invertebrates; these gradually wean them on to adult food. In late spring, the cows having mostly departed and hunger pains due to continual fasting beginning to have an effect, the bulls lose interest in their reproductive urges and return to the sea for food. Virgin females reach sexual maturity between 3 and 6 years of age. They do not haul out but are mated in the water by males who are physically able to mate but not old enough or high enough in the social order to control a harem.

After the breeding season a period of feeding follows before the adults again return to shore for the moult. The moult lasts for a month during which time they fast, and once completed the groups break up until the following breeding season.

Indiscriminate slaughter reduced the southern elephant seal to such small numbers that extinction seemed imminent. Fortunately at the same time commercial exploitation became unprofitable and killing stopped. By the early years of this century the numbers increased and slaughter recommenced, thankfully under some control. Today, in spite of slaughter but as a result of control, the numbers have increased.

### *Monachus monachus*  Herman
PHOCIDAE   MEDITERRANEAN MONK SEAL
First named in 1779. All three species of this genus, commonly known as monk seals, live in tropical waters.

The Mediterranean monk seal has a lovely rich brown back which shades to a pale yellow-grey ventral surface. Both males and females grow to over 2.7 m. in length.

As the name suggests, this Mediterranean seal is found in the Black Sea and along the west coast of North Africa, including Madeira and the Canary Islands. There is no migration of populations. The estimated population is about 5,000.

Strangely for seals apparently so available to the scrutiny of mankind from the earliest civilizations (it is known that Aristotle dissected a monk seal), little is known of its behaviour or breeding habits. The pups are born in September and October. Their rather fine-textured black coat is somewhat thinner than that of pups born to cold water or arctic conditions. This is moulted for a coat more closely resembling the adult pattern when the pup is about 6 weeks of age.

In the past it seems some were hunted by fishing communities for food, oil and hides.

### *Monachus schauinslandi*  Matschie  PHOCIDAE  HAWAIIAN MONK SEAL, LAYSAN MONK SEAL

Named in 1905, this seal is of particular interest as the female is longer and heavier than the male. Females reach nearly 2.4 m. in length while males are rarely over 2.1 m., and although there is much variation resulting from stages of pregnancy, females can exceed the males in body weight by over 68 kg.

Hawaiian monk seals are restricted in range to the islands stretching north-west of Hawaii, including the island of Laysan which gives it its other popular name. No migratory behaviour occurs, all animals remaining close to their islands all through the year. Sealers in the last century seriously depleted the numbers but estimates now suggest that, as a result of protective legislation by the United States, the perilously low population is on the increase and currently stands at 2,500.

A seal that enjoys the pleasures of the sun, it spends most of the day basking or swimming in shallow coastal regions. At night it feeds; food consists of fish and octopus.

Breeding females give birth in April and May. The pup's black fluffy foetal fur is retained throughout suckling and then, at 5 weeks, is shed for a grey-furred back and white belly. As lactation concludes, the mother leaves the pup to its own devices and returns to the water to feed.

### *Monachus tropicalis*  Gray  PHOCIDAE  WEST INDIAN MONK SEAL, CARIBBEAN MONK SEAL

Named in 1850. This species is so rare that there are real fears for its continued existence and a recent survey suggests that it is already extinct, though local fishermen claim that it is occasionally seen.

Columbus reported that this species was abundant during his second voyage in 1494 when these animals were killed for food. Continual slaughter for oil during the past 2–3 centuries has led to its sad decline. Its previous range was throughout the Caribbean Sea and the Gulf of Mexico, as far north as Florida and as far east as the Leeward and Windward Islands.

It has been suggested that monk seals inhabiting European waters were swept across the Atlantic in late Miocene times and then, since there was a watery connection between the Atlantic and Pacific oceans, on across to the Pacific.

It grows to 2.4 m. in length and has a brown back fading to a pale yellow belly.

### *Ommatophoca rossi*  Gray  PHOCIDAE  ROSS SEAL, BIG-EYED SEAL

This species, named in 1844, is rarely seen; when it is, however, its physical characteristics are quite unmistakable.

The body is extremely large and thickset, about 2.3 m. long. The head appears short, with a very thick neck region, and it is wide at the jaws. Large chubby cheeks increase the illusion of a very short stubby head. The eyes are large. The dark grey back shades to a pale belly.

Ross seals live solitary, isolated lives, as far as is known, on the pack ice around the southern polar land mass. Estimates of such a poorly known species are almost meaningless, but it has been suggested that some 25,000–50,000 individuals exist.

What little information there is suggests that squid and octopus constitute their main food, although fish are taken in small quantities.

Virtually nothing is known about their breeding behaviour. Certainly no reports of congregations have been made which could have been related to reproduction. The young are white when born.

Turbid waters and marine bays are habitats for the Amazon manatee, *Trichechus inunguis*. They tend to rest at the surface with just the head exposed, and the tail curved beneath it.

***Pagophilus groenlandicus*** Erxleben
PHOCIDAE HARP, GREENLAND OR
SADDLEBACK SEAL

First named in 1777. Males and females are of similar size, reaching over 1.8 m. in length and weighing over 180 kg. The main part of the body is a very pale grey. The head is black and there is a semicircular black band running along each side and over the shoulders which gives it one of its common names. This saddle is very clear in adult males but tends to be broken up into less distinct, smaller patches in the female and immature animals.

Harp seals are distributed in the open sea from the northern coast of the U.S.S.R. in a band across to the north-east coast of Canada. Their range includes the White Sea, Franz Josef Land, Svalbard, all of Greenland except the most northerly coast, Baffin Island, into the mouth of Hudson Bay and south to Newfoundland. Occasionally isolated animals are seen further south; recordings of sightings have been made around the coasts of the British Isles, the coast of France and the east coast of the United States. Estimates of total population vary from 20,000 to 5 million. It is clear that such margins can have no meaning in reality and one must conclude that the figure remains completely unknown.

Three separate breeding populations have been identified based on the geographical distribution of their breeding sites, although no anatomical variations have been demonstrated. The principal breeding areas are Newfoundland, the north-east coast of Greenland and the White Sea.

After feeding in northern waters during the summer, harp seals collect on the ice to moult. From the autumn mature animals begin their southerly migration to the breeding grounds. Pregnant females haul out very close to the birth of their pups, which mostly occurs during February and early March. Males haul out simply to mate with the females which are receptive about one week after giving birth. The fine fluffy white fur of the pups moults when they are one month of age and then they take to the water.

These seals feed on fish, including herring, haddock and polar cod together with a variety of crustacea. Young seal pups are weaned on to small crustacea which, one eye-witness report suggests, are sucked in.

These attractive animals have long been exploited in Canada, Norway and Russia. The white coat of the pups is valuable, as is the fine grey coat with which they are clad after their first moult. Older animals are killed for oil, meat and leather. The excessive hunting is beginning to deplete the numbers seriously, and there is concern for their conservation. There are various agreements and some international legislation to control slaughter. Time will tell if these are sufficient.

***Phoca vitulina*** Linnaeus PHOCIDAE
COMMON SEAL, SPOTTED SEAL, HARBOUR SEAL
Named in 1758. There are 5 subspecies named as a result of geographical distribution but with few if any structural differences between them though some authorities recognize *P. vitulina largha* as a separate species.

Males and females are similar in size although males tend to be a little larger when mature, reaching up to 8.8 m. in length. Most animals have a pale grey body covered with small dark patches. The number of patches and their size vary considerably. Some individuals are so well covered with patches that they appear almost black; others are lightly flecked and the grey background predominates.

Harbour seals inhabit shallow sandbank areas and river estuaries. They are widely distributed in both the Pacific and Atlantic oceans. In the eastern Atlantic *P. vitulina vitulina* is found along the coasts of Norway, Denmark, southern Sweden, well into the Baltic, along the shores of Germany, France, Spain and Portugal, all around the British Isles and Iceland. It is most common along the southern Scandinavian shores, northern Europe and the eastern coast of Scotland and England, including an important breeding colony in the Shetlands. It does, however, travel far and wide, having been found on all British coasts and considerable distances up into rivers.

In the western Atlantic *P. vitulina concolor* is found; it has a range from the north-east coast of Canada as far south as Florida, and around the southern shores of Greenland. It is only infrequently found at the extremes of its range and

Common seals, *Phoca vitulina.*

rarely ventures into the Hudson Bay, but is common from Newfoundland to Long Island. *P. vitulina mellonae* is an isolated subspecies found inland off the east coast of Hudson Bay.

There are 2 Pacific subspecies, *P. vitulina richardi* in the east, and *P. vitulina largha* in the west. *P. vitulina richardi* occurs all along the coast of Alaska, the western coast of Canada and the United States, as far south as Guadalupe off the coast of Mexico. They are also found on the Pribilof and Aleutian islands in the eastern Bering Sea. *P. vitulina largha*

inhabits coastal waters of Russia, the Sea of Okhotsk and as far south as Korea. Estimates suggest that a total world population of the 5 subspecies is between 200,000 and 400,000 animals.

Harbour seals are fish eaters. They are catholic in their taste, consuming most species of fish found in the area. They also take quantities of crustacea and molluscs by way of variation and substitution as the opportunity or need arises.

Pups of the subspecies *P. vitulina vitulina*, *P. vitulina richardi*, *P. vitulina mellonae* and *P. vitulina con-*

*color* are born on shores between high tides after a gestation period of just under a year and including a period of delayed implantation of the blastocyst, (see *Arctocephalus australis*). The pups are precocious and, having usually shed their foetal fur in the womb, are very soon able to take to the water. The parturition period varies slightly between breeding colonies and is also somewhat dependent on geographical location. However it is usually during May and June. The mother suckles her offspring for about 3 weeks after which she moults, which takes 2–3 weeks, and then mates – an unusual pattern, mating normally preceding the moult. The pup is abandoned by her.

Females of the fifth subspecies, *P. vitulina largha*, produce their pups on the ice in early spring, from February onwards. These pups retain their white fluffy coats for at least 3 weeks and during this time remain on the ice. After conclusion of the suckling, females moult in preparation for mating. All subspecies produce 90 cm. long pups which weigh between 9 14 kg.

Seal pups are not without enemies. Polar bears, sharks, arctic birds of prey and killer whales take a proportion, but man, as usual, is without equal in his ability to decimate a species. Fishermen, eternally bemoaning the seal's right to its natural food, provide justification for an annual cropping of young animals for fur. In some parts of the world the rest of the carcass is salvaged for meat, oil and bone meal.

These seals are not infrequently found in captivity, where they appear to do reasonably well and have lived in contentment for up to 20 years.

## Pusa caspica Gmelin  PHOCIDAE
CASPIAN SEAL

Named in 1788. These small seals rarely exceed 1.5 m. in length. They weigh about 77 kg. The background colour is fawn, decorated with spots of darker brown. Like the ringed seal, *P. hispida*, the spots may be surrounded by a pale border.

Found only in the Caspian Sea, the vast area of inland water north-east of the Black Sea, they are closely related to the Baikal seal, *P. sibirica*, and the ringed seal, and all three species are thought to be descended from a common ancestral form living in the Miocene era. Caspian seals like cold water. For this reason in winter they inhabit the frozen north of the lake, living beneath the ice and breathing through air holes, which they keep permanently open. During summer, as the ice melts and the shallow shores warm up, the seals migrate to the deeper, cooler parts of the lake; they return north as the ice reforms in winter. The present population may well approach the 2 million figure.

Caspian seals eat fish and some crustacea. The pups are born in January and early February. They are clothed in a white fur for the first 3 weeks of life; it is then changed for a shorter coat more closely resembling the adult's. Suckling continues for about 4 weeks. Soon after the pups are born mating takes place, the season being completed by the middle of March. Moulting occurs first in the lactating females, followed by the males and immature animals. Once finished with the moult, all seals migrate south to the cooler, deeper waters.

Commercial exploitation of the species occurs. Pups are killed for white fur, while adults are used for food, skins, and oil. Various systems of hunting are in use. Pups are caught on ice. Some are caught from boats while others are netted during their migration northward for the winter.

## Pusa hispida Schreiber  PHOCIDAE
RINGED SEAL, FLOE RAT

Named in 1775, the ringed seal is found in arctic coastal waters.

Males and females are very similar in size, reaching up to 1.5 m. in length and weighing about 90 kg. This animal gets its usual common name from the characteristic dark patches on the dorsal part of the body which are ringed with pale borders. The background of the body is a pale grey. Along the back the dark spots often fuse to form a continuous area of black.

Based on geographical distribution alone, with no structural variation, some authorities recognize several subspecies. Since ringed seals remain close to home localities such a classification has some justification. *P. hispida hispida* occurs in the arctic regions from Labrador and Baffin Island, through Greenland and Svalbard, to Finland. On rare occasions isolated animals have been found around the coasts of the British Isles and the northern coasts of Europe. Winter visitors to Iceland are also common. *P. hispida krascheninikovi* is restricted to the northern waters of the Bering Sea. *P. hispida ochotensis* is found nearby in the Sea of Okhotsk, south along the Pacific coast of Japan. Two sub-species are recognized from the Baltic lakes, Lake Saimaa and Lake Ladoga, *P. hispida saimensis* and *P. hispida ladogensis* respectively, while in the Baltic Sea itself is found the final subspecies, *P. hispida botnica*.

The world population of ringed seals is esti-mated at 600,000–800,000 animals. They are common in the coastal arctic waters where the sea is not frozen over completely and are rarely found in the open sea. During winter when ice forms, they keep open small areas as escape routes and breathing holes by breaking the ice as it forms with their heads. Ringed seals moult in midsummer when they haul out of the water and lie sunbathing and fasting for the whole period, approximately 30 days.

Although they eat small fish in some quantity, their basic diet appears to be small crustaceans.

The breeding habits of this species are fascinat-ing and somewhat at variance with many other members of the order. Harems form at the usual breeding sites. The mother seal then prepares a cavity in the snow or makes use of a natural hollow in the ice. She also creates a breathing hole which allows her direct access to the pit from the water without coming into view of predators, which might expose her pup to danger. The 60 cm. pups, weighing some 4.5 kg., are born in March and April. The long white foetal fur is not cast for 3 weeks, a relatively long period and related to the habit of remaining on 'land' for such a long post-natal period. The suckling period too, extending for 2 months, is unusually long and clearly relates to the fact that on the ice no other food on which to wean is available.

Males develop a very strong odour, offensive to humans, during the mating period. Mating occurs soon after birth of the pup while the female is still lactating. As usual, development of the blastocyst is delayed and it is not implanted until late sum-mer.

The regular arctic predators, polar bears, killer whales, and on occasions, walruses, feed on these common inhabitants of the arctic wastes, but to man is left the role of population decimator. Eskimos of course reached, over centuries, a good balance with their wintry habitat and nobody would apportion blame to their hunting activities. Harpooning or shooting from kayaks, stealing up to harpoon at breathing holes, and stealthily ap-proaching basking animals on the ice are among a variety of methods employed by Eskimos. They are very resourceful and use all parts of the seal either for food, fuel or clothing. It is the wanton destruction of large numbers in commercial oper-ations for no other reason than to pander to female fashion that should be condemned.

### *Pusa sibirica*  Gmelin  PHOCIDAE
BAIKAL SEAL

Named in 1788. Relatively short and stocky, Baikal seals reach over 1.2 m. in length and usu-ally exceed 45kg. in body weight. Their dark grey fur appears almost black when wet.

They are found only in the huge Russian fresh-water Lake Baikal: the total population is esti-mated at over 80,000. They are fish eaters. During late spring and early summer Baikal seals are evenly distributed throughout the lake but they congregate in herds in the northern regions to-wards the end of June.

Mating takes place while the herds are hauled out in groups during the summer months. When the herds break up and the majority return to the water as the ice forms in October, the pregnant females prepare a warm pinnipedian igloo under the snow. In this the pups are born in early spring – February to March. The rest of the population spends the cold months of the year under the ice keeping breathing holes open for air.

For the first two weeks of life the pups are covered in a long, fluffy white fur coat, but this is then changed for the adult model. They stay with the mother and are suckled by her for 3 months.

It seems likely that both the Baikal seal and its close relative the Caspian seal, *P. caspica*, come from parent stock, which also produced the Ringed seal, *P. hispida*, in Miocene times when there were watery connections to the parts now occupied by the inland lakes.

This species is hunted a little by local people but there is no organized commercial trade.

Baikal seals, *Pusa sibirica*, lying out on the ice.

196

# Sirenia:
## Dugongs, Sea Cows and Manatees

## Introduction

These animals are the only plant-eating aquatic mammals living today. Their bodies are large and bulky but have adopted a streamlined shape well suited to travel in water. They do not come on to land, and are unable to move if stranded.

Sirenian heads are large with rather elongated fleshy snouts. Their fore limbs are modified to form flat paddle-like structures supported by 5 sets of phalangeal bones following the typical mammalian pattern. Some of the manatees retain nails on the fore limbs, but dugongs have none. Hind limbs have been dispensed with during their evolutionary history. Even the pelvic girdle is but a vestigial remnant, functioning only in the male where it gives rise to the penis. The tail is flattened to a paddle shape in the manatees, and almost to a fluke in the dugongs. The tail and hind quarters are the main organs of locomotion. Sirenians have bristles around their mouths, and are covered with fine hair. The skin is thick with little subcutaneous fat.

Like all plant-eating animals, special modifications are necessary to deal with the large quantities of the plant carbohydrate – cellulose – they consume. They have a long, rather large alimentary canal (see Anatomy) where cellulose can be processed by the organisms of the gut. It is important to realize that the living sirenians are dependent for food on the higher water plants, and not on algae, for their nourishment.

As a result of their feeding requirements these creatures are inhabitants of rivers, shallow coastal waters and river estuaries. They are rarely found in the open sea. Apart from the great danger to all wild life – man – they have few natural enemies. Reports of attacks by sharks, caymen, and even jaguars exist but are generally assumed to account for few losses. Some scientists believe that before man's systematic slaughter for profit began, they were confident creatures which may have lived in reasonably large social groups with little to fear from their environment. Starting with the extermination of the largest of modern sirenians, the Steller sea cow, in the mid-eighteenth century, man's behaviour in the name of commercialism can only be castigated. Within 30 years of their discovery in the Bering Sea by a German ship doctor, Georg Steller, the sea cows, which were to take the doctor's name, were hunted to extinction by the whaling and sealing expeditions which frequented the waters. Their flesh, resembling veal, was preferred by the seamen to whale or seal meat. Valued for their meat, oil and hides, as well as medicinal and aphrodisiac properties, all sirenians have been persistently and relentlessly pursued by man in modern times until the survival of the few species that remain is seriously threatened. In 4 years, for example, between 1938–42, Brazil exported thousands of carcasses of the amazon manatee, *Trichechus inunguis.*

Probably as a result of man's hunting activities, sirenians have become shy, retiring creatures. For most of the time they remain still and silent among turbid plant-covered waters, coming silently to the surface to breathe every few minutes through nostrils conveniently placed on top of the snout. Occasionally, during poor weather conditions they form groups, and there is some evidence of a poorly defined spring migration. Observers of groups of sirenians have reported nuzzling and kissing, behaviour which is clearly important as a form of social interaction.

Dugongs are exclusively marine animals found close to the coasts where they feed on sea grass and other water plants. They have mouths adapted to bottom feeding. Their range is from the Red Sea and the coastal waters of East Africa, to the south-west coast of Asia and Australia, and on to some tropical islands of the Pacific. Manatees are the sirenians of the Atlantic, inhabiting the rivers, estuaries, and coastal waters from the Carolinas to Brazil, and similar habitats on the tropical coasts of West Africa. The mouth parts of manatees are less specialized allowing for more varied feeding patterns. Although they are usually found in shallow coastal waters manatees have been seen several miles out to sea, unlike their cousins the dugongs, who seem tightly wedded to shallow coastal regions.

The sirenians have since recorded history been associated with mythology. Indeed the name is derived from the sirens of Greek mythology, whose lilting songs of seduction called ancient mariners to destruction among the rocks.

Man's commitment to the conservation of these interesting and gentle creatures must be continued until their survival is assured. It would indeed be a sin if the catastrophe which befell the Steller sea cow so recently was to be repeated.

## ANATOMY

The order Sirenia has been little studied and therefore information about the basic anatomy is limited.

### Manatee

#### Alimentary canal

The point where the oesophagus enters the stomach is guarded by a strong sphincter muscle. The stomach has the normal simple mammalian form but there is an interesting acid-producing gland which empties into the dorsal curvature of the stomach near the entrance of the oesophagus. The stomach itself produces a similar secretion but this specialized gland seems to provide additional supplies. Leading from the stomach through the powerful pyloric sphincter is the dilated and much folded duodenum. The coiled caecum, producing more acid and having peptic cells, empties into the duodenum and, further along, the bile and pancreatic ducts open separately. A gall bladder is present.

The muscular small intestine is unusual in having no villi, and a squamous cell epithelium rather than more typical columnar cells. The ilium is separated from a caecum by a sphincter muscle. The caecum has 2 small blind appendages. The large intestine also has a squamous cell epithelium rather than a columnar celled one. This unusual lining structure may relate to the water balance requirements of the manatee; the excess absorption of water may need to be prevented since the kidney is not capable of removing large quantities.

#### Circulatory system

The vascular system has the basic mammalian form. There are however several modifications which may relate to the aquatic way of life. The most interesting is the presence of structures known as retial bundles. The main artery breaks up into small arteries and these, running parallel to small veins, are enclosed in connective tissue, the whole structure being surrounded by a sheath. Retial bundles are not exclusive to aquatic animals as they also occur in some species of primate and sloth. They have several different functions and are used in various ways by the particular species. In manatees they are found in the head, thorax, abdominal wall, flippers and the tail.

Two anterior vena cavae and 2 posterior vena cavae enter the right atrium; 2 pulmonary veins join before entering the left atrium. Apart from these features, and a rather rounded shape, the heart has the typical mammalian form.

#### Musculature

A most unusual feature of manatee musculature is the broad, thick sheet of muscle which runs from the vestigial pelvis to the head. This muscle adds essential support to the abdomen and thorax and assists in locomotion.

#### Nervous system

The brain is unusual in that it resembles a foetal brain in having few folds. The olfactory area is quite well developed, confirming the observed reliance on a good sense of smell. The primitive or undeveloped form of the brain is reflected in the poor ability of captive manatees to learn more than the simplest tricks.

## Reproductive system

Knowledge of reproduction in manatees is poor. The gestation period and frequency of pregnancy are unknown. The penis is enclosed in a sheath posterior to the umbilicus and the testicles are abdominal. There are large seminal vescicles and and an erectile prostrate without glandular function.

## Respiratory system

The respiratory system of sirenians has been little studied; the trachea divides into bronchi which lead to unlobed lungs.

## Skeleton

The vertebral column consists of 6 cervical vertebrae, 17–18 thoracic vertebrae, 3 sacral and 20 or more caudal vertebrae. The presence of only 6 cervical vertebrae is an unusual feature which manatees share with sloths; most mammals have 7 neck bones. They have short but strong neural arches. The transverse processes are wide but diminish in size towards the tail. The caudal vertebrae have developed strong ventral processes, probably to provide attachments for muscles used for locomotion.

The ribs are large and strong and very dense; they are said to act as ballast to stabilize the animal. The sternum is unsegmented and is attached to only the first 3 ribs. This gives elasticity to the thorax but, as has been seen in captivity when the animals are taken out of the water means that they prefer to lie on their backs to prevent the weight of the body from crushing the lungs.

The bones of the fore limbs follow the normal pattern although they are rather flattened. The joints are unmodified but are very flexible. There are no clavicles and the normal pattern of 5 phalanges is maintained. Three rudimentary nails are present except in the Amazon manatee, *Trichechus inunguis*, which has none. All hind limb bones have disappeared and only a vestigial pelvis remains.

All the bones are very dense, a feature shared with other aquatic mammals. Long bones and ribs have no marrow. Some bones resemble those of a foetus because they lack certain cells called osteoclasts, which are instrumental in the reabsorption of bone tissue.

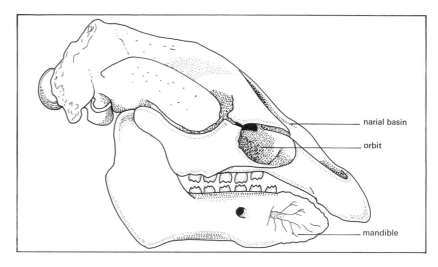

The manatee skull with the large narial basin for accommodating the fleshy snout and the flattened teeth characteristic of a herbivore.

The skull has heavy zygomatic arches, orbits which are well forward, and a large recess for the nares, giving it a characteristic and unusual shape. The mandible is massive with a flat roughened anterior portion.

## Teeth

The teeth of manatees are of particular interest. Only the molars erupt. From 4 to 7 teeth are present in each quarter of the jaw at any one time, and there appears to be a continual replacement of these as they move forward in the jaw. The anterior teeth are the oldest and they are replaced by eruption of new teeth posteriorly. The worn anterior teeth drop out following reabsorption of their roots, and the teeth move forward by a constant process of jaw-bone reabsorption in front and replacement behind.

## Urinary system

In spite of problems associated with water balance, the kidneys are of basic simple structure.

## Dugong

The anatomy of the dugong resembles that of the manatee in most respects. Therefore only the important known differences are listed below.

## Alimentary canal

The pancreatic and similar ducts have a common entry to the duodenum. The caecum has only one appendage.

### Nervous system
The brain is more elongated.

### Reproductive system
The female has rather unusual features. The ovaries are contained in a bursa. The clitoris is large and conical.

### Respiratory system
There is a poorly developed epiglottis and fleshy outgrowths which resemble vocal chords.

### Skeleton
The dugong has 7 cervical vertebrae, and ribs and long bones are slightly less dense and heavy. The zygomatic arch is not quite so massive.

### Teeth
Dugong males have tusks which are in fact modified incisors. They are about 30 cm. long but hardly show below the fleshy lips. Posterior-anterior movement of molar teeth is thought to exist.

### Urinary system
The structure of the dugong kidneys is segmented around a central sinus although externally it is not lobed.

## BEHAVIOUR
Sadly little is known about the behaviour of sirenians. Their elusive lifestyle, spent hiding in solitude or very small family groups among thick coverings of plants in turbid water does not make for ease in field studies.

It seems possible – indeed probable – that man's ruthless slaughter of these animals in recent times has led to marked changes in behaviour. Contemporary reports of both manatees and dugongs in the eighteenth and nineteenth centuries have described large social groups. In some cases these groups were apparently of huge proportions. For example one observer mentions a herd of dugongs about 5 km. in length and 275 m. wide congregated in Moreton Bay on the east coast of Australia. With virtually no natural predators these slow, docile creatures remained fearless when confronted by man. Their fearlessness proved to be evolutionary suicide and they were massacred for their flesh and fat. As a result of the drastic reduction in numbers, surviving individuals may have lost the feeling of security and the confidence which is an integral part of belonging to a large herd. They have certainly become shy, solitary and retiring except on rare occasions. It would be wrong to assume that they learned to fear man but since behavioural adjustment is one of the mechanics of adaptation – one of the tools of evolution – they modified their behaviour to survive.

What little is known and can be still observed recalls herd activities. Body contact in the form of nuzzling, 'kissing', prodding, and flipper 'cuddling' seems well developed. There are recordings of sirenian sounds, supposedly important in communication within the herd. The few gatherings for reproductive activity which have been witnessed strongly suggest group participation. One must not, however, forget the alternative possibility that owing to a paucity of females in a receptive mood, when one is available all the males for miles around respond and congregate.

In Australia, where legislation has to a large extent protected the dugongs, there is evidence that numbers are increasing. Very recent eyewitness reports suggest that herds of up to 100 dugongs can be seen, on rare occasions, in the northern coastal waters of Australia. Aggregations of manatees around warm springs and outflows of warm currents have also been reported. Grazed areas of water plants also suggest important social activities. It will be interesting to see if increasing numbers will lead to the formation of large herds which exhibit less secretive behaviour. Such hopes are not entirely flights of optimistic fancy. Sightings of large herds of up to 500 animals in the late 1960s, exhibiting fearless behaviour, were reported by a reliable observer off the southern coast of Somaliland.

The flippers are used to dig and collect food and then to convey it to the mouth. The rather unusual structure of the mouth with its large fleshy upper lips also assists feeding.

There seems to be doubt about the circadian rhythm or 'built-in clock' of sirenians. The general consensus of opinion considers modern sirenians to be nocturnal feeders. They seem to lie dormant on the seabed, hopefully hidden from attack during the day.

Knowledge of their breeding behaviour is far from complete. They do seem to congregate in groups, possibly a receptive female together with several mature males. Then follow hours of social behaviour, possibly including courtship, during which mating is assumed to occur, although it has not been observed. The most detailed observations to date have been made on the Florida manatee (see *Trichechus manatus*). The length of gestation is believed to be between 350–450 days, and pregnancy restricted to one calf every 3 years. In some areas there are suggestions of seasonal calvings but the evidence is scanty. The calf is born in the water and assisted to the surface to breathe. The mother's behaviour is very solicitous. Young sirenians have been seen riding on their mothers' backs. Three births of manatees have been observed in captivity and it appears the young are suckled in the water with the mother in the normal horizontal swimming position. This leads one to question tales often recounted by homesick mariners of animals seen lying on their backs cradling the young in their flippers to suckle. However two different positions are not impossible.

Some evidence exists that calves may be left in kindergarten groups away from the main herd and close to shore. Young manatees could never be said to gavotte with infantile delight but some have been seen playing; this consists of nudging small objects about with their snouts.

The existence of sirenian migrations has not been established. Aggregations do occur quite regularly in some areas but clear evidence is sparse.

It is only too apparent that our knowledge of sirenian behaviour is limited. Semi-domestication or captivity may provide more readily accessible information but will not replace time-consuming, but essential, natural studies. Hopefully time will not run out with the animals' extinction leaving man the poorer.

## CAPTIVITY

Experience with sirenians in zoological parks and gardens is scanty indeed. Early attempts to keep the animals in captivity consistently resulted in death after a few months. The first records of sirenians being transported any distance from their natural habitats were of 2 American manatees, species unrecorded, one of which went to Philadelphia Zoo and the other to London. Neither survived for long. The longest recorded time a sirenian has been kept in captivity is just over 12 years, from 1912–1924 in the Zoological Garden at Hamburg.

Hard facts as to requirements in captivity are few. Some animals are reported to take a variety of green foods while some keepers record difficulty in getting them to take anything but sea grass. One establishment weighted the food, saying that the animal would not take it from the surface of the water, while others have found sirenians to be more adaptable, even browsing from herbage at the side of the tank and from the keeper's hand. One manatee was said to eat up to 9 kg. of lettuce daily.

There seems to be little agreement concerning the physical conditions of the water. In many cases salt water has been used which was changed at intervals – in some cases daily, in others only weekly. Rangoon Zoo, which has some experience with dugongs, has experimented with various concentrations of salt on the hypothesis that since many of their feeding grounds are covered for long periods by brackish water it might be beneficial. Water temperatures of around 27°C are generally recommended and air temperatures of at least 21°C are thought to be important in preventing respiratory disease.

Observers at Mandapam research camp in southern India, where a pair of dugongs was kept, found them to be much less 'intelligent' than dolphins and said that they failed to recognize the regular keeper.

Behavioural observations on captive sirenians in the Miami Seaquarium have proved of use. A very strong social bond between a pair was established. The male became distressed if he was separated from the female and made vigorous attempts to get to her. Three manatee births have been witnessed in Florida aquaria. The young were suckled with the mother in the horizontal position. Dugongs have been trained to respond to a gong for food like Pavlov's dogs. They appear to enjoy the companionship of a human swimming with them and will allow themselves to be ridden. They can be trained to do simple tricks.

An interesting observation made on captive sirenians which relates to their anatomy concerns their breathing. When their tank is emptied for cleaning they sometimes turn on to their backs. The poor attachment of ribs to sternum means that breathing becomes difficult in the normal position when water support is lost. As the tank fills they right themselves again.

Hopefully there will not be a rush among the increasing number of zoos in the world to exhibit these creatures in an attempt to provide a gimmick which will in turn improve the gate money. The only justification for captivity is serious scientific investigation which will improve conservation.

## CLASSIFICATION
The members of the order Sirenia are most closely related to the elephants (Proboscidea) and the hyraxes (Hyracoidea). Within the order there are 2 living genera, the *Dugong* and *Trichechus*, and usually included is the genus *Hydromalis* to which Steller's sea cow belongs. Sadly it was hunted to extinction in the late eighteenth century.

Taxonomy is far from the exact science its disciples would have us believe. Variations on any basic classification are, it sometimes seems, endless. The form used in this book is one of the most recent and is now commonly accepted.

Some experts do not accept the separation of *Trichechus manatus* into 2 subspecies while others, to confuse the issue, divide *Dugong dugon* into 2 subspecies based on geographical distribution.

Some classifications place the Steller sea cow in a subfamily Dugonginae. In addition within the suborder Trichechiformes there are included at least 2 families which became extinct in the Eocene – Prorastomidae and Prostosiremidae. A family of more primitive sirenians, the Desmostylidae, which probably died out in the Miocene, is placed under a separate suborder – Desmostyliformes.

## CONSERVATION
Our knowledge of the natural history including feeding habits, reproduction, social behaviour and suspected migratory movements of the Sirenia is indeed sketchy. This paucity of understanding handicaps conservation, for detailed information about an animal's environmental requirements is extremely useful in planning conservation programmes. Sometimes a small factor missing from an environment makes the difference between survival and extinction. More commonly however no such simple trick exists and it is important to ensure a multitude of suitable environmental factors if the animals are to exist and breed.

We know for example that one must consider populations and the social behaviour of threatened species. When populations become too small, even though there may be a few males and females of breeding age, the social environment is unsuitable so replacement of population becomes impossible and extinction is guaranteed. In the case of the sirenians we know or suspect that they have markedly changed their social behaviour over past decades. From gregarious animals living in large herds they have become solitary or form small family groups, living silent inactive lives hiding among the weeds. Group behaviour may have been an important factor in stimulating reproductive activity. The loss of such grouping may act against mating and replenishment of population. However, these theories have still to be established.

Fortunately some biologists have studied sirenian behaviour but it is a difficult and time-consuming task because the subjects are so rare and not easy to find.

In our ignorance we can at present do little more than rely on education of the human populations where the creatures exist and back it with legislation to prevent hunting. It must be appreciated however that for native populations with protein deficient diets, conservation is an irrelevant luxury. Certainly few would be prepared to watch their own children starve in the interests of sirenian conservation. The problem is therefore obviously a part of the much wider issue which includes human population control and the provision of adequate food for all. Thus the responsibility for depleted numbers of sirenians lies on the shoulders of 'civilized' man, motivated by commercial profit, and not at the feet of native hunters. Sirenians have lived in balance with an ecology which includes native hunting for a great many years. It is modern exploitation which has threatened them.

With worldwide interest in conservation has come legislation for sirenian protection. However, since the existing population is so widespread and so rare, enforcement is almost impossible in many areas, although some parts of the world have been successful. Australia has stopped the hunting of dugongs, except in certain areas around aboriginal settlements, with the result that numbers have slowly increased. Sri Lanka too has protective legislation for dugongs. The U.S.A. has rigid laws which will hopefully ensure the survival and replenishment of their populations. South and Central American countries vary considerably in the protective legislation they have enacted, but rapid changes of political climates, which are such a feature of that part of the world, do not assist implementation of the laws. A factor of advantage to the sirenians is their habit of remaining in shallow coastal waters within national limits, which means that enforcement of law is easier than for the less fortunate cetaceans.

Less happy is the situation of the river species the West African manatee, *Trichechus senegalensis* and the Amazon manatee, *T. inunguis*. Their river habitat makes them more vulnerable to native hunting and sophisticated slaughter than their relatives in coastal waters. The rarity of the African species, even in historical records of the nineteenth century, suggests that even before exploitation by industrial man they were finding survival difficult.

Conservation always seems more acceptable if it has practical advantages rather than purely aesthetic benefits. Thus Florida is stimulated by the tourist attractions these rare sea mammals provide. The possibility of so increasing the sirenian populations that careful cropping would become possible makes politicians pulsate! Couple this with their suggested use in water plant clearance and people begin to listen.

The vexed question of attempting to keep animals in zoos to establish breeding nuclei from which specimens can be returned to more natural environments applies equally to sirenians. It is certain that some species, Arabian oryx and white rhinoceros for example, have been saved from almost certain extinction by this method. However

the cost of maintaining aquatic mammals in conditions suitable for breeding is very high indeed. The simpler development of marine 'park' areas of natural coasts where life is protected from man's active influence is financially more interesting and provides hope. Such areas have been designated along the Australian and African coasts and around Sri Lanka, which will benefit dugongs. Similar areas also now exist for the protection of Atlantic sirenians.

Conservation is not for cranks. It is the attempt of thoughtful, biologically aware people to safeguard our wildlife heritage for future generations. The extermination of the Steller sea cow resulted from the thoughtless actions of the ignorant. For contemporary man to do the same to the remaining sirenians will be condemned by future generations as a calculated act of desecration.

## DISEASES

Very little is known about the diseases of the Sirenia. Some studies have been made on the parasites, which include roundworms, tapeworms and crustacea, but even these are scanty and incomplete.

They are known to be particularly susceptible to secondary fungal infection and sometimes bacterial infections following damage during capture or transportation. It is assumed that similar infections occur in nature when the skin is damaged.

When in captivity they frequently suffer from general respiratory infections such as bronchitis, pleurisy and pneumonia, as a result of incorrect air temperatures above their water.

Clearly detailed studies must await an increase in natural populations which can then be followed by devoted field work.

## DISTRIBUTION

In the distant past members of the order Sirenia had a much wider distribution than the modern representatives. Fossils of the dugongs in particular show that they had a widespread prehistorical distribution which included European and Atlantic waters. As recently as the eighteenth century a small population of the Steller sea cows lived in the cold waters of the North Pacific.

Today dugongs are restricted to the Indo-

Pacific, from the Red Sea and the tropical east coast of Africa to the northern coast of Australia including the southern tip of the Indian sub-continent and islands of South-east Asia.

All the species of manatee are found in the tropical Atlantic. The west African manatee, *Trichechus senegalensis*, is now rare but the range extends all along the west coast of tropical Africa and into the rivers, estuaries and lakes. The American manatee, *T. manatus*, is found, as 2 subspecies *T. manatus manatus* and *T. manatus latirostris*, again in coastal waters and river estuaries, along the coast of southern North America, Central America and tropical South America. The Amazon manatee, *T. inunguis*, is a purely freshwater animal distributed in the rivers of the Amazon Basin.

Dugongs are thought to be most abundant in the coastal areas of Northern Australia and along the southern coast of New Guinea. In other parts of their range, including the Red Sea, east coast of Africa, Sri Lanka and Malaysia, they are very scarce indeed.

The prospects for the West African manatee, *T. senegalensis*, are indeed gloomy. Its distribution from Senegal in the north to the River Curene remains precarious and local observers are unhappy about its survival for any length of time. *T. inunguis* is today restricted, as already mentioned, to the Amazon Basin tributaries. It is doubtful if it now occurs south of the line of latitude 7°S. In former times it was widespread in Peru. Although legally protected in Brazil and Peru, the enforcement of these acts remains an immense problem.

Of all species of manatee, the American manatee, *T. manatus*, is the most abundant. Several thousands exist in the United States, Guyana and in Belize, but the number is still decreasing. Only careful conservation will reverse the decline and see an increase in distribution to former areas of their habitation.

## DIVING

Unlike pinnipeds and some cetaceans, sirenians dive with their lungs fully inflated. Bradycardia, a slowing of the heart rate, develops rather gradually. The maximum duration of a dive is about 15 minutes. Following the dive the respiration rate rapidly increases to three times its resting rate. Not surprisingly the oxygen content of the blood falls during the dive while the carbon dioxide rises but makes a steady recovery on its completion as the increased respiratory rate clears it from the blood.

Lactic acid, low before the dive, hardly rises throughout the dive but shows dramatic increases when the dive is completed. It seems that the lactic acid formed in the muscles during the dive is effectively isolated from the circulation until the dive is complete when it is released rapidly into the blood. The muscles appear to contain virtually no myoglobin, thus there is no local oxygen store. Compared to the other sea mammals which have large amounts of myoglobin, this is a surprising, and physiologically interesting, observation.

The Sirenia are rather unusual in their adaptation to the aquatic way of life. Their low metabolic rate (See Sirenia – Metabolism) is in marked contrast to that of the Cetacea and the Pinnipedia. Similarly the relatively large blood volume seen in Cetacea and Pinnipedia is not found. The absence of myoglobin and poorly developed oxygen stores are apparently compensated for by the low metabolic rate. The isolation of the muscles from the circulation during a dive, with the inevitable local build-up of lactic acid and unavailability of the circulating oxygen, is an unusual but effective adaptation. In land mammals the lactic acid is passed straight back into the blood and triggers off the mechanism which makes the animal breathe. If it was present in the sea mammal's blood during a dive, the dive could not last very long.

## EVOLUTION

The evolution of the Sirenia is fascinating in spite of our incomplete knowledge. It is interesting to speculate on the environmental pressures which made an important group of land animals return to the water. Modern sirenia are but the remnant of what appears to have been a group far more common and more widely spread than those alive today. Although living sirenia are all plant eaters, there is evidence that some extinct forms were carnivorous.

The sirenia are most closely related to the elephants (Proboscidea) and the hyraxes or conies (Hyracoidea), in addition to the now extinct dinocerates and pantodonts. The forms from which these orders developed, sometimes referred to as paenungulates, probably had heavy bodies and other features common to modern ungulates. It is thought that the elephants, sirenians and hyraxes appeared in Africa during the Palaeocene.

Primitive sirenian fossils, with small hind limbs and typical sirenian characteristics of the skull, also share many of the features of other primitive ungulate fossils from the same period. Sirenian fossils have been found in the islands of the Caribbean and in northern Africa. Evidence from Miocene fossils found in the Pacific region suggests heavy-bodied, tusked animals which were probably semi-aquatic in habit, indicating one of the many steps in reconquering the watery environment.

Fossil evidence shows that the dugongs and manatees had far wider distribution (see Distribution) in the past than is the case today. Dugong fossils have been found widely in Europe, the West Indies and the Pacific Ocean. The Steller sea cow inhabited cold water areas of the northern Pacific well out of the range of modern sirenians and is assumed to have fed on marine algae which distinguishes it from living forms.

It is clear from fossil evidence that this exciting group of mammals is today but a shadow of its former self.

## EXPLOITATION AND USES

The modern sirenians are sometimes presented as rare animals, relics of a former greatness, which were already maladapted to their environment before modern man began to exploit them. The impression of an already failing order dominates but the facts do not justify this myth.

Manatees were abundant in the Caribbean and rivers of Central and South America in the seventeenth and eighteenth centuries, so abundant in fact that ships were chartered to carry the meat from the rivers of the Guianas to the islands of the area. Commercial hunting on a large scale continued throughout these centuries and well into the twentieth century, when canned manatee meat was exported in large quantities. This would hardly have been possible if the animal had been scarce. No scientific programme of cropping was in operation with the result that animals, which had been well adapted to their environment, almost became extinct.

The manatees of Africa have never, in modern times, been so abundant. Commercial exploitation was therefore never undertaken. It is assumed that pressure from native hunting diminished stocks, or that some other environmental change occurred to which they were unable to adapt.

Dugongs, now so rare as to be in serious danger of extinction, only a century or so ago were so abundant in North Australia that an eyewitness reported a herd over 5 km. in length and 275 m. across. The relatively small numbers taken by aboriginal hunting were clearly not detrimental to these animals' survival but modern man, mainly within the nineteenth century, reduced the vast herds to pitifully small numbers. They were netted and harpooned at night as they fed, and yielded oil, hides and teeth, while their bones were made into charcoal for use in the sugar industry. Japanese vessels came to share the spoils and pearl divers killed them for meat.

The natives employed an unpleasant method of harpooning dugongs. The harpoonist stood silent in the bow of a boat while the crew, with muffled oars, approached the victim. With a sudden movement the harpoon was thrust into the thick hide of the creature. After a short flight, it would tire and a man would slip into the water to plug its nostrils with wooden pegs to prevent the animal breathing while others lassooed its powerful tail and hoisted it clear of the water to hasten drowning. Netting is still occasionally used to hunt dugongs but more commonly they are caught accidently in the shark nets erected to protect bathers. Native hunters of manatees also used harpoons.

Modern fishing methods employ huge nets which trap sirenians as well as fish. Entangled in the mesh and unable to reach the surface to breathe, they drown. The use of man-made plastic, in place of older more natural material for nets from which these creatures could break loose, increases the toll.

The sad story of the Steller sea cow is another black mark in man's history of merciless exploitation. The Komandorskie group of islands off the coast of Kamchatka supported a small population of these creatures in delicate balance with their environment. Only 2000 were estimated to live in the region when discovered by Steller, the ship's doctor on a Russian expedition sailing under the Danish Commodore Bering. From that moment, commercial whalers and seal hunters, who preferred the sea cow meat to any others available, continued to slaughter them until the species was exterminated.

The meat of both dugong and manatee makes excellent eating. In Sri Lanka it has been used for religious ceremonies and Moslems eat it in place of pork.

Tanning of sirenian hide is a long and time consuming business. It is so thick and tough that working it is extremely difficult. In spite of the problems, hides of the Amazon manatee, *Trichechus inunguis*, were exported in large quantities from Brazil in the 1940s. They were used for particular industrial purposes which require very strong leather.

Several plant-clearing experiments, utilizing manatees' need to eat large quantities of vegetation, have been tried this century, some with encouraging results. When the water hyacinth, *Eichhornia crassipes*, became a serious problem in the artificial Lake Kariba in Africa, it was proposed that manatees might be used to keep it under control, and at the same time provide a bonus crop of good quality meat. However, too little was known of the environmental requirements of the animal for the project to succeed and too few manatees were available, either in Africa – *T. senegalensis*, or in America – *T. inunguis*. Several American scientists have experimental projects in hand, aimed at using these creatures for biological engineering. Practical conservationists appreciate the advantages of commercial pressure in preserving this threatened species.

In addition to practical exploitation and uses, both dugongs and manatees have been important in the past, and even today, as a source of aphrodisiac and medicinal tokens. Both tusks and the dried penis of the male dugong are highly prized in some parts of the world, and dugong oil attained a measure of importance among the aboriginal population of Australia as a magical panacea.

## LOCOMOTION

All sirenians move by an up-and-down thrusting of the tail and hind quarters. Movement is slow, about 2 knots, with a maximum escape speed, sustainable for short distances, of 5 knots. The flippers are not used for propulsion in adults but act as stabilizers. It is interesting that young sirenians do use their flippers for swimming, keeping their tails tucked up under them close to their bellies.

## METABOLISM

Metabolic studies show that oxygen consumption in resting manatees (and the same is probably true of dugongs) is much lower than that of other aquatic mammals and considerably less than is the case in man. This, coupled with the unusual structure of manatee bones, which closely resemble foetal bones because of the persistence of primary bones, suggests hypothyroidism. Thyroid secretion is needed to ossify the epiphyseal limes and thereby stop growth. Certainly microscopic studies show the manatee's thyroid to be quiescent. This goes a long way towards explaining the sluggish behaviour of sirenians.

## MYTHOLOGY

The scientific name of the order Sirenia comes from the mythical seducers of the ancient Greeks, the tempting sirens. They sang so sweetly from the

It is possible that drawings such as these, from 1491, of creatures half human, half fish were based on early sitings of sirenians.

rocks that mariners, succumbing to their promised charm, turned the rudder and sailed in their direction only to flounder among the rocks. Orpheus, appreciating the dangers, protected his crew from their lilting tones by singing to them himself with such beauty that they felt no need to listen to the sirens. By filling his crew's ears with wax and lashing himself to the ship's mast Odysseus protected them all from their audible charms.

For many centuries tales of mermaids were recounted by mariners. Gorgeous creatures, half woman and half fish, were said to inhabit the deep. It is assumed that many of these tales were stimulated by manatees and dugongs who are said by some observers to have a habit of cradling the young in their flippers, whilst the young suckle from pectoral mammary glands. Such behaviour would have borne superficial resemblance to the mythical creature. The journey must have been long and the mariners' needs pressing for these blubbery aquatics to have assumed human form.

## REPRODUCTION see Behaviour

## RESPIRATION
The mechanisms of adaptability used by aquatic mammals to enable them to dive for extended periods are indeed fascinating.

It might be anticipated that the problem would be solved by increasing the lung volume. In fact this does not happen. Most terrestrial animals only change a small percentage of the air contained in their lungs during each breath. In man this amounts to about 12–18 per cent. In the Cetacea that have been studied there is approximately a 90 per cent change. Manatees are somewhere in between, exchanging about 55–60 per cent of lung capacity. Of the oxygen so inhaled a much higher proportion is utilized than in terrestrial mammals. Research has also shown that the oxygen consumption is much lower for resting manatees than for land-dwelling mammals.

Studies with manatees show that as they dive the heart rate gradually slows down, almost halving in an average dive. Manatees (and probably dugongs too, although no studies have been carried out) also have a low breathing rate, little more than one breath a minute. See Diving.

## SENSES
The development of sensory systems in a species is an indication of some of its behavioural patterns. Sirenians have well developed hearing and smell but are poorly sighted. In addition they make use of the tactile sense, particularly around the head region. The bristles around the mouth are used to assist selection and identification of food.

## SKIN
Sirenia are virtually hairless, having no more than a few bristles around the mouth. The epidermis is very thick and there is a generous layer of blubber beneath the dermis all over the body which varies in thickness, assisting, by filling in the dents and bumps, in smoothing the outline. Certain areas are marked by distinct skin creases, notably the neck and ventral abdomen. They do not shed a layer of skin annually as is the case with the Cetacea.

## TRAINING
Members of this order have not been subjected to training, either for scientific or entertainment purposes, to anything like the extent of cetaceans and pinnipeds.

Manatees and dugongs do become very tame in captivity and have been trained to come for food when a bell is rung. In some cases they have been persuaded to perform other tricks for food rewards. They also seem to enjoy men swimming with them and allow a hitched lift on their tails, so much so that if the rider falls off they are said to wait for him to climb aboard again.

## TRANSPORTATION
The sophisticated techniques which have been developed for the transportation of small whales and dolphins have not been so extensively used for sirenians. The basic problems are, however, similar for all marine mammals totally committed to an aquatic life style. The control of overheating remains one of the major problems. The body must be kept moist and protected from damage which would open the way for secondary infection by fungal and bacterial organisms. The lungs are designed to work with the body in water. Out of water the pressures alter, creating strains which predispose it to respiratory infections.

# Dictionary of Species

## DUGONGIDAE

Characteristically the members of this family, the dugongs, have a crescent-shaped fluke, the trailing margin being concave. There are 7 cervical vertebrae and in adult animals the tusks are large. The family is restricted to the Indo-Pacific Ocean. See *Dugong*.

### *Dugong dugon*  Müller
DUGONGIDAE  DUGONG

Dugongs were well known to the ancient peoples of the Far and Middle East, however Western man did not discover them until the late eighteenth century. They were named in 1766.

They grow up to 3 m. in length and they are rather sleeker and more streamlined than their cousins the manatees. The large head is characteristic. Its huge, dense-boned construction supports a large, well-muscled, fleshy snout which is partially divided into two. These fleshy parts overhang the lower lip. The nostrils, 2 crescent-shaped slits, are placed close together on the dorsal surface to enable breathing to take place without undue exposure of the head. The nostrils are not, as in the Pinnipedia, able to close completely, but musculature around the ducts, which are up to 10 cm. in length, makes a completely watertight closure. The whole of the upper lip is well covered with a large number of long bristles doubtless used for the selection of plants during food-gathering procedures. The male's 2 tusks, which are in fact incisor teeth, are up to 30 cm. long. They are mostly covered by the upper lip and only the tips extend below the lower lip.

The eyes have no lids but are covered and protected by a transparent nictitating membrane. There is no external ear lobe, merely a small hole.

The front limbs are flippers, supported by the typical 5-fingered bone pattern of mammals. There are no claws on the flippers.

Dugongs are bluish grey in colour with a thick rough skin rather resembling elephant skin. The tail is a flattened crescent-shaped fluke resembling the whale's. It is not supported by bones apart from the caudal vertebrae. A thickened ridge runs along the dorsal surface of the tail.

Dugongs are slow moving, solitary creatures. They lie dormant on the seabed among the turgid weed-covered shallows, rising every two minutes or so to breathe. Movement is exclusively achieved by up-and-down movements of the tail and hind part of the body. The flippers act as stabilizers and some say they are used in addition to dig out plants and to assist food to the mouth. They feed at night on seaweed and sea grass *Diplanthera univervis*, the latter being an important source of food in some regions. They do not form social groups beyond seasonal pairings and the mother-offspring relationship. No observations of grouping have been recorded. Sadly the reproductive behaviour of these retiring creatures is unknown. The gestation period is thought to be about 1 year. A single offspring is born in the water and the mother assists it to the surface to breathe. It is about 90 cm. in length at birth. The 2 mammary glands lie close to the flippers. Dugongs seem to be generally excellent mothers, cradling their young in their flippers as they lie on their backs.

Found in shallow marine waters close to coral, dugongs never move into rivers, neither do they venture far out to sea. They are widely distributed in the Indo-Pacific Ocean from the Red Sea and the east coast of Africa, around the southern coast of the Indian subcontinent and Sri Lanka, the south-west coast of Asia to the northern coast of Australia.

Sadly these gentle creatures, with few predators but man, are diminishing in numbers in most places. Laws protecting them are all too rarely enforced. They are prized for their meat, oil and hides, and for their supposed medicinal and magical properties. Necklaces made from dugong teeth are thought by some cultures to have protective properties and other parts of the body are prized as aphrodisiacs.

Their conservation is an urgent challenge to modern man.

## HYDROMALIDAE

This family is now extinct. It contained the single species the Steller sea cow, *Hydromalis stelleri*. The body was large for a recent sirenian, growing to a length of 9 m. It had no tusks, and the flukes had a concave rear edge, divided centrally by a notch.

There were 7 cervical vertebrae. The species has been included in the family Dugongidae. As far as is known, the distribution was restricted to the Bering Sea. See *Hydromalis*.

### *Hydromalis stelleri* Steller
HYDROMALIDAE STELLER OR NORTHERN SEA COW

The Steller's or Northern sea cows must have been a magnificent sight. Their huge bodies, up to 10 m. in length, were covered with a thick skin resembling the bark of trees and inhabited, according to contemporary reports, by large numbers of small crustacea. These parasites were consumed by gulls, which filled the ecological niche of the tick birds which tend land mammals, while the great sea cows wallowed in shallow water with their backs exposed to view.

They were discovered at Bering and Copper islands in the Bering Sea by a German Georg Wilhelm Steller, a ship's doctor who studied them when his vessel was shipwrecked in the area in 1741. He named them in 1774. Eye witnesses estimated that there were at most only 2000 animals in the group. Their fearless behaviour was to prove their downfall. Within 30 years they were exterminated by the thoughtless hunting activities of whalers and sealers who apparently preferred their veal-like meat to a routine diet of fish, whale and seal.

These creatures were unique among modern sirenians in that they lived in water at low temperatures and fed on algae rather than higher water plants. It is assumed that they ate green algae although brown may have constituted some of their diet.

Steller sea cows have never been seen except around these islands. Occasionally reports have claimed sightings since their assumed extinction in the late eighteenth century, but these have never been confirmed. In 1962 the crew of a Russian whaling ship claimed to have seen a group of 6 large animals in the region of Cape Navarin in the Bering Sea. All these men were experienced whalers. They were convinced that the animals were not whales or seals. They described them as being up to 10 m. in length with a large split upper lip overhanging the lower. The animals dived for short periods and on surfacing came high out of the water. From the description it is indeed difficult to confuse them with other species. However further sightings have failed to materialize and only time will confirm or deny these observations. For now it remains only an exciting possibility that these creatures could have survived in the largely unknown waters of the area.

## TRICHECHIDAE

Manatees, the common name for members of this family, are easily distinguished from members of the Dugongidae by their flat oval tail fluke. Their tusks are very small and they have only 6 cervical vertebrae. They inhabit the tropical waters of the Atlantic Ocean. See *Trichechus*.

### *Trichechus inunguis* Natterer
TRICHECHIDAE AMAZON MANATEE

This species, named in 1883, closely resembles others of the genus but has somewhat longer flippers with no nails, and a white patch on its chest. It is a freshwater species found in the lower reaches of the Amazon and its main tributaries. It was previously well known in Peru but, as elsewhere, hunting has been relentlessly pursued. Both Peruvian and Brazilian governments have passed protective laws but adequate enforcement remains a dream. One report claims it to be fairly common on the Jamunda river and lakes on the Lower Tapajoz. As recently as the 1940s large numbers were killed in Brazil to supply an industry which canned the meat and exported the hides. Now the population cannot support the industry.

### *Trichechus manatus* Linnaeus
TRICHECHIDAE AMERICAN MANATEE

Named in 1758, the American Manatee inhabits the tropical shallow coastal waters around the coasts of Florida and the islands of the West Indies, and is known to reach the Carolinas.

Manatees are most easily distinguished from their dugong cousins by the tail. The manatee tail is an oval spade-shaped organ which has been likened to a beaver's, while that of the dugong is fluke-shaped, resembling a whale's. In other ways manatees largely resemble dugongs, being about the same length (3 m.), but they have rather heavier, less streamlined bodies, larger faces with fewer snout bristles, and nostrils which can be closed completely. The flippers are relatively longer than those of dugongs and have 3 nails. These are used in foraging for and assisting food to the mouth. They are not used for swimming but for stabilizing the body during forward motion. The hind limbs, as in all sirenians, have completely disappeared. Only a very rudimentary pelvis remains but no trace of hind leg bones.

Manatees eat vast quantities of green food, but inevitably obtain some animal protein, as small animals, along with the water plants. Almost any vegetation is accepted. Modern manatees are quiet creatures, remaining largely dormant on the seabed during the day, and rising every minute or so to the surface to expose their nostrils to breathe. They feed during the night, feeling and smelling their food. Eyesight in manatees is not nearly as important as the other senses.

Socially they live in very small family units consisting of a male, a female and a couple of calves. Occasionally they form larger groups but these 'herds' appear to be a loose arrangement which breaks up readily. Underwater sounds have been recorded which are thought to be used in communication.

Although mating behaviour has been rarely seen and little studied it appears that groups of males surround a receptive female and indulge in greeting behaviour including a form of muzzle 'kissing'. There follows a period, often several hours in duration, of pushing and shoving, rolling and climbing on and under the female by the males. Fighting among the males has not been recorded. Actual acts of mating have not been observed but it is assumed that they take place by one or several of the males during these activities. There appear to be set times of the year and special areas in which mating takes place. The animals are fearless to the point of stupidity during these times and are easy targets for their enemy, man, since they may approach very close to shore in shallow water.

The gestation period is unknown for certain but is thought to be about a year. A single calf is born in the water. Maternal care is diligent. The mother begins by raising the newborn infant to the surface and holding it during an initial period of adjustment. The respiration, following normal mammalian pattern, is fast at first but later it modifies until, in the adult, it breathes once every minute or two. Interestingly young manatees use their flippers for swimming, leaving their tails tucked under them. Young animals have been observed playing, mainly pushing objects around with their snouts and riding on their mothers' backs.

Sadly, as with dugongs, the meat and hides of manatees are much prized. In addition, various parts of their bodies have been attributed with magical and medicinal properties. Unless hunting can be restricted or arrested altogether, their extinction will soon be certain, for their numbers are small and are rapidly declining.

Two subspecies have been designated. *T. manatus manatus*, the Carribean or West Indian manatee, is found from the West Indies and the islands of the Caribbean to the east of Central America. This species tends to be marine although this probably reflects available environment rather than choice. *T. manatus latirostis*, the Florida manatee, is found along the coast and in the rivers of the Florida peninsula north to the Carolinas. They are said to have a smaller face but wider head than their close relatives, with somewhat longer necks. These differences are, however, only slight modifications, and many authors do not recognise the two separate subspecies.

### *Trichechus senegalensis*  Link
TRICHECHIDAE   WEST AFRICAN MANATEE
This species, named in 1795, varies little from its generic cousins in body form and structure. It is found in rivers and shallow coastal areas of West Africa from Senegal to the River Cunene in Angola, where it feeds on waterplants. It is hunted by some natives both for meat and for ritual or religious significance. Sadly laws enacted for its conservation are not voluntarily observed and are not enforced.

Our knowledge of its natural history is extremely limited and unlikely to be deepened, for its decline to extinction continues unabated.

# The Sea Otter, *Enhydra lutris*

The sea otter is most closely related to other Carnivora, such as the riverine otters, weasels and badgers, also members of the family Mustelidae. It is restricted to a marine environment and lives in rocky coastal waters. It is not able to make long migratory or food-hunting excursions in the open sea, and it does not enter rivers.

## Abundance

The world population is *c.* 35,000–50,000.

## Anatomy

An attractive, lithe animal, the sea otter is small compared to other sea mammals. It grows to about 1.5 m. and can weigh up to 45 kg. The fur is dark brown, with a pale yellow-brown neck; the tail is flattened and is one quarter the length of the body. The fore limbs are not used for swimming but are in constant use for manipulating food and other objects. The sea otter swims on its back at the surface of the water, using its hind feet which are specially flattened for the purpose; the outer digits are longer than the others.

The head is flattened dorso-ventrally and the anterior surface is rounded and blunt. The eyes are relatively small and very dark. External ear pinnae are present which are thick structures, well supplied with blood and with no fur covering.

## Behaviour

The social behaviour of sea otters is not well understood. They appear to form loose transient social groups of anything up to a hundred individuals. Males and females congregate both on land and among seaweed beds where they rest for periods together. Nursing females tend to remain alone but occasionally groups of males have been reported resting together on land. Sea otters are diurnal by inclination (see Reproduction).

## Captivity

Early attempts to keep sea otters in captivity proved disastrous. Experience and research has improved the situation considerably. They appear to be particularly susceptible to cold, but providing they are given clean surroundings, a good-sized pool filled with salt water, and a plentiful supply of fresh food, preferably including some molluscs, they will do well. Because of their high metabolic rate adults must be fed a quarter of their body weight in food a day.

Stress of capture seems to be an important factor in acclimatization. A great deal of the stress is due to transportation (see Transportation). Tranquilizers have been tried, but as is the case with many other captive wild animals, the disadvantages outweigh the advantages.

## Conservation

The distribution of sea otters 200 years ago was more extensive than it is now. From the middle of the eighteenth century the slaughter for pelts continued unchecked, and by the end of the nineteenth century the sea otter was almost extinct. No longer commercially worth exploiting, the species was given protection by law, but far too late to ensure a recovery in numbers. Attempts to reintroduce stock to islands it once inhabited has had only very limited success to date.

## Diseases

Very little is known about the diseases of sea otters. Although they are subject to a number of internal parasites, these usually seem to have little detrimental effect.

## Distribution

Two hundred years ago the sea otter was distributed all along the western coast of North America from Mexico to Alaska. It also inhabited many of the islands off the coast of North America and North-east Asia. Extensive hunting so reduced their numbers that many former haunts were abandoned, and the species was on the point of extinction. Legal protection has improved the situation to a certain extent and some of the vacated habitats have been recolonized, both by artificial reintroduction and naturally, though very few sea otters seem to inhabit the North American coast south of Alaska.

## Drinking

Little is known of the osmo-regulation and water

requirements of sea otters in the wild. Captive animals consume large quantities of fresh water daily.

## Feeding
Sea otters' preferred food are molluscs and sea urchins although when these are in short supply, fish are taken. They dive to depths of 60 m. in search of food which they carry under their fore limbs; thus quite a supply can be collected at a time.

The sea otter has developed the interesting habit of using stones as tools. During a dive it may use a stone to break the shell of its prey so that it will release its hold on the rock and can be collected. Alternatively, floating on its back at the surface, it often rests a stone on its chest against which it can smash the shell of its prey.

## Fur
Unlike cetaceans and pinnipeds the sea otter does not have a protective layer of fat to keep it warm in its cold environment but relies on the air trapped in its thick coat. This is particularly dense, each tuft of fur consisting of a single long guard hair and up to 80 undercoat hairs.

## Grooming
The coat of a sea otter must be in prime condition if it is successfully to act as a barrier between the animal and its surroundings. Grooming is therefore very important and occupies much of the animal's day. It rubs its fur with its paws and even between its paws. It may even clasp a fold of skin in both paws and rub vigorously. When it lands the sea otter shakes itself dry.

## Locomotion
Under water the otter moves by undulating the body, holding the feet and tail out behind. The fore legs lie backwards close against the body. At the surface the animal moves by alternate strokes of its hind feet. Its escape speed under water, which can only be maintained for short periods, is about 5 knots; at the surface it rarely exceeds just under 2 knots. When resting on land sea otters lie flat; when moving, they look like ordinary otters, hobbling along with the back held high.

## Metabolism
The main problem a sea otter faces, spending the majority of its time in water, is heat conservation. It does not have the layer of insulating fat common to most sea mammals and must rely on its dense fur which traps a protective layer of air, and on a high metabolic rate. To keep its metabolism at a sufficiently high rate, its food intake must also be high relative to its body size.

## Moulting
To avoid a period of inadequate insulation, which would occur if it underwent an annual moult, the sea otter moults a little at a time throughout the year; however it loses more fur during the warmer months of the year.

## Reproduction
The sea otter is a non-territorial animal. There are no established breeding areas. A male simply approaches a female in oestrus and courts her. For a few days they play together, hunt together and rest on land together. Copulation occurs several times during the period of oestrus, after which the pair separates. There does not appear to be a particular reproduction season and young are born throughout the year though more frequently in the spring. The gestation period has not been firmly established but is thought to last 10–12 months, after which a single pup is born on land. The pup is protected by a thick fur coat and has its eyes open, but is otherwise helpless. The mother helps it find the 2 nipples on the posterior abdomen, and remains in constant attendance, cleaning and playing with it. The pup soon takes to the water and stays close to its mother at all times except while she dives for food. The weaning process starts after a very few weeks, the pup being handed small particles of food by its mother; this is probably completed some time before the mother-offspring bond is broken in the pup's second year.

## Sleep
The sea otter sleeps both on land and on water. It will lie on its side or back, with the fore feet over its ears or tucked under its chin. When on its back, it maintains equilibrium by reflex movements of its hind limbs, even when on dry land.

## Teeth

The teeth differ from the usual carnivore pattern because the animal does not have to seize and tear its prey apart as it lives on a variety of invertebrates. The premolars and molars are flattened to crush shells, while the lower incisors protrude to form a shovel-like instrument used to scrape out the soft flesh of the victim from its shell. It has one less incisor on each lower jaw than the typical carnivor, the dental formula being $I\frac{2}{3} C\frac{1}{1} P\frac{3}{3} M\frac{1}{2}$.

## Transportation

If they must be moved, sea otters should be transported quickly by air. Careful attention to their heat regulation mechanism must be observed. Deprived of water to cover the fur they rapidly succumb to heat stroke and death, therefore temperatures around 4°C., and water are essential.

# Pollution

In recent years man has belatedly realized that the oceans of the world are not infinite in size nor are they indefinitely able to absorb the large quantities of dangerous polluting materials he has chosen to pour into them. Perhaps too late man has awakened to the problems of the technological age.

Polluting substances are pumped directly into the sea or enter via rivers which carry complex agricultural chemicals, industrial waste products, and human sewage. They may also be discharged into the sea from ships dumping industrial waste or ejecting oil, or they may be dissolved at the surface of the sea from air contamination or washed in with rain.

Once in the marine environment, pollutants affect the whole biological system. There is a danger that they may reduce the efficiency of, or even kill, the plankton which forms over 90 per cent of the biomass; that is everything living in the sea. Plankton is made up of microscopic plant and animal organisms, phytoplankton and zooplankton respectively. The former traps the sun's energy, by photosynthesis, which is then available to the animals which eat it; at the same time it releases oxygen into the atmosphere. The effect of the pollutants on these organisms is not known, but if their numbers or their efficiency were markedly reduced, the consequences would be serious, since plankton is the first stage in marine food chains. The gradual concentrations of dangerous substances have insidious effects such as reducing reproductive efficiency in the higher levels of the food chain, and possibly increasing genetic abnormalities.

Pollution occurs with varying degrees of seriousness. Oil may do no more than harm a local bird population and spoil a stretch of coastline for holidaymakers, while the sudden introduction of large quantities of poisonous chemical or radioactive substances into an area following an industrial accident could produce devastating and wide-reaching effects.

There are many substances which pollute the seas but perhaps one of the most widely studied is the group of chlorinated hydrocarbons, some of which, like DDT and its derivitives aldrin and dieldrin, are well known. Another member of the group is PCB (polychlorinated biphenyl). These substances are carried by the air currents and are washed into the sea by rain. Some also run off the land and into the rivers. Over the relatively short period of their manufacture millions of tons have ended up in solution in the sea. Both DDT and its relatives, together with PCB, are very soluble in fats. In living organisms they accumulate in the storage depots of the body. Occasionally, when large numbers of birds or fish have died suddenly, examination has proved that their body fat contained high concentrations of these chemicals. During times of starvation or famine, the body reserves of fat are mobilized. This releases the dangerous quantities into the blood, with sometimes widespread and disastrous results.

During the last few years chlorinated hydrocarbons have been detected in the blubber of marine mammals on both sides of the Atlantic, and in the Antarctic and Pacific oceans. The recent restrictions on the use and application of DDT and its relatives have resulted in an encouraging decline in the body stores of these substances. The use of PCB compounds has, however, continued and these are found in increasing quantities. How the marine mammals become contaminated with PCB compounds is not known. They may have been taken in as dietary contaminants, or absorbed through the skin.

The most immediate danger to many species of marine mammal is the slaughter of too great a proportion of the population by man. A concomitant and more insidious danger is that by his changing of the structure and composition of the marine environment, life there will become difficult, if not impossible. When and if that happens, the penalties will not be paid by the life residing in the seas but by that on earth, including the species most responsible – man.

# Acknowledgements

## Colour

ARDEA LONDON
F. Collet – Page 111; Kenneth W. Fink – Page 28;
Clem Haagner – Page 94; Edwin Mickleburgh –
Pages 152, 161
HEATHER ANGEL/BIOFOTOS
Heather Angel – Page 112
BRUCE COLEMAN LTD
Des and Jan Bartlett – Pages 125, 151; Rod and Moira
Borland – Page 121; Robert Burton – Page 122;
Francisco Erize – Pages 53, 134 (above and below),
152, 163; Jeff Foott – Pages 173, 192; Michael
Freeman – Page 191; Al Giddings – Page 93 (above);
Sven Gillsater – Page 123; G. Laycock – Page 164;
Allan Power – Page 174; Leonard Lee Rue – Pages 93
(below), 162; M. F. Soper – Page 133; Norman
Tomalin – Pages 81, 82; R. W. Vaughan  Pages 26
and 27; Gordon Williamson – Page 71
THE SUSSEX ARCHAEOLOGICAL
TRUST – Page 25
GEORGE RAINBIRD LTD – Pages 54, 72
SEAPHOT – Page 84 (above and below)
MUSEUM OF MANKIND
Derrick E. Witty – Page 83

## Monochrome

AQUILA PHOTOGRAPHICS
William S. Paton – Pages 178, 179
Gary Weber – Pages 127 (above left), 160, 165
BARNABYS PICTURE LIBRARY – Pages 24, 158
ALISTAIR BIRTLES – Page 210
DR DAVID CALDWELL – Pages 22, 23 (above and
below)
CAMERA PRESS LTD
Africamera – Page 50
John D. Drysdale – Page 131
Fids/Brown – Page 188
Fids/Leppard – Page 61 (above)
IPPA – Page 137
Photoflight  Page 141
Terence Spencer – Page 51
Peter Stackpole – Page 31
Gianni Tortoli – Page 67

TS/RBO – Pages 136, 197
CAMERA AND PEN – Page 30
BRUCE COLEMAN LTD
Des and Jen Bartlett – Pages 100, 103 (above and
below)
Vincent Serventy – Page 109
M. F. Soper – Pages 127 (above right), 172
Leonard Lee Rue – Page 171
Jan van Wormer – Page 127 (below)
WILLIAM COLLINS SONS AND CO LTD
*British Seals* by H. R. Hewer (1974) – Page 126
HAMISH HAMILTON LTD
*Wildlife Crisis* by H.R.H. Prince Philip and James
Fisher (1970) – Page 35
HUTCHINSON PUBLISHING GROUP LTD
*Marine Mammals* by R. J. Harrison and Judith E. King
(1965) – Pages 60, 63 (below), 138, 150, 200
*Whales* by E. J. Slijper (1962) – Pages 12, 17, 19, 33,
34, 38, 41, 45 (above and below), 56, 62, 63 (above),
74 (above and below), 85
KEYSTONE – Page 20
FRANK W. LANE
Arthur Christiansen – Page 194
Gosta Hakansson – Page 130
Marineland of Florida  Pages 76, 115
R. van Nostrand – Page 150
Alfred Saunders – Pages 99, 129 (above)
Lewis W. Walker – Page 186
THE MANSELL COLLECTION – Pages 49, 106,
139, 207
NATIONAL MARITIME MUSEUM,
LONDON – Page 61 (left and below right)
THE NOVOSTI PRESS AGENCY – Pages 15, 17,
52, 65
ROGER PERRY – Pages 159, 183, 184
POPPERFOTO – Pages 117, 129 (below), 168, 185
(right); T. H. I. Phipps  Page 55
RADIO TIMES HULTON PICTURE
LIBRARY  Pages 47 (above left, right and below),
113, 144 (below)
SEAPHOT
Dick Clarke  Page 147
SCOTT POLAR RESEARCH INSTITUTE,
CAMBRIDGE
Artist Edward Wilson (No. 1426) – Page 181
By courtesy of the
VICTORIA AND ALBERT MUSEUM
Derrick E. Witty – Page 58
ZOOLOGICAL SOCIETY OF LONDON – Page 69

# Index

Page references to the species descriptions are in bold type. References to illustrations are in italic.

echolocation, 42–3
elephant seal
   northern see *Mirounga angustirostris*
   southern see *M. leonina*
*Enhydra lutris, 192,* **213** *et seq.*
*Erignathus barbatus,* 140, 149, 156, **177**
Eschrichtiidae, 13, 45, 98
   see also *Eschrichtius gibbosus*
*Eschrichtius gibbosus,* 55, **98**
*E. glaucus* see *E. gibbosus*
Eskimo, *83,* 143, *145*
*Eubalaena glacialis,* 17, 24, *53,* **76**
*Eumetopias jubatus,* 135, 148, **170,** *171,* 175
Evolution
   Cetacea, 43–6, *45*
   Pinnipedia, 143
   Sirenia, 205–6
Exploitation
   Cetacea, 46–50, *47, 49*
   Pinnipedia, 143
   Sirenia, 206

*Feresa attenuata,* 99
finback see *Balaenoptera physalus*
finner, little see *B. acutorostrata*
finner, Japan see *B. borealis*
floe rat see *Pusa hispida*
franciscana see *Pontiporia blainvillei*
fur seal, 144, 154
   Alaskan see *Callorhinus ursinus*
   Australian see *Arctocephalus doriferus*
   Falkland see *A. australis*
   Guadalupe see *A. philippii*
   Kerguelen see *A. tropicalis*
   New Zealand see *A. forsteri*
   northern see *Callorhinus ursinus*
   Pribilof see *C. ursinus*
   South African see *A. pusillus*
   South American see *A. australis*
   sub-Antarctic see *A. tropicalis*
   Tasmanian see *A. tasmanicus*

*Globicephala,* 68
   *macrorhynchus,* **99**
   *melaena,* 21, **99**
   *scammoni,* **100**
Globicephalidae, 14, **99**
   see also killer, pilot whales
Grampidae, 14, **102**
   see also Risso's dolphin
*Grampus griseus,* 31, *54,* 68, **102**
grooves
   Cetacea, 50, *54*

haemaglobin
   Cetacea, 55
*Halichoerus grypus,* 130, 132, 135, 140, 148, *178,* **179**
harbour seal see *Phoca vitulina*

hearing
   Cetacea, 60
   Pinnipedia, 149
*Histriophoca fasciata,* **181**
Hydromalidae, **209**
   see also *Hydromalis*
*Hydromalis stelleri,* 198, **210**
*Hydrurga leptonyx,* 135, 140, *152,* 166, **181,** 182
*Hyperoodon,* 46
   *ampullatus,* 64, **116,** *117*
   *planifrons,* **117**

*Inia geoffrensis,* 31, 64, **113,** *115*

killer whale see *Orcinus orca*
   false see *Pseudorca crassidens*
   little see *Peponocephala electra*
   pygmy see *Feresa attenuata*
*Kogia breviceps,* **104**
   *simus,* **104**
Kogiidae, 14, **104**
   see also pygmy sperm whales

*Lagenodelphis hosei,* **88**
*Lagenorhynchus*
   *acutus,* 54, **88**
   *albirostris,* 19, **89**
   *australis,* **89**
   *cruciger,* **89**
   *fitzroyi,* **89**
   *obliquidens,* 31, 64, **90**
   *obscurus,* **90**
   *superciliosus,* **90**
   *thicolea,* **90**
   *wilsoni,* **91**
learning
   Cetacea, 29
   Pinnipedia, 132
*Leptonychotes weddelli,* 140, 161, **182,** *185*
limbs see anatomy; skeletal system; thermoregulation
*Lipotes vexillifer,* **114**
*Lissodelphis borealis,* **91**
   *peroni,* **91**
*Lobodon carcinophagus,* 140, 146, 155, 156, **181,** *182–3,*
   182
locomotion
   Cetacea, 55, *56*
   Pinnipedia, 145–7
   Sirenia, 207
   sea otter, 214
longevity
   Cetacea, 56
   Pinnipedia, 148

manatee
   Amazon see *Trechechus inunguis*
   American see *T. manatus*
   Caribbean see *T. manatus*